Governor Philip F. La Follette,
The Wisconsin Progressives, and the New Deal

Governor Philip F. La Follette, The Wisconsin Progressives, and the New Deal

John E. Miller

University of Missouri Press
Columbia & London, 1982

Copyright © 1982 by The Curators of the University of Missouri
Library of Congress Catalog Card Number 82–1982
Printed and bound in the United States of America
University of Missouri Press, Columbia, Missouri 65211

Library of Congress Cataloging in Publication Data

Miller, John E., 1945–
  Governor Philip F. La Follette, the Wisconsin
Progressives, and the New Deal.

  Bibliography: p. 217
  Includes index.
  1. Wisconsin—Politics and government—1848–1950.
2. LaFollette, Philip Fox, 1897–1965.
3. Progressivism (United States politics) I. Title.
F586.L3M54   977.5'042'0924   82–1982
ISBN 0–8262–0371–X   AACR2

To my mother and father
Rev. C. E. and Mildred Miller

Acknowledgments

In doing this study, I have benefited from the aid of a great many people, and I wish to thank them for their assistance. The staff of the State Historical Society of Wisconsin was always courteous and helpful, as were those at the Roosevelt Library and the Library of Congress. To my mentor, Professor Paul W. Glad, whose penetrating suggestions and constant encouragement were bestowed so liberally, I owe a special debt of gratitude. Heartfelt thanks also go to Professors Robert C. Nesbit and John Milton Cooper, Jr., for their suggestions and criticisms.

Many persons involved in the politics of the 1930s and 1940s generously opened their doors to me and recalled the events of those years as they remembered them. Particularly helpful were Mrs. Isabel B. La Follette, whose historical-mindedness she shared with her husband, Miss Mary La Follette, Gordon Sinykin, Morris Rubin, Elizabeth Brandeis, and Paul Raushenbush.

To my dear wife Kathy, I owe my greatest debt. Her indispensable encouragement, love, and support carried me through the good days and bad.

Contents

Chapter 1

Introduction

In Wisconsin, as elsewhere in the United States, the sweeping economic and social changes wrought by industrialization and urbanization carried in their wake profound challenges to the political system. Out of the expanding activities of local reformers in the 1890s sprang a statewide progressive movement, which came under the leadership of Robert M. La Follette, Sr., and established the Wisconsin Plan as a model for other states. After La Follette's death in 1925, his sons, Robert and Philip, carried on the progressive tradition in Wisconsin, adjusting it to the new conditions of Depression America and charting a treacherous route through the shoals of radical and third-party political activism.

A paradox lies at the heart of the progressive experience in the United States during the 1930s. At the moment when progressives found their influence at its peak, they began to go into decline. In the 1930s, a decade characterized by heightened ideological awareness and intensified partisan conflict, politics in America revolved around the man in the White House, Franklin D. Roosevelt. Liberal or conservative, friend or foe, a politician's most important decision was how to respond to Roosevelt and the New Deal, and that determination provided the best clue to his position. Its relationship with New Deal liberalism would determine the destiny of political progressivism.

The Wisconsin progressives, like their counterparts elsewhere, enjoyed a revival during the thirties, and much of their success derived from the special relationship they established with the New Deal administration. President Roosevelt, a self-proclaimed progressive Democrat and an admirer of Robert M. La Follette, Sr., worked closely with that distinguished man's sons, Sen. Robert M. La Follette, Jr., and Gov. Philip F. La Follette. Roosevelt shaped some of his legislative proposals in accordance with their requests, dispensed to them political patronage and other favors, and encouraged and cooperated with the new Wisconsin Progressive party, much to the consternation of the state's Democratic regulars. For their part, the La Follettes and their Progressive colleagues

1

supported many of Roosevelt's programs and backed him for reelection in 1936, but they also frequently dissented from New Deal actions and retained considerable freedom of action.

While many progressive Republicans in other states began to drift away from the New Deal by 1937, the La Follettes adhered staunchly, counting themselves among the few enthusiastic supporters of the president's Court-packing proposal of that year. But with the onset of the "Roosevelt Recession" in the fall, Phil La Follette perceived an opportunity to take advantage of the president's declining popularity and in April 1938 launched his short-lived third party, the National Progressives of America. Despite this challenge to Roosevelt's leadership, La Follette ran for reelection to his fourth term as governor as a friend of the national administration.

What rendered the split between La Follette and Roosevelt irreparable was the bitter foreign-policy debate that went on between 1939 and 1941. La Follette became actively involved in the America First Committee and was a vigorous and outspoken opponent of the president's foreign policy until Pearl Harbor, after which he enlisted as an army officer. Cut off from his liberal internationalist friends who dominated national Democratic councils and were increasingly prominent in the leadership of the state Democratic party, La Follette found himself associated with a group of mainly conservative anti-Roosevelt politicians and businessmen. His service in the Pacific during World War II as a public-relations officer on the staff of Gen. Douglas MacArthur seemed to many liberals to confirm La Follette's swing to the right.

Possible explanations for La Follette's course after 1938 include the notions that he underwent a radical shift in political philosophy or that his character was flawed by a propensity to rash and inconsistent action, including the allegedly erratic behavior accompanying his launching of the NPA and his later affiliation with isolationists and conservatives during and after the debate over intervention. I will argue, on the contrary, that Phil La Follette's political pilgrimage evolved naturally out of the conjunction of the events and circumstances of the time with his own ambitions and assumptions. While he did become more conservative over time, a fundamental continuity characterized his ideas and actions. Ambivalence marked his reactions toward Roosevelt and the New Deal from the outset. Before, during, and after his three terms as governor from 1931 to 1933 and 1935 to 1939, La Follette remained a pragmatic progressive politician who both benefited from and was limited by the movement's philosophy of practical idealism. His adoption of a radical tone of rhetoric during the early years of the depression should not blind us to his essentially moderate actions.

In elucidating La Follette's political odyssey, this study will focus on his personal and political growth, his legislative programs and executive leadership, his roles as head of the Wisconsin Progressive party and as advocate of a national third party and political realignment, and his relationship with Roosevelt and the New Deal.

La Follette was shaped by the course of events in his time, but more than most men he exerted a major influence upon them through his energetic style of leadership. As the most powerful political figure in the state during the decade, he more than anyone else set the terms of political debate, initiated the controversies, and influenced legislative outcomes. As Roosevelt established the tone for national politics, La Follette set it in Wisconsin. The major political question facing Wisconsinites in the thirties became whether they stood for or against the La Follettes, and, by 1938, how they stood on Phil La Follette. The governor's personality and actions were the dominant topic of political discussion and the most important factor in state politics.

Part of the governor's success and appeal lay in the artfulness with which he balanced his power with an unassuming, plain-folks style. "Just call me Phil," he insisted, and for the most part people did. "I'm called either 'Phil' or 'that soandso La Follette,' " he grinningly told an Eastern journalist.[1] But one needed only to attend one of his legislative caucuses or closed-door political conferences to be reminded who was in charge. La Follette masterfully grasped the reins of power and was comfortable using them. Political power in his hands was a tool to promote the progressive cause and to advance his own political career.

La Follette appeared cut out for leadership from the very beginning, and the concept of leadership intrigued him. As a boy he started collecting autographed pictures of great men and covered his walls with them. Napoleon was one of his heroes, and he read many works about Abraham Lincoln. His ambition was to become as great a leader as his father had been.[2]

The influence of Robert M. La Follette, Sr., upon his son was profound. Trying to live up to the unattainable ideal established by his father presented both a challenge and a burden. Inevitably Phil would suffer in the comparison. But his parents' high expectations stimulated ambition and a devotion to the progressive cause, which served as a sort of surrogate religion for the family. Phil's mother, Belle Case La Follette, was a remarkable person in her own right, the first woman graduate of the University of Wisconsin Law School, a rock of strength within the family, and a shrewd political adviser and campaigner. On his twenty-fourth birthday, which in 1921 coincided with Mother's Day, Phil wrote her, "I am deeply ambitious—I am overflowing with what seems like boundless energy and vitality, but the rudder of all this ambition and energy is the ideals and principles which you have fostered." In his memoirs, La Follette wrote that three women—his wife, his mother, and her mother—had been the molding influences in his life.[3]

But the testimony clearly shows that Phil, the second son of Robert M. and Belle Case La Follette, born on 8 May 1897, had a personality akin to his father's, while Robert, Junior, born two years earlier, more closely resembled his mother. People noticed that Bob was steadier and more patient, more balanced and less abrasive. He possessed a more sophisticated and cosmopolitan sensibility. Phil lacked Bob's melancholy streak, which, exacerbated by a series of illnesses, brought on bouts of depression. Bob was the more modest of the two and was less speculative and romantic. He seemed polished and suave, while Phil was earthier, jauntier, and seemingly more provincial. Bob dressed meticulously, but his brother frequently appeared in baggy trousers and unshined shoes. The older son seemed to have inherited the judiciousness of his mother, and the younger the fire and zeal of his father. *Assertive, aggressive, nervous, high-strung, dynamic, intense,* and *enthusiastic* were words that described Phii's demeanor. His sister Fola observed in him a "magic gift for living richly in the present" and "the power to plan and to abandon himself to the moment." This characteristic, unquestionably of decided advantage to one weighed down by burdensome responsibilities, sometimes made Phil seem selfishly indifferent to those who could not understand his quicksilver moods.[4]

Phil La Follette always seemed to be in a hurry. He ate quickly, which allowed him more time to talk, and he gave up golf because it was too time-consuming. He enjoyed dancing and watching movies but had few other diversions outside his family. He was a voracious reader, especially of history and biography but also of anything relating to current affairs, and would read an entire book in an evening. He talked rapidly, too, and packed a lot into his speeches, whether they lasted for ten minutes or two hours.[5]

People agreed on Phil La Follette's brilliance, but there was a feeling that Bob exhibited greater discretion and perhaps possessed greater wisdom. Phil as governor was the executive type who liked to attack problems and implement programs. Bob as senator was more suited to the legislative role, with its necessity for bargaining and compromise. He was inherently conservative, anxious to tap every opinion and to investigate every facet of a question before deciding it, and even then sometimes hesitated to act. While Phil was deliberative and normally cautious, he was also confident of his own intuitions and ready to risk defeat if the potential rewards were great enough. Like Bob, he solicited advice from many different people, but one legislator recalled that, while the governor often asked him for advice, he "never believed that La Follette cared one bit what I thought about anything."[6]

Phil La Follette's greatest skill was his ability to communicate. As a child he had enjoyed playacting and pretending that he was a preacher or an orator. He had liked to dress up in costumes and organize family parades with Bob and their younger sister, Mary. Their older sister, Fola, was an accomplished actress, and their father had settled on the law as a career only after rejecting the stage. Like his father, Phil possessed exceptional dramatic gifts. The platform seemed to be his natural habitat, and his speeches, almost always extemporaneous, usually succeeded in arousing his audiences. His fiery oratorical style seemed a copy of his father's, especially the outstretched arm and pointing finger and the habit of making a wry facial expression to indicate his feelings. When he ran his fingers through his hair, tore off his coat, and rolled up his sleeves, some in the audience were ready for Old Bob to reappear in his son. Standing five feet seven inches, Phil was an inch taller than his father, though he had a slighter frame, weighing only 125 to 130 pounds until he started putting on a little weight in his early forties. He combed his brown hair back in similar fashion, and his square jaw and piercing blue eyes reflected the same kind of earnestness and conviction. Wandering freely from the lectern, pounding fist in hand, peering intently at his audience, La Follette could mesmerize people. Posing alternately as impassioned advocate or judicious thinker, he always retained control, a skill that he had developed as a college debater. "He is an actor, undoubtedly," one reporter noted, "but not an insincere one."[7]

Born into a political family, which according to their friend Louis D. Brandeis gave the boys "more political experience in politics than any boys since the days of the Roman senators," groomed as the political successor of his illustrious father, and actively involved in political campaigning by the time he was nineteen, Phil La Follette, in the estimate of one friend and associate, was "a near-one-hundred-percent political animal." Gregarious by nature, he enjoyed meeting, talking, and working with people. While Bob disliked crowds and preferred behind-the-scenes organizational work, Phil loved the give-and-take of the campaign trail. As his wife later said, he "breathed, ate, and slept politics."[8]

Most people saw only one side of Phil La Follette, the hearty, jaunty, exuberant, and outspoken extrovert who possessed clearly reasoned and forcefully argued opinions on most political subjects. In many ways he was a man of unusual candor, but close friends and relatives saw another side of him, the loner who guarded his feelings and ambitions and seldom revealed his deepest thoughts. Isabel Bacon La Follette, called "Isen," who politicked with him and upon whose advice he greatly relied, once noted that her husband was not very loquacious and even she was often not privy to his thoughts when he was in the process of making important decisions. At such times, however, La Follette was more inclined to reveal the doubts and anxieties that he virtually never expressed in public. In his office La Follette disliked small talk and required his staff members to get straight to the point when they were talking with him.[9]

Over the years La Follette acquired numerous enemies and critics who dwelt on the less attractive aspects of his personality. Although generally cautious and deliberate in his actions, the governor was unpredictable enough to give people the impression of impulsiveness and instability; some called him the "wild man of Madison." Headstrong and outspoken, he was frequently thought to be abrasive. His imagination and willingness to innovate led him down unfamiliar paths. His tendency early in the depression to associate with radicals and identify himself as one reinforced the image many had of him as a maverick. And his obvious ambition seemed to provide a motive for demagoguery and mischief.

When in 1938 La Follette did attempt to launch a national third party with the aid of symbolism eerily resembling that of the fascists and when he later joined hands with the predominantly right-wing America First movement, his activities convinced many observers that he was an unstable personality whose unquenchable political ambition had led him to abandon conventional politics for the netherworld of fascism and the far right.

A more satisfactory interpretation of La Follette's behavior is that he simply responded to changing conditions in a manner essentially consistent with mainstream American politics. Though he possessed unusual intellect, creativity, ambition, and leadership skills, he operated firmly within the confines of the philosophy of practical idealism that had characterized the Wisconsin progressives from the earliest days. La Follette can correctly be seen as part of the emergence of modern liberalism, which built substantially upon the progressive foundations laid by his father and others and added a growing sensitivity to the needs of labor unions, urban residents, the poor, and the unemployed. He readily moved beyond the views of earlier progressives but never felt completely comfortable with the expanded governmental role advanced by New Deal liberalism. This ambivalence constrained him throughout the 1930s and eventually contributed to his break with Roosevelt. That relationship between progressivism and the New Deal determined the destiny of Wisconsin progressivism and of Gov. Philip La Follette.

Chapter 2

The Depression, the Governor, and the Progressives

The Great Depression wreaked its vengeance on every section and every class. Wisconsin's economy, however, contracted faster than those of neighboring states, with the state suffering greater fluctuations than its neighbors in durable-goods industries but less in those involving nondurable goods. In 1930 approximately one-quarter of the state's work force was engaged in agricultural occupations, and another third worked in manufacturing industries. The depression hit both groups hard. Net income produced by Wisconsin's manufacturing industries declined from $616 million in 1929 to $173 million in 1932 (in 1929 dollars), and manufacturing employment fell from 309,397 to 179,365. Those fortunate enough to hold their jobs saw their incomes decline by 23 percent during the three years after 1929. These drops significantly exceeded those for the country as a whole. Volume of construction in the state declined from over $160 million in 1929 to less than $30 million in 1933.[1]

Some industries suffered more than others. Between 1929 and 1933 employment of wage earners in metal products declined from 108,322 to 51,970; in lumber from 33,810 to 15,838; in food and tobacco manufacturing from 26,183 to 20,293; in textiles from 21,207 to 13,305; in leather goods from 18,061 to 13,424; in paper from 16,705 to 12,307; in printing and publishing from 7,567 to 5,751; in chemicals and petroleum from 4,387 to 2,816; and in stone, clay, and glass products from 3,214 to 1,848. Some areas of the state and some cities were especially affected. The decline in employment from September 1929 to September 1931 was only 2.5 percent for Watertown but 30.1 percent for Milwaukee, where more than one-third of the manufacturing wage earners in the state worked. Racine, with a 48 percent drop, fared even worse. Other recorded declines included Eau Claire, 24.5 percent; Fond du Lac, 28.9 percent; Green Bay, 24.9 percent; Janesville, 34.5 percent; Kenosha, 33.1 percent; La Crosse, 31.1 percent; Madison, 45 percent; Oshkosh, 30.8 percent; Superior, 17.4

percent; and Waukesha, 50.6 percent. Farmers, if anything, were even worse off, although they did have the advantage of being able to grow their own vegetables. Farm commodity prices dropped 57 percent between 1929 and 1932. Contributing to the farmers' woes was the drought that hit the region during the early thirties, reaching its most serious dimensions during 1934.[2]

The depression provided progressives with an opportunity to reclaim the power and influence that had eluded them during the 1920s, but although they were readier than their conservative opponents to try new approaches, they failed to devise completely satisfactory answers for the economic debacle. Progressives tended to be more certain about what they opposed than about what they favored. Possessing a political temperament that inclined them toward opposition and attack, they forged their identity in bitter conflict with conservatives, whom they preferred to call "reactionaries," and viewed the political world through a dualistic frame of reference that confidently discriminated between us and them, the people and the interests, equality of opportunity and privilege, democracy and plutocracy, or, more simply, the good guys and the bad guys. The depression posed new kinds of problems for political progressivism, which had been forged during prosperous times, and as the old progressives decided what road to follow a new kind of urban liberalism became the primary vehicle for political reform in the United States.[3]

Economic depression stimulated a progressive revival in Wisconsin, too, and none too soon, for the group was suffering from inertia, divisiveness, defeatism, and lack of direction. The late 1920s were frustrating years for the progressives, who began to look anxiously for someone who could unite them in a campaign to oust the stalwart Republicans from the statehouse. From his Washington office Sen. Robert M. La Follette, Jr., worried about organizational weakness and disunity in his state and the defeatism that had infected his progressive colleagues in Congress. As long as the leader of the Senate progressives, Sen. George W. Norris of Nebraska, remained discouraged and reluctant to lead and others remained hesitant to act, the progressive bloc continued to drift.[4]

In Wisconsin, progressive Republican leaders attempted to drum up enthusiasm at planning conferences in preparation for the 1928 campaign, but enthusiasm waned as soon as they returned to their communities to face widespread voter apathy, depleted treasuries, and hostility from conservative Republicans. Strategy was formulated by a small group of leaders in Madison who received occasional advice from Bob and Belle

Case La Follette in Washington. The "Madison Ring," as its critics preferred to call it, included Phil La Follette; Alf Rogers, a law partner in the family firm; newspaperman Fred Holmes; William T. Evjue, editor of the *Madison Capital Times;* Supreme Court justice Charles Crownhart; and several others. Most of them had long experience with the La Follette organization.[5]

The 1928 elections resulted in further frustration and demoralization for the progressives. Norris's victory over Herbert Hoover in the April presidential primary was more than offset by the loss in the September gubernatorial primary of Congressman Joseph D. Beck, a four-term progressive, to Walter J. Kohler, a stalwart Republican plumbing manufacturer. During the general election campaign Phil La Follette joined many other progressives in deserting the Republicans to endorse presidential candidate Alfred E. Smith and other Democrats. Bob La Follette, in his race for the Senate, however, refused to go quite that far, even though the Democrats withdrew their own senatorial candidate from the contest.[6]

Successive defeats in 1926 and 1928 left the progressives determined to find a leader who could successfully return them to power. Their chances appeared none too good in light of Governor Kohler's demonstrated administrative competence and the failure of a court case the progressives initiated against him for allegedly violating the Corrupt Practices Act by overspending during the 1928 campaign. Phil La Follette bided his time, in no hurry to reveal his plans. He could afford to wait. Evjue's refusal to run for governor removed the only strong challenger and gave La Follette progressive endorsement for the asking.[7]

When La Follette celebrated his thirty-third birthday on 8 May 1930, his only political office had been to serve for two years as district attorney of Dane County. Yet no one stood above him within the progressive leadership, and everyone assumed that it was only a matter of time before he ran for governor. Now the time seemed propitious as La Follette watched business conditions deteriorate after the stock-market crash, and he thought that if a building slump occurred that winter it would damage Kohler's popularity. The depression was slow to exert its impact, however, and only gradually did Wisconsinites realize what was happening. Even readers of the *Progressive* received little enlightenment on the matter.[8]

La Follette needed a campaign issue, and he found it in the rising clamor against chain stores and chain banking. The chains resulted from a long process of consolidation; small merchants disliked the competition, and other critics equated chains with monopoly. La Follette identified the issue as one that would appeal not only to Main Street businessmen but also to old-time progressives who had rallied behind his father's battles against the trusts. He made several speeches around the state warning about the threat the chains posed to American individualism and democracy.[9]

La Follette was also concerned about the kind of press coverage given progressives. They could count on few papers other than the *Progressive* and the *Madison Capital Times* for favorable coverage. He especially would have liked to obtain better treatment in Milwaukee to counteract the anti–La Follette stances of the *Journal* and the *Sentinel*. In June he visited William Randolph Hearst in Chicago to discuss the political coverage carried by Hearst's *Wisconsin News*. He was partially encouraged to hear the influential publisher tell him, "Well, we'll see if we can't make the paper more positively friendly."[10]

When no other progressive candidate stepped forward, La Follette announced at the end of June 1930 that he would run for the governorship. He made the chain issue his central theme, asserting that state government had become "a virtual partner of powerful and selfish monopoly interests" and that he would dissolve that partnership. Nothing in his platform sounded unfamiliar to progressive ears. In addition to the monopoly issue, it focused on excessive rates charged by the "power trust" and on alleged stalwart violations of the Corrupt Practices Act. Underlying all three issues, he asserted, was the fundamental question of whether great wealth would control the economic and political life of the state. His rhetoric and strategy were aimed at the same constituency that his father had courted.[11]

La Follette set a whirlwind pace during the Republican primary campaign, touching practically every county, making up to 9 speeches a day (about 250 in all), and drawing record crowds. He and his progressive colleagues rode hard on the issues of chain stores and chain banking, electric power, campaign expenditures, and property-tax relief. They also sought to discredit Kohler by linking him and the stalwart Republicans to Hoover, who was fast becoming one of the most unpopular presidents in American history. Their opponents concentrated on state issues and attempted to dissociate themselves from the national administration, but "Hooverism" hounded them.[12]

The strategy worked. La Follette attracted national attention with his victory over Kohler on 16 September by a margin of 395,551 to 267,687. The result was tantamount to election in a state where Democrats had not elected a governor in four decades. Progressives captured the nominations for the other four state offices and all but one congressional seat. They were certain of controlling the state assembly and threatened to take away stalwart control of the senate. La Follette easily defeated Democrat Charles Hammersley in November with 69.8 percent of the two-party vote. His victory was only one of many in a year that saw a broad national trend toward liberal and progressive candidates, such as Gov. Floyd Olson in Minnesota, Gov. Huey Long in Louisiana, and Sen. Edward P. Costigan in Colorado.[13]

The governor-elect had two months to prepare for office. He spent several days relaxing in Wisconsin's north woods as he and Isen accompanied Bob and his bride, Rachel Young, who were married the day after the election. Phil and Isen were the only witnesses at the simple ceremony at the Maple Bluff Farm in Madison. Rachel had known Bob since their high-school days and had worked as his secretary for a number of years. Phil then left Isen and their children, Bob and Judy, behind in Madison while he spent two weeks vacationing with his sister Fola and her husband, George Middleton, in Santa Monica, California. There he toured some of the movie studios and relaxed in the sun as he contemplated the job ahead of him.[14]

The pressure began soon after he returned to Madison. Four weeks of budget hearings and a series of conferences with business leaders left no doubt that the new governor's primary concerns would be unemployment relief and budgetary constraints. La Follette had aimed his fire at "conservatives" and "reactionaries" during the election, but now he appealed for aid from "constructive conservatives." His solicitation of conservative advice during the budget hearings gratified Speaker of the Assembly Charles B. Perry, who was a highly respected stalwart moderate. Addressing La Follette as "my dear lad," Perry commended him for disarming selfish criticism and stated his hope that a conciliatory attitude would produce cooperation between conservatives and progressives.[15]

In his endeavor to secure support and advice from a wide variety of sources, La Follette followed President Hoover's example of holding conferences with businessmen, bankers, railroad executives, labor and farm leaders, and legislators to discuss the unemployment situation and other problems facing the state. By this time the issue of chain banking, which had figured so prominently during the campaign, seemed far less important than the immediate danger posed by the possibility of a general banking collapse. Melvin Traylor, the president of the First National Bank of Chicago, journeyed to Madison to meet with bankers and registered his apprehensions about a rumored Senate investigation of the banking situation, which he feared might undermine public confidence in the system. La Follette responded, "We are skating on thin ice and now would be a bad time to break through." He was ready to listen to bankers when their advice seemed useful and they were not merely thinking of their own profits.[16]

While conferring with the presidents of the major railroads in the state, La Follette took up the idea of putting men to work on a grade-crossing-elimination program suggested by John Donaghey, chief engineer of the Wisconsin Highway Commission. The railroads agreed to help finance the program and to complete in months what had been scheduled to take three years. La Follette estimated that ten thousand workers could find employment on the project.[17]

The governor-elect also met with representatives from the State Federation of Labor, who brought with them a shopping list of twenty-five labor bills, including one on unemployment insurance. La Follette promised Federation president Henry Ohl and secretary John J. Handley vigorous support for most of their program and assured them that labor would be fairly represented in appointments to state jobs. Organized labor constituted an integral part of the progressive coalition and expected to play a major role in formulating legislation.[18]

La Follette counted on strong executive leadership and meticulous preparation to make his legislative program successful. A conference with progressive legislators divided responsibility among several groups who would cooperate with the governor's office in drawing up legislation. In the areas of electric power, taxation, and corrupt practices, where general agreement existed, progressives serving on legislative committees were to draft bills for immediate consideration. More time would be needed, though, to hammer out satisfactory measures on the harder subjects of banking, unemployment, and education.[19]

La Follette proceeded cautiously, sounding out diverse opinions and inviting cooperation from people who normally opposed progressives, but left no doubt that he intended to provide strong leadership. His father's example would serve as his inspiration; he symbolically illustrated that by positioning the former governor's portrait on a wall directly facing his desk. He also benefited from the advice and aid of two of his father's closest associates, law partner Alf Rogers and Herman L. Ekern, who had been a mainstay in the progressive inner group and a La Follette choice to run for governor a generation earlier. He asked Socialist state senator Thomas Duncan and University of Wisconsin political-science professor John Gaus to help draft his first message to the legislature. From the outset he worked closely with academicians, including Gaus, Law School Dean Lloyd Garrison, philosophy professor Max Otto, and economists John R. Commons, Harold Groves, Elizabeth Brandeis, and Paul A. Raushenbush. Edwin E. Witte, the head of the Legislative Reference Library and later a professor of economics at the university, sent him a steady stream of memoranda on a variety of subjects.[20]

But there was little time to study or theorize about the problems confronting the state. Immediate solutions were demanded. La Follette shared in the general uncertainty of the times, although he seldom admitted it. The question he posed to progressives in his opening address to the legislature on 15 January 1931 was meant to be rhetorical: "Have we, from our forty years of experience, any wisdom to contribute, or is our message obsolete?" But the relevance of the past to the unprecedented problems posed by the depression was hardly obvious. The new governor asserted that the progressives would apply established American ideals to changing conditions, but the necessity of bridging the gap between tradition and modernity left many options open. The question was whether progressives could steer a path that would allow them to address realistically economic and social problems, to retain their attachment to principle, and to fashion a unified political bloc that would be capable of capturing and holding political power.

La Follette joined a coterie that attributed the economic crisis to the disappearance of the frontier, which in the past, he averred, had been the guarantor of freedom and opportunity. Now government would have to assume responsibility for insuring equal opportunity for all Americans. Like most other progressives, La Follette adhered to the purchasing-power thesis of the depression, arguing that a decline in consumption had triggered the business downturn and that an infusion of purchasing power would restore prosperity.[21] The crucial economic problem in his view was distribution, for the problem of production had already been solved. Relief, although temporarily necessary, would provide no permanent remedy, La Follette said. Employment was the cure, and where necessary the government should take the initiative. While his brother led the fight in Congress for federal financing of public-works projects, Phil La Follette proposed a state-sponsored grade-crossing-elimination program. He also requested legislation that would stimulate farmers' purchasing power, authorize the construction of state and local power projects, create an executive council to advise the governor, and establish interim legislative committees that would continue to operate while the legislature was in recess.

La Follette hoped that consensus would prevail—that results could be achieved without turning group against group. His early decision to consult with leaders of diverse interest groups reflected his desire to avoid conflict and to stress mutual needs. He wanted, if possible, to avoid alternatives that might alienate potential supporters. Separate and even contradictory aims could be advocated simultaneously, as when the governor cited the conferences he had held as evidence that it would be possible "for us to inaugurate for Wisconsin the first steps toward a planned development, to be achieved by the free cooperation of individuals with the government of the state." Government planning and individual initiative were not yet perceived as incompatible goals.[22]

For a few weeks it appeared that harmony might indeed prevail in the legislature. La Follette told his family that the legislators' attitudes were good and that things were moving along satisfactorily. The assembly was safely progressive, but the senate was divided. Twelve progressive Republicans had succeeded in organizing the upper house with the aid of two Socialists, a Democrat, an independent Republican, and a stalwart Republican. But the chances were poor that such a jerry-built coalition could hang together as controversial issues arose.[23]

The new chief executive settled quickly into his new job, finding it "easy" and "natural." His years of training had served him well. As usual he was working hard and seemed to thrive on it. "He is really having a marvelous time," Isen wrote Belle Case La Follette. "It would gladden and amuse you to see his imagination work on a thousand different matters. I can see how he was when he was little!"[24]

La Follette's youth, which was much discussed in the press, was an attribute he shared with most of the progressive legislative leaders. The progressives possessed no monopoly on youth, however, and some were considerably older. Entrusted with guiding the progressive program through the senate were La Follette's law partner Glenn D. Roberts (thirty-three), Thomas Duncan (thirty-seven), Orland Loomis (thirty-seven), and Leonard Fons (twenty-seven). The floor leader in the assembly was Robert A. Nixon (thirty), who was aided by Harold Groves (thirty-three), E. M. Rowlands (twenty-nine), John Grobschmidt (thirty-five), Stanley Slagg (twenty-seven), and Carlton Mauthe (twenty-three). On the governor's staff were executive secretary John K. Kyle (twenty-seven), confidential secretary Edward G. Littel (twenty-eight), and legal counsel Samuel Becker (thirty-one). His first major appointment was David E. Lilienthal (thirty-one) of Chicago to the Railroad Commission. Many county committeemen and local chairmen were older men who had fought the good fight with Old Bob La Follette for many years. The old-timers, however, were rapidly giving way to a new generation whose knowledge of Old Bob and the early history of progressivism was only secondhand.[25]

The increasingly activist, interventionist, and urban brand of liberalism that emerged during the 1930s departed substantially from the traditional progressivism that had been so successful during the first two decades of the twentieth century. The readiness of the La Follette brothers to identify themselves with the labor movement, seek relief for the unemployed, and extend government regulation into new areas associated them with urban representatives such as Robert F. Wagner of New York. Simultaneously they maintained their ties to the older and more agrarian progressives in Wisconsin by reiterating traditional demands for more public power, progressive taxation, assistance for farmers, and anti-monopoly legislation. Increasingly, Phil La Follette found himself addressing issues to which the progressive tradition spoke only obscurely, if at all.

Criticisms of Old Guard Republican policies could only go so far; progressives had to fashion workable alternatives of their own if they were to capture broad public support. Worried that a rare opportunity to push forward might be lost, Bob La Follette persuaded Sens. George W. Norris, William E. Borah, Edward P. Costigan, Bronson Cutting, and Burton K. Wheeler to join him in calling a conference of liberals that met in Washington on 11–12 March 1930 to consider measures that could be introduced in the next session of Congress. Two days of discussion with politicians, college professors, labor leaders, lawyers, newspapermen, and others brought forth many ideas but little agreement on what should be done; the results demonstrated that progressives were uncertain about the correct way to deal with the country's basic problems. Phil La Follette was too busy working on his own legislative program to attend the meeting.[26]

Gov. Franklin D. Roosevelt also was unable to be there, but he did send a message of encouragement. Already the New Yorker was emerging as a likely progressive Democratic nominee for the presidency. The deliberateness with which he came to support unemployment insurance, a state program of unemployment relief, and finally federal funds for the unemployed was typical of progressives around the country as they groped for answers.[27]

The Wisconsin progressives prided themselves on being out in front on social issues but, being good politicians, seldom strayed far ahead of public opinion. Their opponents liked to call them radicals, but the term said more about the conservatives' fears than it did about the progressives themselves. La Follette epitomized the practical idealist, carefully testing the political waters before venturing forth. The constraints under which he operated were considerable. To win approval for his programs in the senate, he had to appeal to cooperative nonprogressives and also limit state expenditures. In addition, he could count on opposition from many newspapers, the Wisconsin Manufacturers Association, and spokesmen for other special interests. No wonder that the governor approached the legislative session cautiously.

Governor La Follette seldom betrayed any uncertainty, however, when discussing the economic crisis. His inherent caution and reasonableness contrasted sharply with the ideological dualism that characterized his rhetoric. On the platform he used a slashing style of attack, heaping scorn and ridicule upon the "reactionaries," "standpatters," and "Hoovercrats" who were leading the country to ruin. "From the beginning of history," he asserted, "human progress is traced in the struggles between the great masses of mankind to lift themselves upward and the determined efforts of limited groups of dominant men to maintain their control of the economic and political lives of the many." History manifested a basic continuity, from ancient slavery through medieval serfdom through American slavery to the contemporary power of "colossal, organized wealth." Class domination, the governor argued, was evident in the fact that 504 wealthy individuals received incomes equaling those of 4 million farmers. Such a division between the rich and the poor was not only morally wrong but also economically stupid, La Follette said, and had led to the economic collapse that was plaguing the country. Although such statements contributed to a lively and effective rhetorical style, they seldom resulted in practical policies, which depended less on ideology than on the effects of budgetary constraints, administrative imperatives, interest-group demands, and previous experience. The responsibilities of power insured that La Follette and the progressives would not be utopian dreamers but practical idealists, with a strong emphasis on that qualifying adjective.[28]

Gov. La Follette quickly consolidated his authority as head of the progressive faction and conferred almost daily with his legislative leaders to outline strategy. The results were substantial. They obtained approval for a referendum on a state power program, although failing to pass a municipal ownership bill. The legislature reorganized the Railroad Commission, conferring on it additional powers and duties, and renamed it the Public Service Commission. To help the butter producers, the progressives supported a six-cents-a-pound tax on oleomargarine after failing in an effort to require processors to color it green. They also adopted a new state labor code similar in many respects to the Norris-La Guardia Act passed by Congress the following year. The legislature also expanded old-age pension coverage, created an executive council to advise the governor, and during the special session adopted his proposal to put unemployed youths to work in the state forests.[29] The achievement was substantial, adding luster to Wisconsin's reputation as a legislative pacesetter and marking Governor La Follette as an interesting politician to watch, but not nearly as exceptional as some progressives suggested.

Looking for ways to reduce spending, La Follette preferred to postpone consideration of unemployment relief until a special session of the legislature could be called later in the year. The sticky problem of banking legislation he also deferred until later. The progressives treaded lightly on the chain-banking and chain-store questions during the regular session, prompting frequent sarcasm regarding their evasiveness from the opposition. When the U.S. Supreme Court gave its approval to an Indiana chain-store tax, the decision heartened taxation advocates in other states. La Follette opposed a senate-passed graduated tax on chain stores of from $1 to $1,000 based on total sales and recommended instead a maximum $25 tax similar to the Indiana law. He said that his objective was simply to eliminate inequality in taxation between the chains and independent merchants, not to drive the chains out of business. Going back on previous statements about the menace of chain stores, he contended that he neither favored nor opposed chains in themselves but rather was chiefly interested in "the kind of economic society we are going to build and preserve." Many legislators determined to curb the chains' growth disagreed with him.[30]

La Follette also retreated from his earlier censure of chain banking. Now that his concern was not to get elected but to govern, he needed the cooperation of businessmen and bankers. The crucial problem for the short run, he believed, was to restore public confidence in the banks and to preserve the stability of the banking system. When he assigned the banking and unemployment issues to special interim committees, who were to report to the special session of the legislature, conservative Republicans taunted him for reneging on his campaign pledge to eradicate the chain threat.[31]

The governor had to admit that he had changed his mind. Speaking to the legislature just before adjournment on 4 June, he observed that passing legislation adverse to bank chains without any positive program to accompany it might undermine financial stability. Such a law would discharge his platform commitment, he said, but "it would not fulfill an even higher obligation to meet great problems with constructive alternatives. To deal only with the negative aspects of this problem would be playing politics with banking." La Follette's admission reflected his growing maturity and realism in office and also illuminated the oversimplifications of the previous year's campaign.[32]

La Follette also made one of the most important political moves of his career when he appointed Thomas Duncan, a Socialist state senator from Milwaukee's Sixth District, as his executive secretary after the regular session ended. "Tommy" Duncan, who had graduated Phi Beta Kappa from Yale and then served as secretary to Milwaukee's mayor Daniel Hoan, was one of the cleverest political operators in the state and functioned as La Follette's trusted adviser and political troubleshooter during his years as governor until Duncan's 1938 conviction for manslaughter in an automobile accident forced him to resign. The Milwaukeean's sharp wit, organizational ability, and tactical brilliance contributed greatly to La Follette's success. Duncan's Socialist background and abrasive manner, on the other hand, stimulated terrific abuse from his detractors.

In the third year of a four-year senate term in 1931 after spending six years in the assembly, Duncan viewed his position in the legislature as a political dead end. Never doctrinaire in his Socialist views, Duncan had frequently cooperated with the progressives during the 1920s and rapidly emerged as one of La Follette's most reliable supporters, playing an especially important role as chairman of the Joint Committee on Finance. As his importance in directing the progressive program through the senate grew, his Socialist friends became increasingly indignant, accusing him of selling out the cause of the workingman.[33]

Many political observers assumed that Duncan harbored higher political ambitions, but his selfless devotion to the progressive cause after joining the governor's staff revealed instead a personality driven by a strong impulse to do good. The Socialists forced him to resign from the party because of his work for La Follette, but Duncan continued to maintain close ties with labor and Socialist associates and served as a valuable link between them and the governor. La Follette leaned heavily on him in formulating his legislative programs, especially the financial ones, and in directing progressive strategy in the legislature. Many progressives considered Duncan to be too far left, and others did not care for his methods, but no one denied his effectiveness in obtaining results.[34]

La Follette had a five-month breather in 1931 during the June-to-November legislative recess. He continued his search for ways to provide unemployment relief without having to raise taxes. Ordering the University of Wisconsin president, Glenn Frank, to eliminate unjustifiable spending was one way of impressing people that he was doing everything possible to cut expenditures.[35]

La Follette admitted that he possessed no sure remedy for the depression. He told a *New York Times* correspondent, "I am not convinced about the means, but there surely must be a way and that way has got to be found." He refused to disclose his position on unemployment insurance until the special session. Some of the expedients he suggested for attacking unemployment were shortening workweeks, limiting production, and obtaining better statistics on the business cycle. "The government has got to help industry find a way out, and we are going to start in Wisconsin!" he promised. "A way will be found to meet unemployment. I am sure of it. We merely need organization, determination. Industry needs foresight. . . . Especially we should look to the future and provide the means of control in producing and distributing our wealth." His intentions, like those of many others, were good, but he was as baffled by the enormity of the economic problem as anyone else.[36]

Governor La Follette's speech opening the special session of the legislature on 24 November 1931 attracted unusual attention and widespread praise for its bold thinking. "A great message," the *Nation* called it. Historian Charles A. Beard wrote to a friend, "In all the history of American public documents there has not appeared a more important or more reasoned state paper." Years later La Follette likened it to his crossing the "political Rubicon." Asserting in his speech that the nation was facing its greatest domestic crisis since the Civil War, he drew a sharp distinction between those who favored and those who opposed collective action to deal with the emergency. He outlined four main areas needing action: the extension of public ownership of utilities, the creation of governmental machinery that would allow business to "govern itself," the wider use of social and economic research and planning, and the equalization of the tax burden.[37]

Public ownership of utilities was an item on which almost all progressives could agree. It comprised the first plank of the progressive platform that was carried on the editorial pages of both the *Capital Times* and the *Progressive*. "Have we no other impulse in our national life except profit?" La Follette asked. He did not challenge the concept of profits per se but rather the excesses of a system that favored the wealthy and worked against the poor.[38]

La Follette's advocacy of self-governing business reflected the growing popularity of the idea of planning among liberals and conservatives alike. Soon after his speech, La Follette met privately with Alfred Sloan, the president of General Motors and an outspoken advocate of planning. What La Follette, Sloan, Charles Beard, Stuart Chase, John Dewey, and other enthusiasts meant by planning was often less than clear, however. Bob La Follette was calling at the time for a national economic council that would collect economic data and furnish expert advice, but Phil La Follette's references to planning remained rather abstract. He retained the hope that government, business, labor, and agriculture somehow could pull together to solve their common problems. He never intended for planning to replace the market system and never fully considered the implications of the concept; his commitment to planning, like that of many others, was faddish, and as its popularity waned during the early New Deal years, La Follette's enthusiasm for it also declined.

His primary method for redistributing income was taxation, whereby he proposed to stimulate purchasing power in order to bring about economic recovery. The goals of achieving greater progressivity in taxation and of reducing the overall burden of taxation, however, could not always be reconciled.

The governor's speech set the tone for a highly productive special session. The governor obtained eight million dollars for relief and public works, half of his original request. The program was to be financed by a surtax on incomes, a dividends tax, and a chain-store tax. Although La Follette became known as an ardent proponent of relief for the unemployed, he advocated it only as a last resort, always emphasizing the need for the creation of useful jobs. In addition, the progressives sought to relieve distress by reducing state-imposed property taxes and by providing aid to mortgage holders.[39]

Surprisingly, it was not until he addressed the special session that La Follette gave clear support to unemployment compensation. During the 1920s, compensation schemes had run into legislative roadblocks several times. In 1930, when he was campaigning for governor, he had asked several friends on the University of Wisconsin faculty—Paul A. Raushenbush; Raushenbush's wife, Elizabeth Brandeis; and Harold Groves (whom he induced to run for the state assembly at the same time)—to work on an unemployment-relief bill that could obtain legislative approval. All three of La Follette's friends had studied economics under John R. Commons, the distinguished labor historian, and were vitally interested in the issue of unemployment insurance. La Follette let them work completely on their own until the special session, when he endorsed the employer-reserves plan that Groves had drafted.[40]

Passage of the bill near the end of the session occasioned a great deal of self-congratulation among progressives, who advertised it as another example of the state's innovative record; no other state enacted such legislation before Congress passed the Social Security Act in 1935. But there was nothing radical about the Wisconsin law, which was basically a preventive rather than a compensatory measure. Governor La Follette, along with Groves, Commons, Raushenbush, and Brandeis, conceived of its central purpose as being to reward and extend the best practices of businesses who managed to maintain steady levels of employment. Those employers with stable employment could reduce their contributions to the system. The profit motive thus would be harnessed in the interest of stabilizing capitalism and preventing unemployment. The "Wisconsin Plan" considered unemployment, like industrial accidents, to be an industrial hazard that increased production costs and should be prevented if possible but compensated where unavoidable. Commons commented, "It is extraordinarily an individualistic and capitalistic scheme."[41]

The Wisconsin Plan, or "American Plan" as it was sometimes called, came in for strong criticism from advocates of the "Ohio Plan," who wanted to create a true insurance system that would pool contributions and risk rather than maintain individual employer reserves. They denied that individual firms could do much to affect overall employment levels. Since they believed that business cycles and unemployment were inevitable, they concentrated on providing adequate compensation for the unemployed by pooling risk in a single fund contributed to by both employers and employees. Some advocates of that plan also supported government contributions. To La Follette and other progressives, the scheme sounded too much like a "dole." Later on, Wisconsinites, including Raushenbush, Arthur Altmeyer, and Edwin E. Witte, played a major role in developing and administering unemployment insurance at the federal level. During congressional consideration of the social-security bill in 1935, the governor stated to President Roosevelt his concern that comprehensive federal legislation might disqualify the Wisconsin program, but Roosevelt, who strongly favored federal-state cooperation in this area, reassured La Follette that a wide area for state initiative would remain open. Later Bob La Follette secured acceptance in the Senate Finance Committee for an amendment to the bill which permitted states wide latitude in establishing separate schemes. After 1935 Phil La Follette often cited Wisconsin's law as an excellent example of how states could function as laboratories for social experimentation; ironically, considering all the help President Roosevelt gave Wisconsin on the issue, the governor frequently claimed that Wisconsin's plan was superior to federally sponsored programs.[42]

Banking was the third major issue facing the special session. Governor La Follette emphasized the need for stabilization, and the legislature passed a stabilization bill that had been put together by the interim banking committee. It failed, however, to approve a proposal aimed against chain banks when the two-thirds majority required for banking legislation could not be reached. La Follette subsequently muted his attacks on the chains, although he still occasionally warned against the "absentee ownership of credit." Shelving his populist, anti–Wall Street rhetoric, he solicited advice from bankers both inside and outside the state, including Melvin Traylor of Chicago's First National Bank and Reeve Schley of the Chase National Bank of New York. La Follette boasted that during the first half of 1932 bank suspension rates were lower in Wisconsin than in surrounding states.[43]

The results of both the regular and the special sessions were gratifying, considering the precarious position that the progressives occupied in the legislature. The governor's accomplishments owed a great deal to the atmosphere of crisis in the country, but also important were his vigorous leadership, his willingness to compromise, and his ability to conciliate various interest groups in the state.[44]

After the legislators left town, Phil traveled east to talk with Bob and some of their friends. Conversations with a wide variety of people in Washington and New York left him "less sanguine" than he had been earlier. Nobody seemed to have answers for what ailed the country.[45]

The governor again revealed his uncertainty about the future in a speech on the National Broadcasting Company's "National Radio Forum" on 14 March 1932. Creating the kind of graphic word picture he often relied upon, he likened the country's situation to being lost in a forest and suddenly realizing that the trusted guide no longer knows which way to turn. "The forest looms about, its stillness intensifying the terror that lurks within you," La Follette said. "Such is the situation of America today. We have lost confidence in leaders because leaders have lost their own way." Some method was needed to control "unplanned and unregulated growth." He suggested the same prescriptions he had given the legislature in November—public ownership of utilities, social and economic planning, business self-government, and progressive taxation. Wisconsin in his view had demonstrated the wisdom of balanced budgets and pay-as-you-go taxation. "In the true meaning of the word 'conservative'—to conserve and preserve—the only real conservatives in America today are the progressives," La Follette concluded.[46]

The governor continued during the remainder of 1932 to discuss his ideas with bankers, businessmen, academicians, journalists, and others. He revealed his pessimism in a letter to his brother in May: "Economic conditions are getting rapidly worse. Unless something drastic is done both in the direction of furnishing employment and inflation, I doubt if things will hold together. We may be faced with the necessity of action any time to avoid serious conflict. There is little or nothing we can do locally without works and funds to finance them, until and unless things break out badly. Then, of course, we shall be compelled to act." Phil told Bob that conservatives were getting so worried that some of them sounded "almost red."[47]

On 22 May he dined at the home of the Sears-Roebuck president, Gen. Robert E. Wood, in Chicago, where he discussed the deteriorating situation with several businessmen, including Sewell Avery of Montgomery Ward, Gerard Swope of General Electric, and F. J. Sensenbrenner, a Wisconsin paper manufacturer whom La Follette had named to his executive council. A week later he joined a group at the Chicago Club that included Gov. Floyd Olson of Minnesota and farm editor Henry A. Wallace and outlined for them a five-point recovery program created with

the help of John Gaus. It included a national economic council to facilitate
government planning and business self-government; shortened
workweeks to extend employment; reductions in railroad and utility
rates; balanced budgets; and a federal works program to create jobs for
everyone able and willing to work. These meetings provided excellent
opportunities for gauging elite opinion and for testing ideas against elite
criticism.[48]

An especially perplexing issue facing Bob La Follette that summer was
the bonus bill, which was designed to provide early payment of bonuses
that Congress had granted to war veterans after the First World War but
had not scheduled for payment until 1945. When Bob asked his opinion on
the matter, Phil replied that while he was no great enthusiast for inflation,
he believed the bonus bill would be a practical way to boost purchasing
power and aid veterans at the same time. The senator decided not to take
his brother's advice, however, and voted against the bill when it came up
in the Senate.[49]

The depression posed new and unfamiliar questions for Phil La Follette
and his fellow progressives. The solutions he advocated were seldom
very radical or original, but because he argued eloquently for planning,
public works, and aid for the distressed, La Follette acquired a reputation
for boldness and imagination. Being uncertain about what would work,
La Follette talked about collective action but maintained flexibility
regarding methods.

In preparation for the September primary election, Governor La Follette crisscrossed the state in May, patching up organizational deficien-
cies and attempting to raise enthusiasm for the campaign. The people he
talked to sounded confident despite numerous warning signals. The
presidential primary in April gave evidence of a broad shift to the
Democrats as the party dramatically increased its totals in Wisconsin,
giving twenty-four of its twenty-six convention delegates to Governor
Roosevelt of New York. The progressives had endorsed Sen. George W.
Norris of Nebraska, who captured eleven of the Republican delegates,
the other sixteen going to President Hoover.[50]

Although progressives enjoyed seeing President Hoover blamed for the
country's economic woes, popular dissatisfaction with the Republicans
worked against them too, since it took a large bloc of votes into the
Democratic column. The progressives faced a dilemma. They felt uncomfortable in a Hoover-led Republican party, but they found the conserva-
tive-dominated state Democratic party no more congenial, although they

had formed temporary alliances with the Democrats in 1928 and on several other occasions.

Roosevelt possessed considerable appeal for them, however. In New York State he had promoted conservation of natural resources, unemployment insurance, progressive taxation, and public-power projects. He was already beginning to establish a relationship with the La Follettes. His office had requested copies of all of Phil La Follette's speeches. In 1930 Roosevelt had been the La Follettes' alternate choice to deliver the address at the annual memorial service for their father in the event that Senator Wheeler was unable to do it. Roosevelt's increasing momentum seemed to be a sign of the liberal turn that the country was taking.[51]

The national Democratic revival stimulated the virtually moribund state party to renewed efforts. One progressive leader, sizing up the implications of the anti-Republican trend, told Phil La Follette, "If this Democratic trend turns out to be very strong it might conceivably elect Democratic state officers in Wisconsin this year. Stranger things than that have happened in politics."[52] From 1922 to 1928 the Democrats had failed to capture a single seat in the state senate; they had obtained one in 1930. Their representation in the assembly during this period had averaged two or three seats, considerably fewer than the Socialists had. They usually had obtained respectable totals in general elections for state offices, largely because many adherents of whichever Republican faction had lost in the primaries would refuse to vote for the Republican nominee in the general election. But in gubernatorial primaries from 1922 to 1930 the Democrats had received substantially less than 10 percent of the total vote. Political decisions therefore had been made for all practical purposes within the Republican primary. The progressives depended on the votes of "fair-minded" Democrats to help them defeat stalwart Republican candidates in the primary elections. Some observers estimated that there were only thirty thousand to fifty thousand "hard-core" Democrats in the state before 1932, but the presidential primary of that year demonstrated that in fact tens of thousands of Democrats were ready to vote in their own party's primary when offered an attractive candidate and a feasible chance of winning.

Governor La Follette clearly recognized the challenge posed by a progressive Democrat such as Roosevelt. Isen predicted, "If Roosevelt gets the nomination I think we will have a hard fight on up to the November election, but if they nominate someone else, as I begin to think they may, I don't think we will have such a fight against the Democrats in

Wisconsin." One week after the Wisconsin presidential primary, on a trip to New York City, the La Follettes visited the Roosevelts at their Sixty-fifth Street apartment, and the Wisconsin governor came away favorably impressed with his counterpart from New York.[53]

The stalwart Republicans seemed to go out of their way to push the progressives into the embrace of the Democrats. In June, Wisconsin's progressive delegates at the Republican National Convention in Chicago were labeled "un-Republican, un-American, and unpatriotic" by their conservative counterparts for remaining seated during a Hoover demonstration in which a huge American flag was unfurled. They cast their votes for Sen. John J. Blaine, as Hoover easily captured the nomination on the first ballot. Many stalwarts welcomed the idea of a progressive exodus. Their attitudes found expression in the statement of one party regular at the convention: "If a bunch of Methodists went to a Baptist meeting and were thrown out, the people would just laugh."[54]

The Democrats followed the Republicans into Chicago two weeks later, and except for two Smith supporters the entire Wisconsin delegation voted down the line for Roosevelt. Conservatism, dullness, and inertia had characterized the party's leadership for years, but now leaders such as Otto La Budde, Charles E. Broughton, and F. Ryan Duffy enthusiastically backed the liberal candidacy of Governor Roosevelt. The popularity of the New York governor with the electorate did not carry over, however, to many party leaders, who remained wedded to a more traditional point of view. The question now was whether old-line conservatives or a newer group of liberals would actually control the party.[55]

The progressives adopted a strategy during the primary election of defending their own record, pinning the Hoover label on the stalwarts, and avoiding all mention of the Democrats. During the early going La Follette remained optimistic. "I don't see any sign of a swing to the stalwarts *at all,*" he wrote Bob. "And I sense that the swing toward the Democrats, some weeks ago in the Roosevelt sentiment, has considerably abated." Nevertheless, he sensed that people were worried and did not know which way to turn. "There is no question that the general economic distress has made the people (and justifiably) distressed, disturbed, and discontented," he remarked.[56]

On the hustings La Follette defended the progressives, reciting the list of legislation they had passed benefiting laborers, farmers, businessmen, and property owners. He accused the stalwarts of being merely negativistic when they asked in their platform for "the enactment of the fewest possible laws; repeal of useless and obsolete laws and those which restrict individual initiative and the home control of local government." Pointing to his own record in reducing taxes and cutting costs, including a personal 20 percent pay cut, he called a stalwart promise to cut costs a "high-sounding but hollow phrase used to conceal the utter bankruptcy of their record and platform." He alleged that his opponents were representatives of the rich, who were trying to buy office to gain special privileges. He emphasized three issues during the campaign—taxation, relief, and public power—as areas where the progressives were forward-looking but responsible advocates of sound, constructive change.[57]

The progressives' best hope for victory lay in the chance that President Hoover's unpopularity would rub off on the stalwarts. The conservatives, who were well aware of this, sought to disengage themselves from the Hoover image without appearing too disloyal. Their gubernatorial candidate, former governor Kohler, ran a low-key campaign of advocating sound business principles in government. Aspiring to the United States Senate was a brash, outspoken young newspaperman from Ashland with no previous experience in government, John B. Chapple. Flinging absurd charges with abandon, Chapple spent most of his time blaming the progressives for the radicalism, atheism, and immorality that he alleged were rampant on the University of Wisconsin campus. The incumbent, Senator Blaine, who before going to Washington had spent three terms as a progressive governor, assumed like almost everyone else that Chapple posed no serious threat to him, so he spent most of his time campaigning for Phil La Follette and the other progressive candidates.

As the weeks wore on, Governor La Follette gradually came to the conclusion that he would lose. Sensing a Democratic upsurge on his swings around the state, he studiously ignored it, reminding the voters that they were not voting for a president in September. When one reporter asked for his opinion about the Democratic situation in Wisconsin, he cut the question off with "I don't know much about it." And to a query about Roosevelt's nomination, he replied, "I had nothing to do with it." On the day before the balloting La Follette lunched at the Loraine Hotel in Madison with some of the members of the progressive inner circle, including Secretary of State Theodore Dammann; law partner Glenn D. Roberts; Thomas Davlin, a state official; Thomas Duncan; and William T. Evjue. Most of them seemed confident that the final week's campaigning in Milwaukee would put them over the top, but La Follette did not have much to say. He was worried and so was Evjue. They did not believe the newspapers' predictions that the progressives would win.[58]

Their fears were well-founded. The balloting on 20 September dealt a heavy blow to the progressives and set in motion forces that would eventually transform the state's party system. Kohler received 414,575 votes to La Follette's 319,884. The three Democratic candidates polled a total of 131,930 votes, 114,890 more than the party had received two years earlier. The Socialists captured only 31,836 votes. Even more surprising was Blaine's loss to Chapple by about 11,000 votes. Among the progressive candidates for state office, only Secretary of State Dammann survived the political hurricane. Spokesmen for the White House said they were encouraged by the news from Wisconsin. The Democrats in turn waxed optimistic over their increased turnout. Their gubernatorial nominee, Albert B. Schmedeman, mayor of Madison and former ambassador to Norway, asserted that there were still some 200,000 missing Democratic votes and expressed his confidence that come November they would be found in the Democratic column.[59]

The increased Democratic turnout did not by itself explain the progressive defeat. Incumbents everywhere, blamed for the depression, were turned out of office in 1932. In addition, Wisconsin's stalwart Republicans ran a much better financed and more professionally organized campaign than their opponents and had most of the state's newspapers behind them. La Follette managed to retain majorities in most of the rural districts, but in urban centers and smaller towns, Kohler generally obtained larger pluralities. Milwaukee County was crucial to the stalwarts' success; having lost there by 5,447 votes in 1930, Kohler ran up a margin of 48,023 two years later.[60]

Letters expressing surprise, shock, and encouragement poured into the governor's office during the days after the election. People urged him to carry on the fight in politics. They told him that he was simply a victim of circumstances and that Wisconsin was not tired of progressivism but that a lot of people were tired of not having a job. Prominent liberals around the country also expressed their disappointment. The *Nation* called the outcome "a hard blow to liberals everywhere." La Follette put up a cheery front, telling people he was not dispirited and repeating a favorite expression: "Truth has lost many a battle but never a war." He said that although one round had been lost, "this contest shall go on until it is won. Every progressive will face the enemy, tighten his belt, and prepare for the next round." He blamed his defeat on the opposition of the press and the utilities industry.[61]

Despite the tough-sounding words, La Follette was tired and deeply disappointed. As he vacationed for several days in northern Wisconsin, his sister Fola noticed that he looked worn. "Sometimes when he was sitting alone in the room and I would come in unexpectedly he looked so much a boy and yet his face bore the marks of such tension and strain that my heart aches," she wrote their sister Mary. "I wish he could and would break down and then come back slowly after letting go, instead of being almost too brave." It was not La Follette's nature, however, to pour forth his emotions. Whatever disappointment and frustration he felt remained inside.[62]

The progressives never seriously considered backing the stalwart nominees during the general election. At one enthusiastic rally of progressives who squeezed into the capitol's assembly chamber preceding the statutory platform convention, La Follette emphasized that their goal should be to elect as many progressives as possible and that they had no obligation to Kohler or Chapple or any of the other stalwart nominees. The platforms adopted the following day by both the Democrats and by the controlling faction of stalwart Republicans included pointed appeals to the progressives. The Democrats' welcome came in the very first sentences of their document: "Wisconsin Democracy has always been thoroughly progressive in theory, spirit, and action. . . . We earnestly appeal for the support of all liberal and progressive minded citizens of Wisconsin for both the national and state Democratic platforms and for the national and state candidates."[63]

Two realistic alternatives confronted the progressives: endorsing the Democrats or remaining neutral. Evjue spoke for most of the leaders when he declared that backing Hoover would constitute "the worst kind of moral depravity." Some decided to vote for Socialist Norman Thomas, but the vast majority marked their ballots for Roosevelt and Garner. La Follette's friend Robert M. Hutchins, who was the president of the University of Chicago, urged a vote for Thomas because Hoover and Roosevelt were basically indistinguishable. "I will bet you ten bucks that you will be as sick of Roosevelt in two years as you have been of Hoover—or sicker," he wrote La Follette.[64]

The progressive leadership waited a month before officially announcing their position. Governor Roosevelt improved the Democrats' chances with a speech on 30 September in Milwaukee, where he described the profound impression that the Wisconsin progressive tradition had made upon him:

> Back in the days when I was in college and began to ponder the great principles of political life, I learned much and profited much by what was going on in Wisconsin. The things that you were doing were not only contributions of immeasurable value to the state of Wisconsin, but they were inspiring to the youth of all the land.
>
> I stand here today quite conscious of the fact that these great basic principles were not only useful to me in forming the lines of my political life, but that when as governor of New York I met these problems in practice, I found that our own state of New York had in many respects profited by the pioneer efforts of Wisconsin.

Roosevelt asserted that his fight for public power paralleled Wisconsin's and urged his listeners to cast aside party allegiance when they entered the voting booths that fall.[65]

Following the lead of Hiram Johnson in California, Norris in Nebraska, Cutting in New Mexico, and other progressives around the country, the *Capital Times* endorsed Roosevelt on 18 October. The following day Bob La Follette announced his support for Roosevelt, Schmedeman, and Duffy, and the rest of the progressives followed suit. They also backed other Democrats where no progressives were on the ballot. Phil La Follette doubted whether any substantial differences separated Republicans from Democrats, but he told people that a choice between Hoover and Roosevelt dictated a vote for the latter.[66]

Although the progressives concentrated mainly on their own candidates, there was a wholesale crossover into the Democratic column on 8 November. A good example of the switch occurred in Bear Lake Township in Barron County. In the primary election it had given 94 votes to La Follette, 18 to Kohler, and 8 to the Democratic candidates; in the general election, 26 votes went to Kohler, 132 to Schmedeman, 16 to Hoover, and 145 to Roosevelt. The election witnessed a resurgence of the Democratic party in the state, but quite clearly progressive votes turned the tide for Roosevelt, Schmedeman, and the rest. The Democrats elected a governor, a United States senator, a lieutenant governor, an attorney general, and a state treasurer and increased their contingent in the state senate from one to eight and in the assembly from two to fifty-nine. As usual, many Democrats had gone into the campaign not expecting to win.

One of them later recalled, "In our county, six of us Democrats were running for coroner. But it was decided that we must have a full ticket to offer the voters so we agreed to pull straws, and the one receiving the short end would have to run for the assembly. I lost, but I was elected."[67]

Afterward, La Follette sounded pleased with the results. Governor Roosevelt thanked him for his assistance and asked him for continued advice and cooperation. "We have won a great victory, in appearance at any rate," Cutting wrote La Follette. "I hope that the Democratic party is capable of taking advantage of the situation but I doubt it very much."[68]

Progressives in Wisconsin were hopeful but skeptical about Roosevelt's desire to push for a truly progressive agenda of reform. They were in an unfamiliar situation, having a reformer friendly to them sitting in the White House. Frustrating as it had been, the succession of conservative Republicans in Washington had made things easy for progressives in one way: they had possessed the luxury of defining their position in basically negative terms, simply reacting to the policies of conservatism. That made it easy to ascertain what they opposed, but they were not so sure about what they were for.

Having a progressive Democrat in the White House was a welcome but threatening change. In the past, the La Follette progressives had frequently had to decide whether to maintain Republican regularity or to go it alone. Temporary accommodations with Democratic candidates, however, had not prepared them for the possibility of a powerful, popular, progressive Democrat who aggressively courted their favor. Now they would have to decide how far they should go to accommodate themselves to a president who advocated many of the reforms they themselves supported but who also disagreed with them on many details of public policy.

As the New Dealers packed their suitcases to head to Washington, Phil La Follette watched with interest from the sidelines, hesitating to commit himself wholeheartedly before Roosevelt provided further signals about the direction he intended to go. La Follette would adopt a wait-and-see attitude and continue to promote his own ideas. Perceiving that the politicians and so-called experts had failed, La Follette felt that he was as well qualified as anybody to understand the economic calamity. After he left office, he continued his search for solutions and for a vehicle that would return him to power.

Chapter 3

A New State Party

For Phil La Follette, defeat could be only a temporary setback; progressives had known adversity before but had always rebounded from it. The new political scenario, in which the White House would occupy center stage for progressives and liberals, provided new opportunities. La Follette, like several other prominent progressives, turned down a chance to mold policy in a high administrative post in Washington, opting instead for the role of independent critic. Hesitation and ambivalence marked his earliest responses to New Deal actions and contributed to his decision in 1934 to help establish a Progressive party in Wisconsin. The La Follettes did not take the lead in the movement, however; former congressman Thomas R. Amlie and other radical farm and labor spokesmen pushed more established leaders toward the decision to break away from the Republicans. The friendly attitude of the national administration played a significant role that fall as not only both La Follettes but also a large part of the entire Progressive ticket were successful in their bids for electoral office. The relationship between the Progressive party and the New Deal played a dominant role in the decisions that Wisconsinites made about political realignment.

One of Roosevelt's first decisions after the election was to name several progressive Republicans to his cabinet, both to reward them for the support they had already given him and to provide incentive for further cooperation. La Follette heard many rumors about the likelihood of his being offered a major post in the new administration, and the speculation was based on fact: on 11 January 1933 Roosevelt told one of his brain trusters, Raymond Moley, that La Follette, Hiram Johnson, and Cutting were his top choices for secretary of the interior. La Follette remained skeptical about all the talk but said that he thought progressives who were in contact with the president-elect should endeavor "to show our cordial disposition to be strongly back of him *if* he takes a progressive line."[1]

Having heard nothing from Roosevelt by the first of the year, La Follette and his wife went ahead with plans for a European vacation and sailed from New York on 5 January. It did not seem worthwhile to postpone the trip to wait for an invitation that might never materialize. When Bob La Follette received word several days later that Roosevelt wished to talk to his brother about a job, Bob considered it poor coordination on the part of Roosevelt's staff to have let Phil slip through their fingers if they really wanted him.[2]

On 19 January at the Mayflower Hotel in Washington, Senator Johnson turned down the Interior position. Later that day Roosevelt met with Bob La Follette and Senator Cutting, to whom he offered the position. The New Mexico senator replied that he would be more likely to accept the offer if a place was available for Phil La Follette in the cabinet. Roosevelt indicated that as a matter of fact he was considering either La Follette or Felix Frankfurter for the attorney generalship. "I want Phil in my official family. I do not know just where yet, but he must come in," he told the two senators. Actually, Roosevelt had already invited Sen. Thomas J. Walsh of Montana to head the Justice Department but expected him to refuse the job.[3]

Roosevelt talked to La Follette and Cutting again three days later at his retreat in Warm Springs, Georgia. He emphasized his commitment to progressive principles and praised Phil La Follette, indicating that the former governor would be offered the job of attorney general if Walsh declined it. He inquired about other positions that might interest Phil if Walsh did decide to take the job, and he reiterated his earlier statement that he needed Phil La Follette's aid during the crisis that the country was in.[4]

By the first week of February, when it appeared that Walsh would in fact take the cabinet post, Senator Cutting continued to insist that Phil La Follette go into the cabinet with him. Roosevelt asked Bob La Follette to find out whether Phil would consider the chairmanship of the Federal Power Commission or an appointment to the Federal Trade Commission. Phil wired back from Budapest that unless Bob, Cutting, and their friends in Madison thought differently, he preferred not to consider either position.[5]

Perhaps Roosevelt would have tried harder to persuade Phil La Follette to join his administration had they been in direct communication during the early weeks of 1933. But Phil and Isen had decided on an extensive European tour when their friend James Causey, a New York investment broker, had offered to help finance it. La Follette's fourth visit to Europe would provide him a respite from politics before he resumed his law practice. He negotiated an agreement to write a series of articles for the Hearst press based on his observations. The rest of the family agreed that being away from Madison while the Democrats took over had certain advantages. Most importantly, the trip would be educational. La Follette eagerly anticipated sounding out politicians, academicians, and other experts about their views on the depression.[6]

As their itinerary carried them to London, Brussels, Berlin, Moscow, Warsaw, Budapest, Vienna, Rome, and Paris, La Follette spent less time sightseeing than he did talking to scores of public officials, businessmen, newsmen, academicians, and other people. Many of them welcomed a chance to meet the governor of an American state; in addition, friends La Follette had made on previous visits and letters of introduction he had obtained from Nicholas Murray Butler, president of Columbia University, provided him with numerous contacts. A conversation with one person often led to other interesting meetings. Among those he talked to were Prime Minister Ramsay MacDonald, Permanent Undersecretary for Foreign Affairs Sir Robert Vansittart, *Economist* editor Walter Layton, and Bank of England official Sir Josiah Stamp in London; former chancellor Heinrich Brüning, Reichsbank President Hans Luther, and "two of Hitler's chief advisers" in Berlin; *New York Times* correspondent Walter Duranty and Russian intellectual Karl Radek in Moscow; Amb. Nicholas Roosevelt in Budapest; Chancellor Englebert Dollfuss in Vienna; and Pope Pius XI in Rome.[7]

What impressed La Follette most was the shadow of war looming over the Continent. He returned home predicting that unless economic conditions improved, war was inevitable. La Follette possessed acute powers of observation and had acquired a wealth of information, but everything was filtered through his own assumptions, and nothing he saw or heard forced him to reformulate any basic ideas. Instead, he discovered further evidence to support his long-held assumptions. For example, Stamp won his approval by giving an explanation of the depression based on a version of Frederick Jackson Turner's frontier thesis. La Follette praised England's system of unemployment insurance; the "dole" made sense to a progressive advocate of redistribution. "Britain is better off today," he contended, "because Britain has deliberately and consciously sustained the purchasing power of her domestic market. She has conscientiously distributed her national income, instead of letting individuals hoard it."[8]

Elsewhere, too, La Follette found evidence to support his beliefs. British politics illustrated how divisiveness among liberals could work to the benefit of conservatives; a huge but apparently inefficient automobile factory in Moscow demonstrated how excessive size could hamper productivity; and a visit to a German power plant provided a "marvelous demonstration" of what a publicly operated utility could do.[9]

He also saw much that looked unfamiliar, especially in Germany and Russia. Although La Follette denied that Americans could learn anything from Russia about organizing society, he left there convinced that the country would play a crucial role in any future war. Its potential military power impressed him, and he predicted, wrongly as it turned out, that "the hour of danger will be when a hungry Russia is led by an angry Germany." Russia's immediate importance, La Follette believed, was as a huge market for American industry and agriculture. He asserted in one of his newspaper articles, "Trade with Russia, China, Central and South America, coupled with a domestic program of public works to aid industry, would answer the American problem of unemployment and agricultural depression."[10]

Turmoil in Germany left the most lasting impression on the La Follettes. They arrived two days after Hitler became chancellor and witnessed chanting throngs, unruly demonstrations, and huge rallies of Nazis and Socialists. La Follette had a term for the Nazis: *futilitarians*. Their methods of suppressing political opposition troubled him. Polarization and political extremism seemed to have emerged directly from the economic miseries and misguided policies visited upon Germany by the victorious Allies. One scene especially ran through his mind—the thousands of miserable huts on the outskirts of Berlin where people had gone to resume a sort of primitive subsistence existence, scratching a living from the land. Meanwhile, in the city To Rent signs hung in the windows of many apartments that people could not afford to occupy.[11]

Hitler obviously distressed La Follette; Mussolini, on the other hand, held some fascination for him. Later on, some people raised their eyebrows when they saw the dictator's portrait on La Follette's wall along with the dozens of other autographed pictures that he had collected. The former governor professed no sympathy for fascism, but he had written a friend that he would go to Italy with an open mind. He thought that "some of the specific things, as corporate development, that we have been proposing here in Wisconsin, as specific projects (as distinguished from Fascist *method* of control) have much in common with the Italien [*sic*] projects. We did not playgerize [*sic*] from the Fascists, but worked out the same plan from experience. They have, of course, been able to put into practice projects that we have only begun, and deal with a wider economic unit. But, as you suggest, this is a field for almost unlimited study."[12]

La Follette obtained an appointment with Mussolini, which later was unexplainedly canceled. By that time it was early March, and as La Follette strolled through the Roman Forum contemplating the past, events in the United States were accelerating as inauguration day approached. Bob La Follette was experiencing difficulty in relaying messages to him, and now the question of a cabinet position resurfaced. Senator Walsh died on 2 March, two days before the inauguration, and Bob thought that Roosevelt might again seriously consider making Phil his attorney general. On 6 March he wired Phil in Paris, suggesting that he return immediately to discuss the situation with the president, so Phil and Isen canceled their stops in Denmark and Ireland and sailed home a week earlier than planned, arriving in New York on 16 March.[13]

Few American politicians could boast of the extensive knowledge and experience that La Follette had acquired in Europe on this and previous journeys. He continued to correspond with several of the people he had met there, and he watched developments on the Continent with considerable interest. Despite his eager curiosity, genuine interest in events, and apparent cosmopolitan attitude, however, La Follette perceived no need to alter any fundamental assumptions, and, if asked, would have declared that his father's brand of isolationism remained relevant despite changing world conditions. As for most Americans and their elected officials, his central concern in 1933 was the state of the American economy, not foreign affairs.

La Follette's first action after arriving home was to clarify his situation with President Roosevelt. He and Bob visited with the president in the White House for about an hour on 21 March. Roosevelt listened to Phil describe some of his impressions of Europe and then got down to business. Saying that he was anxious to have the former governor in his administration, he wanted to know what jobs seemed appealing, suggesting as possibilities the Federal Power Commission, the Federal Trade Commission, or something in transportation or relief administration. La Follette replied that he would take no position at that time because he had deep roots in Wisconsin and believed he would be of greater service at home "on the firing line." Modestly, he suggested that there were plenty of other men who could perform the jobs better than he. He suggested that while the president seemed to have many friends at the moment, if he fought for a progressive program, as La Follette believed he would, the contest would become very bitter—it would be like a war. At that time, if no one was available to perform a particular task as well as he could, La Follette said he would gladly consider it. Roosevelt urged him to speak up if he wanted anything. "I am going to count on your keeping in close touch with me," he said. "Come and see me often." "All you have to do is let me know and if I have the railroad fare I will come," La Follette replied.[14]

In June, Roosevelt informed Bob La Follette that he was considering Phil for a place on a three-person advisory board that would report directly to himself under the provisions of the proposed industrial recovery act. For the moment Phil La Follette would watch and wait. Like many other progressive Republicans, he found the role of outsider more natural and comfortable than that of insider. Joining the administration would have closed off most of his political options. Like Harold L. Ickes in the Interior Department and Henry A. Wallace in the Agriculture Department, he would have become an administrator and apologist for Democratic actions. "There is real danger that by going into his cabinet we would become prisoners of his future," Phil had told Bob. The continued development of an independent progressive movement would be jeopardized, and the political futures of La Follette and his colleagues in Wisconsin would be endangered. La Follette wanted to maintain his options, to retain the right to be critical, and to wait to see just how progressive Roosevelt would be before committing himself. By avoiding one alternative, he would keep others open.[15]

During 1933 Phil La Follette rebuilt his law practice, delivered some speeches both inside and outside Wisconsin, maintained contacts with other progressive politicians, and followed political and economic developments. "The luckiest thing that ever happened to you came last September," his law partner Glenn D. Roberts told him. Some progressives believed that two years of Democratic rule in the state would drive people back into their arms. Their task was twofold: ideologically they needed a sound program that would appeal to the populace; politically they had to find an electoral vehicle capable of carrying them back into office.[16]

"I see," La Follette wrote in July, "only three alternatives for us here in Wis.: the old Republican route, going into the Democratic party, or a third party." The wretched political prospects of the Republicans and the Democrats' long record of conservatism rendered the first two options distinctly less desirable than the third one, which also entailed serious liabilities. "It would be a gamble to go into a new party," La Follette admitted. What strongly recommended it, however, was that they would not have to worry about fighting stalwarts for the nomination any more. By establishing a new party, their crucial test would come in the general election, into which they could funnel all of their resources.[17]

La Follette remained hopeful that the New Deal would follow progressive policies, but he was not ready to give it his unconditional backing. In the United States Senate Bob La Follette criticized Roosevelt's banking plan and budget cuts, which he feared would launch an "engine of deflation." Phil La Follette joined a chorus of protests against crop restrictions imposed by the Agricultural Adjustment Administration. Such a philosophy of limiting production, he warned, would necessitate elaborate and stifling government controls.[18]

Even the National Recovery Administration (NRA), which embodied two of the La Follettes' favorite ideas—economic planning and public works—aroused their dissent. An initial interest in the concept soon gave way to disenchantment. By September 1933 Phil La Follette was expressing "very grave doubts" about the NRA. In July, August, and September, the *Progressive* carried several articles critical of it. Bob La Follette was especially concerned about the slow pace of expenditures on works projects under the direction of Harold Ickes.[19]

The progressives remained ambivalent toward the New Deal. On the one hand, they liked to claim, as the *Progressive* did in one editorial, that "the national administration has taken its policies and principles for its recovery program direct from the platforms of Progressives in Wisconsin." On the other hand, they criticized numerous aspects of administration policy and were disappointed in its failure to pass further legislation. They especially wanted to see more done to expand mass purchasing power. Their relationship with the New Deal remained tentative—hopeful but critical, supportive but doubtful. As Bob La Follette put it, they would not be "blind followers" of President Roosevelt but rather would scrutinize each program on its own merits.[20]

The rapid-fire activity of the first hundred days of the New Deal was as bewildering to the progressives as it was to other people, and they were not always sure what to make of things. Isen La Follette attempted an analysis in her weekly column in the *Progressive:* "All of us who listen to radio and read the papers know that something has been going on down there that is new." Her general impression was that the New Deal constituted a "program of opportunism" rather than a "definite economic program." Yet, considering the situation, it might have seemed the only possible course for President Roosevelt to follow. Whatever its merits, she concluded, it certainly provided exciting drama.[21]

Three months into the new administration, Wisconsin's progressive Republicans were more uncertain than ever about their future course. Roosevelt was wooing them, and legislation establishing relief, public works, agricultural subsidies, industrial cooperation, mortgage relief, and public power responded to demands they had been making. Yet tradition and experience seemed to argue against amalgamation with the Democrats. The idea of a national third party seemed more congenial to most progressives, who had counterparts in states all around the country.

A decade had passed since Robert M. La Follette, Sr., had made an independent run for the presidency, and memories of that venture furnished the progressives with both an inspiration and a warning. It kindled the hopes of people who looked forward to a new party, but other advocates of political realignment drew from the 1924 experience the lesson that third-party efforts were destined to futility unless they were preceded by protracted, painstaking organizational efforts at the grass roots. A movement imposed "from the top" would go nowhere, they believed.

In an effort to coordinate the various groups that were considering a new party, a group of intellectuals, social-gospel ministers, followers of John Dewey, and moderate Socialists created the League for Independent Political Action (LIPA) in September 1929. Not intended to be a third party itself, its purpose was to provide encouragement, publicity, and coordination for state and local organizations. Paul Douglas, a vice-chairman, and Robert Morss Lovett, a member of the executive committee, were faculty members at the University of Chicago, but most of the leaders were easterners. The organization's eastern, middle-class, intellectualistic orientation contrasted sharply with the kinds of people it aimed to lead.[22]

From the outset the LIPA suffered the effects of political inexperience and inadequate finances. Its leaders could afford to devote little time to it and relied heavily on the energies of the executive secretary, Howard Y.

Williams of Minneapolis, a former minister. The principles they espoused appealed to many progressives, but many particular items provoked disagreement. The most important obstacle to the organization's growth was the reluctance of progressive officeholders to align with it. Many progressives were vaguely committed to the creation of a new party, but when election time rolled around, they shied away from efforts that might damage their reelection chances.

The LIPA received a shot in the arm in April 1933 when the youthful editors of *Common Sense* magazine, Alfred Bingham and Selden Rodman, assumed a larger role in the league's activities. Bingham, the twenty-eight-year-old son of an Old Guard Republican senator from Connecticut, was in charge of the political end of the magazine. Rodman, the managing editor, only twenty-three and like Bingham a recent Yale graduate, concentrated primarily on cultural and literary matters. Established in December 1932, *Common Sense* now became the unofficial organ of the league and provided a forum for the kind of "new American radicalism" that Bingham and Rodman hoped would capture the country's imagination.[23]

Phil La Follette turned down an invitation from Williams to sign a call for a two-day conference of third-party activists in Chicago in early September 1933, replying that he was interested in the idea but that most people still wanted "to give Roosevelt a chance." The president had made some questionable moves, La Follette observed, but after four years of Hoover people were "impressed with the fact that he is *acting.*" A conference might become appropriate later if the administration appeared to be in a rut, so he asked Williams to keep in touch with him, and in July the two did confer in Madison.[24]

La Follette also failed to follow through on Bingham's request for an article on a national farmer–labor party from the Wisconsin perspective, but he did allow himself to be listed as a contributing editor of the magazine. Bingham stopped in Madison to see him and urged him to identify with their cause, suggesting that the former governor was "probably the most logical person to take leadership in such a movement."[25]

La Follette's hesitancy dismayed the idealistic editors, and they relied on former congressman Amlie to lead the third-party effort in Wisconsin. By early 1933 the Elkhorn lawyer had become thoroughly radicalized, having concluded that capitalism was obsolete. Losing his seat in 1932 after serving a single term in Congress, he first unsuccessfully sought a job in the Roosevelt administration and for a while urged people to cooperate with the president, who he thought was "a progressive at heart."[26]

It was not long, however, before he was telling people that liberalism had failed. In his view the New Deal and the progressives would have to make way for a truly radical brand of politics and eventually the complete socialization of industry. He hoped that the La Follettes and other progressive leaders would see the light, but he doubted that they would, since "those gentlemen feel that they have a vested interest in the present setup, and besides they do not have a very clear conception of what is really happening to the capitalistic system."[27]

In September 1933 at the LIPA's Chicago conference, Amlie electrified the gathering with a rousing speech on the failure of the economic system, and when the organization was reconstituted as the Farmer Labor Political Federation (FLPF), he became its chairman while Bingham, as executive secretary, was left to administer its day-to-day operations.[28]

Amlie called himself a disciple of Thorstein Veblen and assimilated many insights of Marxian economics without becoming a thoroughgoing Marxist. His congressional experience, however, had made him a prudent and practical politician as well as an ideologue. More than anyone else in Wisconsin he combined the idealism and the pragmatism that constantly tugged the progressives in different directions. He provided a link between the FLPF radicals and the progressive leadership, since only he was prominently placed in both groups.[29]

Amlie had a green light from the FLPF to organize third-party activity in Wisconsin. Support came from Williams, operating out of an office in St. Paul. Citing "caution born of long experience," Amlie avoided needlessly antagonizing progressive leaders whose support he would need to have. Suppressing his radical inclinations, he proceeded cautiously, waiting until some of the progressive leaders were convinced of the necessity for a new party. Skimpy financial resources also hampered his efforts. The FLPF office had few funds at its disposal, and Amlie had to spend more time than he would have liked in tending to his law practice in order to support his family.[30]

Converts were few in the beginning. La Follette was one of the few progressive leaders who was warmly receptive to his message. Amlie believed that the La Follettes would back a third party once it was shown that widespread support for it existed and that the rest of the progressives would go along with the La Follettes. Thus, he avoided any appearance of challenging the brothers' predominance. In a long discussion with La

Follette in September, Amlie stated his hope that the former governor would assume direction of the third-party movement but indicated that whatever happened he intended to continue his own work with the farm and labor groups and the Socialists. La Follette expressed interest but hesitated to push ahead too fast; he also noted the serious legal obstacles that stood in the way of getting on the ballot. La Follette preceded most progressives in concluding that a separate party was desirable, but he wanted a clearer feel for public opinion before committing himself on the question. He accompanied Amlie to several meetings that fall but remained on the sidelines, letting the former congressman carry the ball.[31]

Amlie often wearied of trying to convert people to his cause. Reasonable arguments often seemed less effective than appeals to people's prejudices and emotions. Amlie noticed how effectively the Nazis, disagreeable as they were, utilized the approach of negative emotionalism. Something might be learned from the fascists, he wrote Rodman: "First, because these methods are highly efficacious; and secondly, if we are realistic, we will not let those methods lie around unused, for sure as shooting the capitalists will organize and finance a fascist movement that will immediately pick up all of those weapons and use them to our great sorrow." Amlie failed to carry through on these ideas, however, and had the good sense not to discuss them publicly.[32]

Wisconsin and Minnesota were the most likely starting points for a national third party, in the eyes of its leading advocates. Amlie enthusiastically applauded the adoption by the Minnesota Farmer-Labor party of a thoroughly left-wing platform at their convention in April 1934. He expressed his hope to Gov. Floyd Olson that Wisconsin would soon follow Minnesota's example. While Bingham and Rodman waited expectantly for results from Wisconsin, Amlie continued to reassure them that La Follette was "absolutely all right" and that he would be able to control the situation. The former governor's attitude might have gratified Amlie, but whether he would be able to carry other progressives along with him depended largely on how willing they were to be led. Many progressive Republican officeholders and leaders were plainly apprehensive about venturing outside the party that had served them quite well in the past. The potential dangers of a third-party movement, not its undesirability, were the main reasons for their hesitancy.[33]

Even before entering the governor's office, La Follette had taken a great interest in the notion of political realignment. After the 1928 election he had urged his brother to consider the idea of starting a new party before the next campaign. The progressives might lose, he had written, but "it would tend to solidify our forces and stop the 'boring from within' that is always going on when the fight is factional within one party. It is just a question of whether the time is approaching for this step or not." Apparently they decided the time was not ripe, but again in 1931 Phil La Follette's interest in a third party picked up. Evjue was preaching the need for one, Sen. Burton K. Wheeler, a liberal Democrat from Montana, was predicting one, and John Dewey of the LIPA was seeking a leader for his third-party movement. To his family La Follette confided his lack of enthusiasm for running for reelection on the Republican ticket and indicated that he had been thinking about trying to persuade nearby states to join Wisconsin in establishing a new party. His mother discouraged the project, however, fearing that it would jeopardize everything they had already accomplished. In discussing the matter, though, she admitted that she could not say what her husband's opinion would have been under such circumstances.[34]

The same conditions of economic malaise that fed public discontent and urged radicals toward a new national party also established the conditions for the emergence of Roosevelt's New Deal. The very success of the national Democratic administration in responding to demands for major reforms undercut the appeal of the radicals. In 1932, Roosevelt's reputation as a liberal reformer had reduced the Socialist vote and discouraged efforts for launching another national party. Then during "the Hundred Days" and after, many people thought it desirable to "give the president a chance." As long as he retained his appeal for reformers and other left-wingers, the chances of establishing a viable radical party were minimal. Clearly, at the national level third-party hopes depended on the political fortunes of the New Deal. At the state level, on the other hand, in those places where Rooseveltian liberalism failed to penetrate the local Democratic hierarchy other options were available.

The problem of how to react to the New Deal, therefore, related directly to progressive thinking about a third party. During early 1933 La Follette counseled a wait-and-see attitude. He did not actively encourage Wisconsinites to take jobs in Washington but was pleased to see former Sen. John J. Blaine appointed to the board of directors of the Reconstruction Finance Corporation and David E. Lilienthal of the Wisconsin Public Service Commission named as a director of the Tennessee Valley Authority. Further evidence of Roosevelt's solicitude for the progressives came in his appointment of State Sen. Harold Groves as a tax consultant to the Treasury Department, but pleasure turned to dismay when the appointment was later withdrawn. Progressives scrutinized such actions for signs that would indicate what direction the national administration was heading.[35]

Playing the role of private citizen left La Follette feeling somewhat out of place while his brother participated as a major actor in the drama unfolding in the nation's capital. He would have preferred to be in the center of action himself, but under the circumstances his opportunities to act were limited. He told Bob that while he did not want to appear to be an "officious intermeddler," he had developed a proposal for expanding public-works expenditures and for reviving exports that he wanted the president to study. He worried that Roosevelt was not receiving enough "leftish" advice. On a trip to Washington in May, La Follette phoned presidential assistant Marvin McIntyre, who failed to return the call. The next month, when Phil returned to the East Coast, Bob relayed to him the message that the president "wants to see you a little later but it is not necessary for you to come on this trip."[36]

From the vantage point of Madison, it was difficult to assess the situation. "I think things are improving," La Follette observed in June. A month later he was pessimistic, as he reported, "The 'new deal' has not arrived here." As fall arrived he feared that, unless drastic remedies were applied, the country was headed for "some sort of reaction."[37]

His concern also showed in his speeches. Addressing a Kiwanis meeting in Waukesha in September, La Follette warned that constitutional government was in danger. People still seemed to believe in "witch doctors," he noted cryptically, observing that government continued to "pick at the scab" rather than attack the source of the malady. Plowing under crops would solve nothing, nor would paying people to remain idle on relief. Put people to work, let them earn money, stimulate consumption—that would restore people's self-respect and the national income as well. La Follette stopped short of naming offenders, but he clearly implied that the New Deal was concentrating on the wrong things.[38]

In November, La Follette outlined a five-point recovery plan that differed somewhat in details from those he had previously proposed. Everything in it was designed to restore mass purchasing power: distributing the "so-called surplus" of food to the needy and exporting it to Russia, China, and South America; spending over a billion dollars to modernize railroads and replace other industrial equipment; offering public-works jobs to all who needed them; restoring to depositors losses sustained in bank failures; and providing old-age pensions. The billions of dollars such a plan would cost would be obtained, La Follette said, from the "people who've got it."[39]

Along with many other progressives, La Follette grew increasingly skeptical about the New Deal and increasingly sympathetic to the radical viewpoint. Yet he would not go along with Amlie's call to scrap capitalism. Ambivalence and indecision characterized his thinking and that of many other progressives. The uncertainty was reflected in a statement of principles emanating from a conference of progressives that La Follette invited to meet in Chicago on 3 December 1933. This small gathering agreed that Roosevelt was moving in the right direction but also declared that his leadership left much to be desired.[40]

Late in the year President Roosevelt sought to placate farm-state radicals with his gold-buying and dairy-support programs and various other activities, but La Follette awaited further signals. In December he vocalized his misgivings to Treasury Secretary Henry Morgenthau, indicating that Roosevelt could get the progressives behind him "*if* he would definitely, and promptly make his choice." In January the La Follettes were further disturbed to learn that the president was planning to phase out the popular but short-lived Civil Works Administration, which had employed large numbers of the jobless. Phil La Follette's major criticisms of the New Deal centered on his concern that federal spending had not gone far enough and that misguided efforts were being made to limit production.[41]

Misgivings about the New Deal augmented La Follette's receptivity to third-party talk, but his primary concern remained the health of the progressives in Wisconsin. By early 1934 the prospects for a new state party improved daily. The New Deal was attracting increasing criticism. Despite some improvement in business conditions, the depression continued. After the events of 1932, winning nominations in the Republican primary appeared problematical, and teaming up with the Democrats would have required fundamental shifts in attitudes. Amlie's spadework was paying dividends among farm and labor groups. La Follette quietly encouraged those who were working for a new party while simultaneously urging them to consider realistically the dangers in such a departure. Although he did not want to harm his brother's chances for reelection, he let Bob know that he thought the time was ripe for such a move.[42]

In retrospect it is obvious that the decision to poll progressive sentiment on the third-party question by holding a statewide conference constituted the real turning point on the path to establishing the Progressive party. La Follette had sounded out many progressives on the question, and it was becoming increasingly evident that if he and Bob failed to act, others would proceed without them. The Wisconsin Federation of Labor and several farm organizations, including the Wisconsin Milk Pool, were on record in favor of a third party. Some progressive leaders, such as Evjue and Groves, were openly advocating the idea. Opposition to the move was rallying behind Secretary of State Theodore Dammann, who had been the only progressive state officeholder to survive the Democratic tide in 1932. At a meeting in Milwaukee he criticized Amlie for sowing confusion and for defying the established leadership. His discussion with twenty-one progressive assemblymen revealed that only a couple of them considered it prudent to venture outside the party that had facilitated their success for more than thirty years. The legislators forecast defeat for themselves and their colleagues if they were forced to run as third-party candidates.[43]

The progressive leadership decided that only a conference with every county represented would resolve the confusion. During the last week of February, invitations went out to county and local leaders around the state to attend a conference in Madison on 3 March. Signing the call were Bob La Follette, State Sen. V. S. Keppel, Assemblyman Robert A. Nixon, veteran wheelhorse Herman L. Ekern, and Secretary of State Dammann, who cooperated in arranging the conference despite his opposition to a third party. Although his name headed the list of signers, Bob La Follette possessed scant enthusiasm for a new party. Worried about his reelection chances and unenthusiastic about leaps into the unknown, he preferred to continue along familiar paths.[44]

Word that the Wisconsin progressives were planning something stimulated interest among New Dealers. On 25 February, Phil La Follette informed Secretary of the Interior Ickes, who had been advocating progressivism in Chicago for decades, that Roosevelt had not worked hard enough to hold progressive Republicans in line and complained that Democratic patronage policies had been harmful to the progressives as well as to Roosevelt's own best interests. He implied that these dissatisfactions were feeding third-party sentiments in Wisconsin. The following day Bob La Follette met with the president himself, who tried to explain the difficulty of his position. He wanted to help, he explained, but the

Wisconsin Democratic organization was pressuring him to maintain party regularity. His notion that Governor Schmedeman, if reelected, could pledge a progressive administration drew La Follette's response that the governor was linked to the most conservative elements in the state. Although Roosevelt indicated that he could more easily aid his friend's reelection campaign if La Follette ran on a third-party ticket, the senator drew little satisfaction from the meeting, inferring that, while the president genuinely desired to help him, he also wished to avoid stirring up the Democrats. "To sum it up, my view is that we can pretty well count on Roosevelt's not doing anything in Wisconsin which will be at all effective so far as we are concerned," he concluded.[45]

The senator journeyed to Wisconsin as undecided as ever about what position to take. "I am in just as much of a quandary as before I left," he wrote his wife. "Perhaps it will help in making a decision to see and talk with people from over the state. I hope so!" On the evening before the conference he and Phil met with about thirty top progressive leaders at the Maple Bluff farm. Only about a quarter of the group seemed favorable to the idea of a new party, and after the meeting Fola La Follette received the impression that her brothers doubted whether there would be enough enthusiasm to put a new party over the next day. However, only a few of the people who would be attending the conference had expressed their opinions up to that time.[46]

Only later did it become fashionable to say that branching out in a new party was inevitable. There were certainly incentives for making the break, but the drawbacks were equally substantial. Hardly anybody seriously considered the possibility of going over to the Democrats. That party continued to be dominated by conservative, anti-Roosevelt leaders; in addition, the long-term prospects of winning on the Democratic ticket appeared bleak. The only realistic alternatives in 1934 were to remain within the Republican fold or to form a new party. The relationship with the stalwart Republicans was one of continual strife, but the two factions had coexisted within the same party for more than a generation. Although the outflow of Democratic votes would render it more difficult to capture nominations in primary elections, many if not most of the progressives believed they stood a better chance of success by remaining within the Republican party.[47]

But doubts were brushed aside at the Park Hotel gathering on 3 March as the delegates enthusiastically voted for the establishment of a new state party. Bob La Follette opened the meeting by telling the delegates that the decision was in their hands. He stressed the urgent need for political realignment but observed that it did not necessarily have to come in the form of a new party. Evjue, who chaired the conference, let representatives from every county state their positions on the question. The roll call showed thirty delegations in favor of a new party, fourteen in opposition, and seventeen undecided. The enthusiasm and excitement generated by the third-party proponents outweighed the glum warnings of skeptics such as Dammann, who argued that voters would be more likely to cast ballots for progressive candidates who campaigned within the familiar confines of the Republican party. Spokesmen for the farm and labor organizations were conspicuous and vociferous in urging a radical departure. Henry Ohl, president of the State Federation of Labor, pointed out that organized labor in Milwaukee had been on record for months on the issue. The Farmers' Holiday Association and the Cooperative Milk Pool also spiritedly supported a new party. Speaking for the radicals, Amlie declared, "I don't believe that the Roosevelt progressive program of Wisconsin Progressives is adequate to meet the economic problems of the day." Evjue, who had been a member of the progressive inner circle for almost two decades, retorted that progressive principles remained as relevant as ever and rejected Amlie's censure of the New Deal, but he heartily agreed on the need for a new state party.

Phil La Follette stepped forward only to stress the importance of progressive unity and to mention the problems that might emerge in trying to get a position on the ballot on such short notice. Since the law was vague, the delegates voted to adjourn after directing a special temporary committee to initiate an action before the state supreme court to determine exactly how many signatures they would need in order to run candidates that fall.[48]

Although final action had been temporarily deferred, it was obvious that, barring unforeseen legal difficulties, the new party would become a reality. "It was a howling success from our own point of view," Amlie happily reported. "And under the leadership of Phil La Follette I am certain that it will be a left-wing movement." La Follette had favored a third party from the start, he said. *Common Sense* editor Bingham was delighted at the turn of events and talked about holding another conference that spring. Now he thought that "the La Follettes seem ready to take leadership nationally."[49]

His growing doubts about the direction of the New Deal reinforced Phil La Follette's conviction that the progressives were making the right decision. "Out here it looks none too good," he wrote a friend in the East. People were growing more discouraged each day. "Unless material change for the better comes before long," he predicted, "they will sour on the 'New Deal' thoroughly." When Leo Crowley telephoned La Follette later that month to suggest that Bob run for reelection on the Democratic ticket and indicated that Roosevelt would probably cooperate with the plan, Phil stated his lack of enthusiasm for the idea but did pass the message along to his brother.[50]

Phil La Follette took charge of the progressive lawsuit to determine the potential legal status of a new party. The state supreme court, acting quickly, ruled on 1 May that a political party could get on the ballot by merely obtaining in at least ten counties a number of signatures equal to one-sixth of the total presidential vote during the previous election. The progressive temporary committee convened in La Follette's law office three days later and signed a call for a conference to meet in Fond du Lac on 19 May. La Follette then grabbed a train to Washington to discuss the situation with Bob and the other progressive congressmen.[51]

As reports filtered in from county meetings, Phil was gratified to learn that the delegates selected to attend the Fond du Lac convention consisted almost entirely of trusted veterans in the county organizations rather than novices or radicals who would be more committed to their own pet schemes than to the progressive movement. Hubert Peavey, a six-term congressman from Washburn, was one of the few progressives who announced that he would stay in the Republican party. "Blaine men" generally opposed the move, and before his death Blaine himself had reportedly indicated his disapproval of the switch. A more common sentiment among many of the older progressives was voiced by former congressman and longtime associate of Old Bob La Follette, Joseph D. Beck, when he confided to his wife, "I do not know what to think of the new party. Guess we'll have to go along with it though."[52]

The news from Wisconsin attracted national interest. "All week I have been bothering everyone about Bob La Follette," Rexford G. Tugwell recorded in his diary.

> Jim Farley hadn't done anything up to yesterday and I tackled him at the Cabinet meeting. What Bob is to do in this fall's election is being settled out in Wisconsin today and I wanted him to come out for him. He belongs in our camp and I don't want a bunch of conservative Democrats in Wisconsin to run away with the administration's prestige. What will come of it, I don't know, but Farley is incorrigibly regular and will probably make the obvious

mistake; though I must say Cummings and Swanson spoke up immediately for Bob and Farley seemed impressed.

While attention outside the state focused on the implications that the progressive move would have on national politics, the progressives themselves were primarily interested in the state movement. Tugwell and Farley could rivet their attention on the meaning of the move for the New Deal or the impact on national third-party hopes; the progressives, for the moment at least, were worried mainly about their own election chances that fall.[53]

Evjue again wielded the gavel when more than one thousand delegates gathered in Fond du Lac on 19 May 1934 to chart the future of the progressive movement. They faced three questions: whether to create a new political party, what to name it, and how to organize it. Debate on the first question, whose outcome was a foregone conclusion, was limited to one hour. For one last time Dammann argued that progressive success depended on holding fast to traditional party ties, but he admitted that his was a lonely voice. "I know that in the steam-roller convention the question before the house will be steam-rollered and a uniform decision made," he complained. Walter Graunke, a plainspoken, loquacious delegate from Marathon County, jumped up to respond, "There is only one thing that is going to steam-roll—it is not going to steam-roll, it is going to stampede—this convention, public opinion only." The advocates of change appealed primarily to principles and ideals, but they also argued that practical necessity dictated the move if progressives were to have a chance to win elections. Only four other delegates, three of them from Milwaukee, joined Dammann in questioning the wisdom of the move. Chairman Evjue then turned the floor over to speakers who wanted to argue in favor of the proposition. The vote for a new party was 252 to 44.

The real fireworks at the conference occurred during the debate over what to name the new party. Conflict on this question reflected divisions that already existed between the militant left-wingers, who had pushed hardest for a new party, and more traditional progressives. Congressman George Schneider, Jack Handley of the State Federation of Labor, Samuel Sigman, Amlie, and Graunke supported the name *Farmer-Labor*. The labor contingent wanted the new party to be more than simply a continuation of the old progressive movement, Handley warned. But Walter D. Corrigan, one of the longest-serving veterans in the movement, urged the convention not to abandon the name that had rewarded them with success for so long. *Progressive* was a well-established trademark around the country. To abandon it for a title rooted in class divisions would violate American ideals and traditions, Corrigan argued. La Follette, who served as tally clerk for the convention, echoed that point, stating that progressives had always worked for common, not class, objectives and that their traditional name would be most effective in carrying their message to other states. "We are hopeful that we may have here today laid down a cornerstone for a real political realignment in American public life," he said. The debate revealed how important a symbol a name can be, and the overwhelming vote in favor of retaining the familiar *progressive* label reflected the continuing strength of traditionalism within the movement.

The question of a provisional organization was quickly disposed of when the temporary committee in charge of the court action was reconstituted as a temporary state central committee with Phil La Follette as chairman. Thus, the La Follettes and other familiar faces would control the party's activities during its crucial formative stages.

The radicals had hoped to discuss principles and platforms, but Chairman Evjue ruled a motion to do so out of order, indicating that it would be necessary to hold a platform convention later. Nor were the radicals encouraged by Bob La Follette's closing speech, which extolled the progressive tradition of following a middle way and avoiding all extremes. His father's principles remained as relevant as ever, he contended, but such vague pronouncements did not satisfy the left-wingers.[54]

Mending the fissure in the party required skillful diplomacy on the part of Phil La Follette. To keep all factions at least partially satisfied demanded sensitivity, tact, and carefully calculated appeasing gestures. La Follette had originally believed that the Fond du Lac convention should adopt a statement of principles that could serve as a basis for the Progressive party's platform, but his realization that opening debate on such a document could lead to conflict and disappointment induced him to reconsider the idea. The decision to postpone the platform discussion disappointed left-wingers such as Amlie, who observed, "I am perfectly satisfied with the name if we could only have an adequate statement of principles." He anticipated a struggle with "middle-of-the-road" Progressives to determine "whether the Old Guard within the Progressive movement is to remain in control." Nevertheless, he appreciated the reasoning behind La Follette's desire to avoid such a confrontation at

Fond du Lac, for had the radicals taken charge there, the "elder states-
men" would simply have walked out. Amlie's sentiments fluctuated
between idealism and political realism. Although he sometimes
complained about La Follette's dilatory tactics, he recognized the
wisdom of trying to accommodate the various factions within the
party and advised his colleagues to stifle their grievances for the time
being. No good would result from antagonizing loyal La Follette
supporters who had faithfully served the cause for the reward of a
handshake, a word of thanks, or their own satisfaction.[55]

Considerable resentment existed among organized labor and farm
groups, whose desire for a truly radical party had been betrayed for
"some more old-time La Follette progressivism." Ohl and Handley of
the State Federation of Labor were disgusted with the events at Fond
du Lac. Farmers' Holiday Association leader Walter Singler warned
that farmers would not leave their plows to vote Progressive unless it
became a genuinely radical party. Many critics were convinced that
the La Follettes would block anything that smacked of radicalism.[56]

The left-wingers went beyond criticism and proceeded near the end of
May 1934 to form the Farmer Labor Progressive League (FLPL), which
they modeled on the Minnesota Farmer-Labor Association and designed
as a permanent dues-paying organization, which would write platforms,
endorse candidates, and impose party discipline on elected officials. Sam
Sigman, a lawyer who had been active in the Outagamie County Farmer
Labor Progressive League, former congressman George Schneider of
Appleton, who had previously served as vice-president of the International
Brotherhood of Papermakers, and former state senator Anton Miller
were key members in the small group that organized the initial meeting in
Appleton on 27 May. They enlisted the aid of the Wisconsin State Federation of Labor, the Farmers' Union, the Wisconsin Cooperative Milk Pool,
and the Farmers' Holiday Association and set about writing a statement
of principles. "We have had enough of political organizations controlled
by party bosses and fearful lest the rank and file may have some influence
in the political strategy, purposes or slate of candidates," Sigman grumbled. But insisting on an acceptable platform was easier than writing one.
The process quickly bogged down and threatened to split the few who
were working on it. Moreover, it could be contradictory to demand that
the platform be both radical and responsive to the wishes of the rank and
file; the two objectives were not necessarily harmonious.[57]

La Follette declined immediate comment on the new organization. He also desired a radical program, he asserted, but one couched in careful terms. He conferred with FLPL leaders and agreed to address their statewide conference to be held in Fond du Lac on 30 June, hoping he could appease the radicals without conceding too much. Meanwhile, John C. Schmidtman, a longtime La Follette follower, took charge of the new Progressive headquarters housed in the La Follette law offices at 115 West Main Street in Madison. By the end of June more than one hundred twenty thousand signatures, far more than were necessary, had been collected on the circulating petitions.[58]

At Fond du Lac on 30 June, La Follette argued against the endorsement of candidates. He stated his firm commitment to the open primary and his opposition to nominations controlled by a group of radicals. He further disappointed the FLPL by insisting on letting the statutory state convention draft the party's platform. In effect, this meant that a small group of leaders, composed largely of familiar faces, would continue to control things. La Follette had good reasons for opposing the upstart organization on these points: he did not want to see his own influence diminished, he realized that moderate Progressives would resist a radical takeover of the party, and he personally disagreed with many radical ideas. Moreover, imposing party discipline to enforce convention decisions smacked too much of the kind of manipulation that had served as the target in his father's campaign for the direct primary around the turn of the century.

The FLPL, which represented only a small minority within the party, needed La Follette more than he needed it. He sought to establish cordial relations with its members but resisted their bid to assume the power to endorse candidates and write platforms. Sigman swallowed his disappointment and thanked La Follette for cooperating with his group. He and his fellow FLPL organizers were embarrassed by their inability to agree on an acceptable platform by the time the conference met. The delegates adopted instead a rather innocuous declaration of principles, which despite having been written largely by Amlie, Sigman, and Prof. Harry Dexter White was quite acceptable to moderate Progressives.[59]

La Follette responded to inquiries about the FLPL by saying that it would be a great asset to the party, but he quietly worked to discourage membership in it. Its sluggish growth pleased him, since its presence, in his opinion, could only complicate his work. By the time of the primary election its total membership receipts, derived mostly from candidates who were running for office, amounted to only about seventy-five dollars.

The following year, 1935, it was absorbed by the new Wisconsin Farmer-Labor Progressive Federation (not to be confused with the Farmer Labor *Political* Federation, created in 1933).[60]

With the approach of the primary election, the question of a gubernatorial candidate became increasingly insistent. La Follette seemed to be the logical choice, but many Progressives questioned the advisability of having two La Follettes on the same ticket. Bob La Follette also was inclined to believe that someone else should be given a chance to run. During a series of discussions at Maple Bluff Farm, though, most of the Progressive leaders agreed that Phil would make the strongest candidate and lend the greatest support to the rest of the ticket. But the former governor wanted to do nothing to endanger Bob's reelection bid and also knew the difficulty a new party would face in its first electoral try. He told Isen that he really was not anxious to run, and he offered to back Amlie if he decided to enter the race. Despite his denials, however, La Follette probably wanted to be the candidate, and when neither Amlie nor anyone else stepped forward, he announced his candidacy on the last day for filing.[61]

This was a new kind of campaign for the Progressives. In the past the decisive contest had been with the stalwarts during the primary, but this time the primaries would constitute a perfunctory warm-up for a three-way battle with the major parties in the general election. Because of this, crowds during the primary campaign generally were small, and apathy seemed to reign.[62]

The future of the Progressive party, it became immediately obvious, depended greatly on its relationship with the New Deal. Whether the party would be able to assume a position of national importance, the *Progressive* editorialized, depended largely on one man—Roosevelt. If he adhered to a progressive course, a national third-party movement might be deferred; but if he caved in to conservatism, it would push rapidly forward. The Progressive party had emerged largely because Wisconsin's Democrats had nothing to offer liberals, the paper asserted. Thus, the Progressives confronted a perplexing dilemma from the very beginning: logic, sentiment, and rhetoric seemed to dictate a national third-party effort, but such a drive would undermine the New Deal, which most of them still agreed constituted the greatest practical hope for the advance of liberalism. It was ironic, therefore, that for progressivism to advance, the New Deal had to succeed, but for a national third party to emerge, it had to fail.[63]

Appreciating how useful presidential approval would be, the Progressives eagerly sought Roosevelt's endorsement. They possessed a useful ally in Tugwell, who urged upon Roosevelt and party chairman James Farley the wisdom of lining up behind Bob La Follette. "We need these Progressives with us," he believed, especially since midwestern Democrats were, for the most part, hopelessly reactionary and useless to the administration. Progressives hoped that their work for Roosevelt in 1932 would be rewarded. Farley, however, displayed no intention of ditching local Democratic organizations and quietly opposed Senator La Follette's candidacy, an action that greatly upset Phil La Follette.[64]

Although Roosevelt disagreed with Farley's attitude, he did not wish to antagonize the party regulars unnecessarily. He informed Sen. George W. Norris of his interest in retaining Bob La Follette in the Senate and indicated that if no arrangement could be made with state Democrats, he intended to announce his preference for the Wisconsin Progressive. Talking off the record to White House correspondents, Roosevelt also remarked, "Personally, I would love to see Bob La Follette back here because he is an old friend of mine and has been very helpful. But, as you appreciate it, I cannot go ahead and the National Administration cannot go ahead and compel some party organization in a particular state to do something at the command of the National Administration. It just cannot be done." He added, "I am trying to get across the idea that if we have the right kind of people, the party label does not mean so very much. I have to keep that off the record too." Roosevelt's desire for political realignment was evident, but he was not yet ready to mount a major challenge to the Democratic organization.[65]

The president's major opportunity to make his wishes known occurred on 9 August during a stopover in Green Bay, which was celebrating its tercentennial. Secretary of Agriculture Wallace had taken care earlier to praise the work of the La Follettes during a speech to a Madison audience. As the presidential train rolled through North Dakota and Minnesota on its way to Wisconsin, state party leaders pleaded with Roosevelt not to endorse Senator La Follette. The *Milwaukee Journal* featured a front-page cartoon entitled "Out to Welcome the Roosevelt Special," picturing the La Follette brothers waiting on the platform for the train to pull in, a smiling Bob holding a flower in one hand and tipping his hat with the other while a menacing Phil gripped a club behind his back. The anti-La Follette newspaper was trying to spread the notion that the brothers were in fundamental disagreement.[66]

Roosevelt's comments in Green Bay dismayed the Democrats but also failed to satisfy the Progressives. The president obviously had them in mind when he criticized people who were inspired by progressive objectives but unwilling to cooperate with others. Then Roosevelt carefully uttered the words for which everyone had been waiting: "Your two Senators, Bob La Follette and Ryan Duffy, both old friends of mine, they and many others have worked with me in maintaining excellent cooperation between the executive and legislative branches of the government. I take this opportunity of expressing my gratitude to them. . . . I thank Governor Schmedeman, another old friend of mine, for his patriotic cooperation with the national administration." The president added, "I. am glad to be in a state from which I have greatly drawn in setting up the permanent and temporary agencies of government."[67]

Exegesis began immediately. Roosevelt's failure to mention Phil La Follette was regarded by some as a snub or even a "trenchant blow." Several reasonable explanations existed for the omission, however: unlike the other three, the former governor was not present on the speaker's platform; his role was as an ordinary citizen, while they were the three top officeholders in the state; and he was not yet a declared candidate for office. Besides, Roosevelt did not want to go out of his way to alienate state Democrats.[68]

Discouraged by the episode, Democratic leaders set out to undo the damage. They denied that Roosevelt's statement constituted an endorsement of Bob La Follette. But their efforts to document Progressive disloyalty merely drove the Progressives closer to the New Deal standard. Insinuations that Bob La Follette was seeking Roosevelt's backing while Phil La Follette was undermining the president were false and unfair, the *Progressive* claimed, demanding that the Democrats cite a single instance when Phil La Follette had attacked Roosevelt. "The record shows that President Roosevelt came to Wisconsin for many of his liberal and progressive ideas which have since taken their part in definite sections of the New Deal," the paper reported. "Progressives of Wisconsin openly and frankly supported him in 1932 and have stood behind his efforts to inculcate a new liberalism on the national scene." Critics were seeking to blow up remarks Phil La Follette had made about certain phases of the Triple-A into a blanket condemnation of the New Deal, the *Progressive* remarked, pointing out that some officials within the administration had also opposed the same policies. The weekly paper listed a series of New Deal programs that had found their inspiration either wholly or partly in the Wisconsin experience, including the NRA, TVA, CCC, the Federal Emergency Relief Administration (FERA), the Public Works Administration (PWA), old-age pensions, public power projects, mini-mum-wage standards, labor codes, and unemployment insurance.[69]

The assertion that the CCC was hatched from Phil La Follette's forestry project failed to take into account a variety of similar programs in other states and President Roosevelt's deep personal interest in conserva-tion. La Follette's planning proposals and his enlistment of Wisconsin lumber manufacturers in a voluntary limitation of production were simi-larly cited as precursors of the National Industrial Recovery Act. His railroad bridges, snidely referred to as "roller coasters" by critics, were paraded by the Progressives as inspirations for New Deal public-works projects. Although the Wisconsin experience provided part of the context in which New Deal policies were established, it would be hard to demon-strate a single instance in which the state's example was decisive, except perhaps with regard to Social Security.[70]

Roosevelt's friendly posture in Wisconsin enhanced Progressive pros-pects. "I hope all goes well with you," he wrote Bob La Follette after Green Bay. "Do not hesitate to keep in touch with me." When the brothers sent a telegram praising one of his speeches, he thanked both of them and invited Bob to visit him after the election. He never actually gave the senator a formal endorsement, however.[71]

Many progressives from outside Wisconsin lent their aid to the new party's campaign. Among those who visited the state to speak for Pro-gressive candidates were Gerald P. Nye, Edward P. Costigan, Burton K. Wheeler, Frank P. Walsh, Henrik Shipstead, George W. Norris, Fiorello La Guardia, and Lynn Frazier. Like Roosevelt, they were more in-terested in Bob's candidacy than in Phil's, but Bob urged them to "give Phil a particularly strong boost."[72]

The strategy adopted by the Progressives in 1934 differed little from the route they had taken during previous campaigns. Representing the con-test in familiar dualistic terms, Phil La Follette contrasted his own brand of liberalism with the reactionary attitudes of his opponents. Workers, farmers, and small-property owners were ranged against the forces of plutocratic wealth. Redistribution of wealth continued to be La Follette's basic remedy for the depression as he took credit for being the authentic representative of New Deal liberalism in the state. He cited parallels between progressivism and the New Deal but also criticized crop controls and allegedly wasteful make-work relief projects. The Progressive platform convention on 2 October forwarded a telegram to Roosevelt expressing its "enthusiastic endorsement of your declaration that America is going to restore the opportunity for able-bodied men and women to earn their own living."[73]

An adequate work-relief program was the foremost of twenty-two proposals in La Follette's personal platform, which was in favor of government-owned banks, farm marketing organizations, collective-bargaining rights, old-age pensions, increased school subsidies, government-owned munitions plants, a soldiers' bonus, and public ownership of utilities, and which opposed a sales tax. La Follette contended that governmental expenditures should aim to stimulate business, thereby expanding wealth and income. A single state could not solve the depression but could alleviate its effects by cooperating with the federal government in some areas and by working on its own in others. La Follette's preamble and statement of principles, with only slight modification, were later incorporated into the Progressive party platform.[74]

The rest of the Progressive platform derived largely from the Farmer Labor Progressive League's draft, whose principal author was Harold Groves. Despite its occasionally radical tone, it was designed to appeal to every shade of Progressive opinion. It began by asserting, "Our economic system has failed," and went on to contend that the "old order" was irrecoverable and that the country stood at the "threshold of a new age"; its specific proposals, though, were generally within the mainstream of liberal–progressive thought. The Progressives' acceptance of the notion that the economic system had failed, like the radical tone of the Minnesota Farmer-Labor party platform, provided convincing evidence of a leftward swing in public opinion.[75]

The fall campaign found La Follette speeding around the state in his usual whirlwind style, sometimes speaking to eight or nine audiences in a day. He continued to stress the need for redistribution of wealth and recommended a variety of programs that would benefit various interest groups, while also demanding frugal and efficient government to keep taxes down.[76]

Bob La Follette's victory in November surprised no one, but the success of his brother and others on the Progressive ticket stunned many observers. Phil La Follette, anticipating defeat, had drafted a concession statement, which now could be preserved for curious historians. Of the dozen or so who participated in the White House election pool, only two, not including the president, had bet on Phil La Follette. But his victory had depended on a three-way split in the vote as he captured less than 40 percent of the total in defeating the incumbent, Gov. Albert B. Schmedeman, 373,093 to 359,467. Howard Greene, the Republican, trailed with 172,980 votes. The Republicans' poor showing led some observers to predict their imminent demise.[77]

As liberals fared well around the country, the Progressives, in their first electoral try, successfully elected a governor, a U.S. senator, a secretary of state, seven of a total of ten U.S. congressmen, forty-five assemblymen, and eight new state senators, who, added to the five holdover senators who had joined the party, gave them a total of thirteen in the upper house.

After vacationing for several days in the Florida sun and swinging through the East on a quick speaking tour, Phil La Follette reported that he had discovered "tremendous interest" in their new party. The immediate task was to concentrate on the situation in Wisconsin; La Follette said that it was impossible to predict whether a national Progressive party would emerge by 1936. "Changes come fast these days," he observed, "and it is impossible to outline an exact course of action during the next two years. The best you can do is chart the direction you are to follow."[78]

During the campaign he had deliberately soft-pedaled his doubts about the New Deal in order to win Democratic votes. Recognizing the strength of Roosevelt's popularity and accommodating himself to that basic political fact, he indicated his approval for the president's policies "in general" but continued to find fault with agricultural-production limitations, inadequate veterans' benefits, and other specific programs. It remained clear that La Follette's political future and that of the Progressive party would hinge on the course of the New Deal and the relationship that existed between the New Deal and the Wisconsin movement.[79]

Chapter 4

The Wisconsin Works Plan
and a Recalcitrant Legislature

The central problem confronting Phil La Follette and other Americans during the 1930s was unemployment. Taking office for a second time in 1935, Governor La Follette was determined to formulate a works program that would employ all of the jobless seeking work and could then serve as a model for other states. He obtained federal approval for operating a separate state plan, free from Washington's supervision. But a coalition of conservative Republicans and Democrats in the state senate rejected the Wisconsin works plan by a single vote and went on to block every other major gubernatorial initiative. The legislative battle over the works plan helped to cement the political alliance between Roosevelt and the La Follettes, consolidated the conservative anti-La Follette coalition in the legislature, and provided the governor with a ready-made issue for his reelection campaign.

Unemployment posed a baffling, frustrating problem for all Americans, but for La Follette the issue carried special implications. On the question of work, perhaps more than on any other, his private values paralleled his public responsibilities. Being himself a relentlessly hard worker sustained by endless energy and drive, he attached to work an almost mystical importance. Work would provide salvation for the individual and revitalization for the economy. There was nothing that hard work could not achieve; nothing was more destructive of individual initiative and respect than not being able to work. People wanted and deserved a chance to work; to make his point, La Follette spelled the word out in his speeches: "W-O-R-K!" He believed that government had a responsibility to find meaningful work for people and that Wisconsin could establish a model program. This became his top priority when he moved into the governor's office for a second time. The Wisconsin works plan constituted La Follette's most significant and imaginative response to the depression, and he always felt that it would have provided a superior alternative to federal work-relief programs.

61

Relations between Washington and Madison on the subject of relief for the unemployed had steadily deteriorated during Governor Schmedeman's term in office. Harry Hopkins and his deputies in the relief administration had grown increasingly frustrated with Wisconsin's record of inefficiency, political favoritism, and inadequate state funding. After strenuous efforts, federal officials had secured a pledge from Schmedeman that after the 1934 elections he would call a special session of the legislature for the purpose of appropriating further funds for relief, but Hopkins and his aides seriously doubted whether the Democrats would follow through.[1]

Schmedeman's defeat that November caused no mourning in the offices of federal relief officials, who anticipated establishing a much better relationship with La Follette. The new governor quickly agreed with them to request five million dollars in supplemental state funds from the next session of the legislature, a sum that Hopkins had indicated would be required if Wisconsin were to remain eligible for further aid from the Federal Emergency Relief Administration. La Follette waited to get Hopkins's stipulation in writing before forwarding his budget request to the legislature. Disconcerted by La Follette's friendly relationship with administration officials in Washington, Democrats in the legislature grumbled and counterattacked. State Sen. Morley Kelly questioned Thomas Duncan about the Hopkins letter:

> KELLY: "Who told you we owed that money?"
> DUNCAN: "Hopkins did; we received a letter from him which has already been published in the Senate Journal, and which is on your desk right now."
> KELLY: "That may be so. But those are only copies. I want to see the original of the letter. And besides, didn't you people get Hopkins to write that letter?"

Duncan of course denied that they had solicited the letter and said that the federal government would be satisfied if the legislature now passed the five-million-dollar relief bill.[2]

The bill easily cleared both houses after unsuccessful Democratic efforts to amend it. Democrats accused La Follette of trying to concentrate too much power in Madison, and they sought to transfer substantial administrative authority to local offices. Hopkins strongly opposed the idea and thanked the governor for cooperating with FERA's request, but one Democratic senator growled, "We might as well have a dictator and a czar in Wisconsin and let the legislature go home. The administration has become both the executive and legislative branches of government."[3]

La Follette possessed no great liking for relief, considering it a necessary but distasteful temporary expedient. His real concern was to provide jobs for people, and it soon became apparent that he would deal directly with Roosevelt and Hopkins on the matter rather than operate through normal bureaucratic channels. "I get most of my information on the governor's program from Washington," noted the head of the FERA regional office in Chicago, Howard O. Hunter.[4]

La Follette realized that the Roosevelt administration was hammering out a new work-relief program, and he hoped to obtain presidential approval for a unique scheme that would allow Wisconsin to operate independently. When the La Follette brothers visited the White House on 7 December 1934, Phil mentioned the idea to the president, who encouraged him to proceed with the program and to keep Roosevelt personally informed about its progress.

Politics were also discussed, and Phil La Follette said that the Progressives would support the national administration if the president pushed a program "worth fighting for." Phil said that he felt obliged to cooperate with third-party proselytizers but hoped they would do nothing to complicate the 1936 election and return a reactionary Republican to the White House. Roosevelt stated his concern about left-wing elements arrayed around Huey Long, Milo Reno, Dr. Francis Townsend, and Upton Sinclair, which had "potentialities for dangerous development—some well-intentioned but visionary leadership — some dangerous and selfish leadership." Afterward, Phil wrote Isen, "My general impressions were (1) He was more direct and *less* 'yep-yep'—none at all in fact— (2) He is not overconfident about 1936— (3) He thinks he will need or may need our help— (4) He intends to work with us and probably more freely than with other governors or states."[5]

During the transition period before his inauguration, La Follette had the Wisconsin Regional Planning Committee begin an inventory of public-works projects that could put people to work in the state. Under chairman Martin W. Torkelson the committee had already compiled considerable data on the state's population, educational and transportational facilities, health resources, and industry. To devise machinery for financing his works program and to circumvent constitutional limitations on state building projects, the governor enlisted the aid of Milwaukee lawyer Ralph Hoyt.[6]

When the La Follettes visited the White House again in mid-January, President Roosevelt reiterated his willingness to consider a special state plan and indicated that he would not be averse to giving Wisconsin a lump sum of money rather than channeling the funds through the federal bureaucracy. At a news conference he indicated that Wisconsin, Alabama, and New Jersey were submitting alternate plans, "which should be sufficient to choose from to put everybody on relief in those states to work."[7]

Allowing Governor La Follette to develop his own program coincided with Roosevelt's willingness to encourage state experimentation and also made good political sense. He wanted to head off the establishment of a third party that might enlist progressives such as Cutting, Nye, and the La Follettes, who were "flirting with the idea of a third party ticket anyway with the knowledge that such a third ticket would be beaten but that it would defeat us, elect a conservative Republican and cause a complete swing far to the left before 1940." Some sort of understanding emerged between the president and the La Follettes, because by mid-March he informed Treasury Secretary Morgenthau that they had promised him their support for 1936. As the secretary recorded it in his diary, "Somewhere during this conversation he let it slip out and tried to cover it up that the price he paid for the La Follette support was that he was going to turn over to them for their Administration in Wisconsin the proposed works program."[8]

By late April, La Follette had his program ready. He spent the first week and a half of May in Washington explaining his program to administration officials and seeking their approval. On 2 May, Roosevelt had work-relief directors Frank Walker, Hopkins, and Ickes come to the White House to listen to the La Follettes' presentation. The governor assured them that Wisconsin could employ every person on relief and still eventually repay 30 percent of the hundred million dollars that the federal government would make available. He said that he planned to remain in the capital until they approved his proposal. "It looks like a well-thought-out and intelligent plan and we were all favorably disposed toward it," Ickes wrote in his diary.[9]

Wisconsin Democrats, however, were furious. What were the La Follettes up to and why was the president playing along with them? They felt betrayed. On 3 May Charles E. Broughton, the national committeeman, James Corcoran, the state chairman, and Senator Duffy went to the White House. They claimed that La Follette had lifted his plan from Regional Planning Commission reports compiled during the Schmedeman administration and that therefore the Democrats deserved credit for the idea. They said that they wished success for the program and hoped that bipartisan cooperation would prevail; more to the point, however, they demanded that politics be eliminated from hiring and warned against the use of funds for "political fence-building."[10]

At his next press conference President Roosevelt called the Wisconsin plan "a good piece of workmanship" and indicated that the chances for its approval were good since it promised an "actual saving" for both the state and federal governments. Responding to Democratic complaints, he tried to play down La Follette's originality, remarking, "It was a plan started last summer by Governor Schmedeman who appointed a State Planning Commission. Back in January, I think it was, Governor La Follette went over the plan and of course made certain minor changes, and brought it down here for us to study." In fact, Schmedeman never contemplated anything remotely comparable to La Follette's bold scheme for state administration of public works, but Roosevelt apparently felt that he could appease the Democrats in this fashion.[11]

Enthusiasm for the Wisconsin proposal was not unanimous within the Roosevelt administration. Rexford G. Tugwell discussed it twice with La Follette, and while he concluded that the governor possessed "a really brilliant mind" and was "an equally brilliant administrator," he questioned several provisions in the "interesting" plan. If the state obtained discretionary spending power, who would protect the national interest? And, while it might seem politically expedient to cooperate with the La Follettes, what if someone like Huey Long or Eugene Talmadge requested the same privilege?[12]

Such questions, however, did not prevent Ickes, Hopkins, and Walker from approving the plan before Phil La Follette's departure on 11 May. All that remained was the president's formal assent. His high personal regard for Bob La Follette and the senator's cordial relationship with Hopkins and other federal officials certainly helped facilitate the decision. While awaiting the formal announcement from Washington, Governor La Follette unveiled his plan during a series of meetings with legislators, newsmen, union officials, and farm leaders. On 16 May came official word of a hundred-million-dollar grant to the state. Questioned about it by reporters the next day, Roosevelt observed that Wisconsin had made "such an attractive offer we felt we could not turn it down."[13]

The Wisconsin works bill overshadowed every other political issue in the state during 1935. La Follette considered it superior to federal work relief, but realizing that Democratic votes would be necessary to get it through the legislature, the Progressives emphasized the cooperative attitude that the president had taken toward Wisconsin. Assertions that the plan was merely a warmed-over version of ideas hatched during the Schmedeman administration were called "amusing and ridiculous" by the *Progressive*. Even before the bill reached the legislature, however, the Democrats had switched gears and, instead of claiming credit for it, began to accuse the governor of shortchanging the state in order to gain personal control over work relief. They argued that Wisconsin was entitled to between $125 million and $130 million under the federal program, but Duncan retorted that Wisconsin stood to get only $88 million under normal procedures, $12 million less than the amount obtained by Governor La Follette. Senator Duffy reported Hopkins's belief that under ordinary procedures Wisconsin would have received about the same $100 million as under La Follette's plan. The battle over numbers signaled the acrimony that lay ahead.[14]

La Follette clearly recognized the difficulty of his task with the legislature. His first step was to educate the public about his bill and persuade them to influence their legislators. Even before the bill had been printed, petitions with thousands of signatures endorsing it were obtained. The governor approached the voters directly in a series of fifteen-minute radio talks describing the goals and methods of his plan. It was designed, he said, to provide jobs to all who needed them. Work would be done repairing and building highways, conserving soil and forests, liming fields, repairing and planting trees, promoting health, and improving education.[15]

To bypass state constitutional prohibitions on borrowing funds or undertaking internal improvements, La Follette envisioned the creation of a Wisconsin Finance Authority (WFA), modeled on the federal government's Reconstruction Finance Corporation, as the financing agency. Its directors, to be appointed by the governor, would be authorized to issue a hundred million dollars in special notes that would circulate only in Wisconsin; they could be exchanged for federal currency at certain banks and would be used for paying wages and for purchasing materials. The plan would encourage the use of the state's own products as a means of stimulating its economy. Spiraling employment, sales, and profits would stimulate increased tax revenues, which could be used to redeem notes issued by the WFA. In the long run, therefore, the program would be self-liquidating. The WFA would finance the program and the State Planning Board would manage it. Everything would be done on a businesslike basis, La Follette promised, and the plan would be budget balancing in the best sense of the word.[16]

A temporary surtax would be levied on increases in income over the 1934 base. "If your government can help you earn more money," La Follette told people, "then out of the extra money that you make you will be in a position to pay a fair share of your increased income to help finance the program." Refuting those who argued that his plan would bankrupt the state, the governor answered, "I know that this program will be attacked by those who say we cannot 'spend' our way out of the depression. But we most certainly cannot starve ourselves out of the depression." Something different had to be tried, and he was going to do it.[17]

The governor viewed his plan as an expansionary alternative to the New Deal policy of "reduction and destruction." It possessed in addition, he believed, the advantages of decentralization, less red tape, and more useful jobs. Under the federal program, he asserted, "We are likely to end up having spent an enormous sum of money and having little or nothing to show for what we have done." Despite the rhetoric, however, the uniqueness of the projects and procedures envisioned by La Follette was not so apparent to unbiased observers. Only experience would sufficiently test the governor's claims.[18]

The rationale for the works plan was couched in the language not of redistribution but of expansion. Before, La Follette's reliance on the purchasing-power thesis had led him to emphasize the need for transferring resources to the needy and underprivileged. Now, his emphasis was shifting to the supply side of the equation. La Follette urged the need for expanded production, arguing that increasing the size of the economic pie would benefit rich and poor alike. His transformation from redistributionist to expansionist proceeded gradually, though, and only later did the implications of the change become apparent.[19]

The distinction between redistribution and growth seemed to make no impression on the governor's detractors. Hostile legislators wasted no time in attacking the Wisconsin works bill as extravagant, dictatorial, and socialistic. The most important opposition newspaper was the *Milwaukee Journal,* which warned that the governor was proposing a virtual dictatorship. Businessmen who testified before the Joint Finance Committee were especially concerned about the new tax. Labor, on the other hand, worried about wage scales on the projects, but after receiving satisfaction on this point they backed the proposal as preferable to the federal attempt to "prime the pump with an eye dropper." Many bankers declared that they would refuse to accept the warrants issued by the Wisconsin Finance Authority, and the Democratic state treasurer, Robert K. Henry, indicated that his office would not accept them until the state supreme court had confirmed their constitutionality. Many mayors also held reservations about the plan. The Wisconsin League of Municipalities requested eighteen clarifying amendments before acting on it. The Socialists, like their conservative counterparts, assailed the bill for granting dictatorial powers to the governor.[20]

Resistance especially focused on the financing provisions. Whether $130 million, $100 million, or some lesser amount would have to be raised, the effect might be to bankrupt the state, many people believed. Even sympathetic observers had reservations about scrip issues. The bill itself and its interpretation by Duncan and the governor's office were vague and confusing. Growing concerned about public reaction on this point, Governor La Follette sought to reassure people by suggesting that the WFA's notes should not be considered scrip but rather would be treated like "certified checks" that people could use to pay taxes or convert into cash at designated banks. The WFA, he promised, would be more liquid than any bank in the state. But he failed to add that its solvency depended on the willingness of people to keep the notes in circulation rather than to cash them in at the first opportunity. Success would hinge on human decisions that no one could accurately predict.[21]

Conservative Democrats raised legitimate questions about the details of the program, but they clearly were mainly worried about its political implications. A Democratic president had conferred on it his blessing, and administration officials were favorably disposed. The Democrats realized that passage of the bill would strengthen the governor's hand in the state and would cement further his bond to the national administration. Opposition to it, on the other hand, would appear disloyal to the president and would probably give La Follette an issue for the next campaign; in fact, a few people thought that the governor secretly hoped his plan would be defeated for that very reason. Also, the prospect of being deprived of their "rightful" patronage galled the Democrats. Some of them suggested that Leo Crowley be given responsibility for work relief in Wisconsin. However, Crowley, who had become director of the Federal Deposit Insurance Corporation, visited the governor on 1 June and later told newsmen and party officials that he and the national administration favored the passage of 443-S. Now the state Democratic organization looked ridiculous; after originally claiming credit for the bill and then denouncing it, they obviously were mere spectators to the Roosevelt-La Follette alliance.[22]

On 13 June the state senate defeated the Wisconsin works bill by a vote of nineteen to fourteen. La Follette, by converting three senators to his side, could still put his plan over. Without hesitation, he transmitted a revised bill to the assembly, where it would be sure of passage. "It would be very fatal to admit defeat now," he wired Bob, and he phoned Hopkins to say that he was going "to open both barrels now." Hopkins replied, "There is no reason why we can't mark time here, Phil. We are not going to lose anything and you're not going to lose anything if the worst comes to the worst." To facilitate its passage, La Follette stripped the bill of controversial school subsidies and supplemental taxes and also eliminated the scrip provisions. He admitted that these changes might reduce the program's effectiveness but said that its basic features would remain.[23]

Determined to put the heat on the legislature, La Follette mapped out a whirlwind speaking tour into the districts of senators who had voted against his plan. Taking a chapter from his father's book, he planned to "read the roll call" of the recalcitrant senators. In evening meetings in Milwaukee, Kenosha, Racine, Oshkosh, and Appleton he lashed out at the obstructionist tactics of the nineteen senators who had voted against him and urged people to write, telephone, or visit their senators and force them to change their minds. "This is your battle and you are the real voice of power," he exhorted. "No battle is won without fighters." The governor's pugnacious words and animated gestures stirred enthusiastic responses from most of his audiences, and hecklers' catcalls just urged them on. La Follette was counting on public opinion to directly affect legislative votes.[24]

Democrats and Republicans lashed back at La Follette. Calling him the "wild man of Madison," opposition senators denounced the governor's "deliberate campaign of falsehoods and misrepresentations." They strongly resented his personal attacks, which seemed only to stiffen their resolve. La Follette sensed this, and after his first week on the road he canceled his remaining appearances in Beloit, La Crosse, and Superior. Continuing the tour seemed as likely to damage his cause as to help it. Of the remaining districts' senators, two offered scant hope of conversion and the third, Phil Nelson of Superior, had already indicated that removal of the tax measures from the bill would allow him to vote for it.[25]

On 28 June, two days after the assembly approved the revised works bill by a vote of sixty-three to thirty-one, the senate rejected it a second time, this time by a single vote, seventeen to sixteen. One postmortem analysis ascribed the crucial vote to Sen. Mike Mack of Shiocton, who reportedly had been ready to vote for the bill until Governor La Follette went into his district. The speaking tour had outraged conservatives, hardened their intransigence, and united the coalition of conservative Democrats and Republicans more tightly than ever before. Former governor Kohler expressed his thanks to Harry W. Bolens, who had led the opposition in the senate, for standing by his guns. The fight, which had stirred more bitterness than anything the legislature had witnessed in years, set the tone for La Follette's second stint in office and marked the battlelines between the pro-La Follette and anti-La Follette forces.[26]

Wisconsin would now have to operate like every other state under the new Works Progress Administration (WPA), which had been established by Congress in 1935. La Follette told Roosevelt and Hopkins that they could make whatever use of his plan they desired. If Wisconsin Democrats thought that they had put the work-relief issue to rest, however, they were wrong. As soon as they learned that Governor La Follette was planning a meeting with the president, they begged Hopkins to name a nonpartisan panel to administer the WPA in the state and informed James Farley that they would tolerate no more flirtations between the La Follettes and the national administration. Roosevelt failed to heed the message. Only four days after the works bill went down to defeat, Hopkins named as head of the state's WPA Gen. Ralph M. Immell, the state's adjutant general. He was a Progressive and a good friend of La Follette, having met him during college. The Democrats raised an immediate howl, charging a double cross. Nothing could disguise the presidential rebuff. Complaints that Immell's appointment was purely political sounded hollow, however, coming from men whose concern in the matter was almost entirely politically motivated.[27]

Democrats continued to charge that the WPA in Wisconsin was a Progressive machine. A potential confrontation in the United States Senate over Immell's confirmation was averted when Hopkins agreed with Governor La Follette to let the state pay his salary. A special investigating committee chaired by Democratic State Sen. William H. Shenners unsuccessfully sought to find evidence of wrongdoing in his office, and a federal inquiry absolved the state administration of charges of nepotism, political favoritism, and excessive red tape. In fact, administrative jobs were so few and bureaucratic holdovers from the dismantled FERA so many that Immell received heavy criticism from disgruntled Progressive job seekers.[28]

Democratic peevishness with the national administration's handling of work relief in the state fanned long-smoldering resentment generated by President Roosevelt's continuing cooperation with the La Follettes. One widely circulated rumor had Bob La Follette taking Vice-President Garner's spot on the Democratic ticket in 1936. Many Democrats blamed Governor Schmedeman's defeat on the president, and they were pained by stories of the La Follettes' constant shuttling back and forth to the White House. A few Democrats, such as Congressmen Raymond J. Cannon and Thomas O'Malley, were willing to cooperate with the Progressives, but Democratic state legislators, and especially a group of staunchly conservative senators led by Bolens and William D. Carroll, were virtually unanimous in their opposition to the idea. Senator Duffy, state chairman Corcoran, and national committeeman Broughton were all loyal to the president but had little success in trying to steer the party along more liberal lines. Roosevelt's actions alienated state Democrats, but they also realized that their political fortunes were intertwined with those of the president.[29]

Roosevelt faced similar situations in other states that contained sizable progressive factions. In each case he sought to cultivate their friendship without alienating the regular Democratic organization. So fearful were Wisconsin's Democrats of an embarrassing incident if Roosevelt spoke at the national convention of the Young Democrats to be held in Milwaukee on 23 August 1935 that they urged him not to attend. Meanwhile, Governor La Follette sent word through Crowley that any presidential statement on his relationship with the Progressives might be misinterpreted or blown all out of proportion. Some unforeseen congressional business provided the president with a proper excuse for staying away that evening.[30]

The defeat of the Wisconsin works bill spelled doom for the rest of Governor La Follette's legislative program; it was clear that the anti-La Follette forces in the state senate had been solidified by the battle and could block any La Follette proposal they disagreed with. Disappointed but not surprised, the governor did the best he could under the circumstances. Although numbering only forty-five in the hundred-member lower house, the Progressives had been able with the aid of several Democrats to organize the assembly, electing Jorge W. Carow as speaker and Paul Alfonsi as floor leader. They held twenty-two of the twenty-three committee chairmanships. A Democratic-Republican coalition, however, had easily organized the senate, installing Bolens as president pro tem. Outnumbering the Republicans fourteen to six, the Democrats had taken six committee chairmanships and had given the Republicans the other three. The thirteen Progressive senators seldom were able to attract more than one or two others to their side on roll calls.[31]

La Follette devoted most of his attention during the first part of the legislative session to his works bill. His hopes for winning over opposition senators had led him to adopt a hands-off policy with the legislature, so he had held only infrequent caucuses with his party's representatives and had maintained a low profile for the most part. A tripartisan committee got the assignment of hammering out compromise budget and tax bills that would not offend anyone too much. Each party wanted to get the credit for economies and expenditures that benefited various interest groups. Since most state funds were already earmarked, the budget debate generally overplayed the choices that actually were available. The only major reduction that conservatives could find was a proposed six-hundred-thousand-dollar slash in the university's budget, but that was later restored, mainly under pressure from Progressive legislators. As finally agreed on, the compromise bills sailed through both houses with scarcely a dissenting vote. But on measures that would have resulted in fundamental changes in state government the Progressives got nowhere.[32]

Next to the debate over the works bill, the university generated the largest controversy. Cultural, not economic, differences determined the line between the Progressives and their opponents on this issue. John B. Chapple's continued efforts to expose antireligious and anti-American activities on the Madison campus had captured notoriety and the Republican senatorial nomination. Early in the session a group of conservatives, composed mainly of Democrats, attempted to link the Progressives with the radicalism, atheism, and immorality allegedly rampant on the campus. Red probes, including one at the University of Chicago, were also popular elsewhere that year. The special investigating committee, chaired by State Sen. E. F. Brunette, a Green Bay Democrat, had its real origins, charged Walter Hunt, a Progressive from River Falls, in "a crowd of organizations which includes the American Liberty League, the

D.A.R., a group of splendid women who love to trace their ancestry back to the Revolution by a drop of blood, the 100 percent Americans, the war profiteers, the Taxpayers' Alliance which wants the poor to pay the taxes, the power trust, and the international bankers.'' Progressives scoffed at the committee's accusations and staunchly defended the university.[33]

When a mob of athlete-led students broke up campus meetings of the League for Industrial Democracy and the National Student League and ducked four of their leaders in nearby Lake Mendota, Progressives charged that the Brunette committee had provoked the incidents. The committee's report related few facts but called for the expulsion of students and organizations expounding un-American doctrines. The Progressives' defense of the university's reputation against such fishing expeditions reinforced the conviction of some people that the university, in league with the Progressive party, constituted a menace to American institutions by fostering disrespect for religion and traditional family ties, denigrating red-blooded Americanism, and disseminating radical political and economic ideas.[34]

The conservative Democrats' enthusiasm for such witch-hunts distinguished them from New Deal Democrats, who themselves became targets of Red-hunting expeditions. The gulf inside the party was further illustrated by the attitude that most Democratic legislators took toward labor unions. Their cooperation with Republican legislators to defeat a Progressive-sponsored bill that was modeled on the National Labor Relations Act led Henry Ohl to denounce the Democrats as enemies of labor. They also defeated several bills introduced by Governor La Follette on the recommendation of Interior Secretary Ickes that would have facilitated federal programs in the state, including Public Works Administration projects. ''We had a program to go straight ahead with Roosevelt but not with Ickes and his aides,'' rationalized one assemblyman. The session demonstrated, if anybody harbored any doubts on the question, that the state's Democrats were not New Dealers.[35]

When it became clear that he could not win over the opposition senators, La Follette abandoned his efforts at conciliation and began to read the roll of those who were blocking his programs. The narrow majority held by the conservatives merely hardened the battle lines, instilling in the Progressives a cohesion they might otherwise have lacked and likewise reinforcing the willingness of Democrats and Republicans to cooperate against the ''Madison ring.'' Tension and bitterness marked the 1935 session, which ran nearly nine months, the longest in state history. One typical exchange witnessed Democratic Sen. Morley Kelly asking a Progressive speaker to yield to a question during a floor debate. "I don't think I want to yield," Herman Severson retorted. "I refuse to engage in disputes with the feeble-minded." Kelly screamed back, "Only the feeble-minded would refuse to yield."[36]

The proceedings left the governor increasingly frustrated. "These reactionaries will continue to talk about loyalty to the Constitution," he told a Constitution Day audience. "They will continue to talk about the menace of Communism, all the time failing to see that if our system of government is ever seriously in danger, it will only be because people's faith in the ability of Constitutional government to meet our critical problems has been undermined." He sometimes doubted how well legislatures could ever respond to crises, and he became increasingly convinced of the necessity for strong executive action. He decided that, given another chance, he would respond more decisively. His thoughts turned to 1936, when he could win reelection for himself and build a legislative majority that would act.[37]

Even after the defeat of his works bill, the governor had to devote much of his time to the unemployment problem. The works bill might be resurrected, he hinted, if the federal program failed to do the job. As the Works Progress Administration slowly began to absorb people on the relief rolls during the latter half of the year, La Follette fired off a barrage of telegrams demanding faster action from Washington. In August he accompanied Immell to the capital in an effort to obtain faster release of federal funds. The following month, shortly before the widely reported showdown between Hopkins and Ickes on relief spending, Roosevelt personally reassured the La Follettes that every effort was being made to speed the flow of funds to the states. And federal officials remarked that Wisconsin had little to gripe about since it was receiving larger relief grants in proportion to need than any state in the region.[38]

When people complained to him about relief, La Follette placed the responsibility on the federal government. "This whole picture would have been different if the Wisconsin program had been adopted," he told them. He also pinned the blame on reactionaries in the state senate. After the final FERA grant in November 1935, the Wisconsin Emergency Relief Administration was dismantled and replaced by a new Public Welfare Department, headed by Alfred Briggs. When a delegation of mayors demanded the calling of a special session of the legislature to avert a relief crisis, the governor refused and suggested instead that they contact the senators who had killed his works program. "I am just as much convinced that we can't answer the problem by just putting salve on the sore spots," he said, "and relief is nothing but an economic palliative—a salve." La Follette continued to seek larger grants from the federal government and talked to the president again in December about the problem. At that meeting the La Follette brothers made the curious suggestion that all relief, WPA, and PWA projects be suspended with the explanation that this was what businessmen wanted. Perhaps the idea was proposed tongue-in-cheek, but the president seems to have taken it seriously. Not being as well acquainted with Phil as he was with Bob, he did not always understand the governor. For his part, Phil La Follette also arrived at his judgments about Roosevelt's personality and intentions on the basis of slight evidence garnered from their infrequent encounters. Thus, it is not surprising that both retained suspicions about the other's goodwill and intentions.[39]

La Follette's arguments about the inadequacy of federal relief and public-works programs would have elicited agreement from most federal administrators, who well knew how much more could have been done. Hopkins was the first to admit, "We have never given adequate relief." But he added that they had done the best they could with the available funds. Much that La Follette wanted could have been obtained had there been more money. From Madison it was easy to demand increased expenditures, but he advocated that for the federal government, not for Wisconsin. Such a point of view was only natural for a state official who hoped to transfer as much of the burden as possible to the federal government.[40]

The 1935 session of the legislature was extremely frustrating for Governor La Follette, who saw a conservative coalition of Republicans and Democrats block every one of his major proposals, including the Wisconsin works bill. The works plan was his favorite panacea, his central effort during the year, and a program he continued to believe would have provided a superior alternative to the federal one. The defeat of the works bill did entail one advantage, however; it provided Phil La Follette with his major campaign issue for reelection.

Chapter 5

Uneasy Alliance with the New Deal

Just two years after its formation, the Wisconsin Progressive party achieved its greatest electoral success. Confronted with a choice between supporting a futile third-party bid and cooperating with an increasingly popular New Deal administration, the Progressives opted for success rather than consistency. Despite their continual calls for political realignment and pledges of support for a national third-party movement, they postponed those goals. Phil La Follette sought to remain in good standing with Alfred Bingham and other third-party advocates, but they grew increasingly impatient as they watched the La Follette-Roosevelt connection solidify. The president's flirtation with the Progressives also frustrated Wisconsin's Democrats, whose conservative leaders prevented a cadre of Roosevelt men, such as Duffy and Broughton, from reorienting the party along more liberal lines. By backing the La Follettes, Roosevelt decreased the likelihood that the Democrats would soon become the vehicle for liberalism in the state. Instead, the La Follette-Roosevelt alliance helped speed the process whereby the Progressives adopted a more urban, industrial cast. Especially after the formation of the Farmer-Labor Progressive Federation in late 1935, the coalitions of voters supporting the Progressive party and the New Deal were very similar.

Although the 1934 midterm elections indicated a decided move toward the left among the electorate, Roosevelt appeared indecisive during the early part of 1935. His efforts to steer a middle course between critics on the right and the left seemed to satisfy nobody. "I really believe he enjoys puzzling people," sighed T. R. B. in the *New Republic*. Ironically, one action that was interpreted as a symptom of his conservative inclinations was his approval of several Wisconsin-inspired provisions in the social security bill being considered by Congress.[1]

Relief and public works remained sore spots with the Progressives. The La Follettes considered the president's $4.8 billion work-relief request to be inadequate, but when Senator La Follette tried to double the amount, his colleagues in the Senate defeated the proposal by a vote of 77 to 8. The

La Follettes also favored the McCarran prevailing wage amendment to provide workers on government projects with more than a security wage, which, against Roosevelt's opposition, narrowly passed the Senate in February. Tugwell complained to Bob La Follette that the Progressives' refusal to accept discipline or leadership was endangering the administration's program, and he warned the senator that their unwillingness to compromise on minor points threatened to jeopardize the entire reform agenda and might drive the president closer to the conservative Democrats, who seemed to be his most reliable allies. One evening as the Senate reconsidered the amendment, Roosevelt invited Senators La Follette, Wagner, and Costigan in for a chat. "Are we Progressives going to stand together or do I have to go to the country and explain that it was you three who wrecked my administration?" he asked, warning them that the McCarran amendment would mean state socialism because everybody would want a government job if the government paid more than private business did. Bob La Follette deserted most of his progressive colleagues and acceded to the president's wishes by voting against the amendment in March.[2]

In April, Thomas Corcoran jokingly remarked to Ickes that unless things improved soon, he would prefer to leave Washington and wait for Bob La Follette to come along in another ten or twelve years. "The New Deal is over," the *Nation* announced after a fireside chat in which the president outlined a watered-down reform program combined with further work-relief spending. Bob La Follette appeared at the White House in mid-May, along with Senators Norris, Wheeler, Costigan, and Johnson, as well as Ickes and Henry Wallace, to urge the president to assert more forceful leadership. Justice Brandeis sent word through Felix Frankfurter that it was now "the eleventh hour."[3]

Other concerns contributed to Progressive dissatisfaction with Roosevelt. Senator Cutting's death in a plane crash on 6 May saddened and angered Progressives, many of whom held the president at least partially accountable for the tragedy. His refusal to support the New Mexico Republican's reelection bid and his willingness to go along with Democratic Congressman Dennis Chavez's challenge to the election results after Cutting's narrow victory appeared to be motivated by personal animosity. Cutting's plane had gone down over Missouri on a return flight from New Mexico, where he had been collecting affidavits in connection with the contest. Phil La Follette had considered Cutting his closest friend among the progressives from outside Wisconsin. The wealthy senator had contributed generously to progressive campaign chests and in his will had designated bequests of $50,000 for Bob La Follette and $25,000 for Phil.[4]

For many reasons the progressives were restive in early 1935. The growth of the insurgent bloc in the House of Representatives, the growing national movement for a third party, and the enthusiasm encountered by the La Follettes in their visits to other states all attracted considerable attention in the press. Additional evidence of discontent lay in the growing popularity of Sen. Huey Long, Father Charles E. Coughlin, and Dr. Francis Townsend.[5] Although their movements, like that of the progressives, fed on dissatisfaction with the established parties, they also were competing with the progressives for members. Most Wisconsin Progressives focused on their differences with these movements rather than on common objectives. Hoping to limit their appeal in the state, Phil La Follette studiously ignored them. Of the three, Huey Long impressed him as being the most dangerous.[6]

Superficial resemblances between the flamboyant senator's "Share Our Wealth" program and Progressive calls for redistribution convinced few Wisconsinites of the worth of the Louisianan's panaceas. Progressive State Sen. Roland Kannenberg of Wausau increased his reputation for independence and eccentricity when he defied his fellow Progressives and called Long "a fine statesman." Long's following in Wisconsin, however, was miniscule, and La Follette hoped it would stay that way. When the senator fell victim to an assassin's bullet in September 1935, La Follette did send a message of condolence to his widow.[7]

Father Charles E. Coughlin's potential following in highly Catholic Wisconsin was considerable, but after the National Union for Social Justice incorporated in the state in June 1935 it registered no great success. The *Progressive,* which ran several favorable articles on Coughlin, soon turned more critical, and La Follette kept his distance.[8]

The Progressives were more vulnerable to the appeal of Townsendism. Throughout 1935 its influence grew, and in November Democratic Congressman Raymond J. Cannon of Milwaukee announced his support for Townsend's pension plan. Most officeholders maintained a prudent silence on the issue, however, being unwilling either to accept Dr. Townsend's arguments or to estrange the voters who did. One person with no worries about reelection was Edwin E. Witte, University of Wisconsin economics professor, who lectured frequently around the state on the unsoundness of the Townsend plan, calling it the "most outrageous deception ever perpetrated upon the old people of this country.'' Progressives generally focused on the proposal's huge cost and regressive tax features.[9]

The fear that the good doctor struck in the hearts of politicians was evident in the praise Senator La Follette gave him in form letters sent out to constituents explaining why the plan could not work. Amlie voted for the Townsend bills in the House of Representatives while continuing to argue for the need for more fundamental economic reforms. Phil La Follette, who was as concerned as the others to tap the support of older voters, stayed mute on the issue but constantly reiterated his concern about the need for adequate old-age pensions. Townsendite adherents warned the governor that unless he got off the fence on the question, he could lose 75,000 votes in the next election.[10]

Governor La Follette told a joint meeting of Wisconsin Progressives and Minnesota Farmer-Laborites in August 1936 that nothing could be gained by attacking people like Coughlin, Townsend, or Congressman William Lemke, who was running for president on the Union party ticket. Thousands of old people believed in the Townsend plan, he observed, and it was admirable that they considered America rich enough to give them adequate social security. But the governor urged Progressives to push their own programs in order to demonstrate that solutions were possible without resorting to "fantastic schemes." In this area La Follette showed himself to be a prudent but not overly courageous politician.[11]

The question of how to respond to the entreaties of the Farmer Labor Political Federation posed a more difficult problem for Phil La Follette, who wanted to retain the good will of the third-party advocates without making any specific commitments. FLPF executive secretary Alfred Bingham grew increasingly impatient with the governor's evasiveness. Amlie considered it ironic that the La Follettes had made the *Nation*'s annual honor roll for their work in establishing the Progressive party when in fact other people had provided the impetus for it. He told Bingham that he was miffed that his own work for the FLPF had been slighted. The magazine later published a letter from Bingham that complimented the La Follettes for their leadership but asserted that both brothers had been somewhat embarrassed by the third-party agitation. Amlie and the FLPF deserved the credit for establishing the Progressive party, Bingham contended. Phil La Follette, "like a good general who cannot afford to leave half his army behind," had committed his full energies to the party only after its popularity had been demonstrated at the 3 March meeting. Ernest L. Meyer, a journalist and former college classmate of La Follette's, also credited Amlie with having been the mainspring behind the new party's organization "though the orchids went with little justification to Phil La Follette."[12]

Although Bingham complained privately about having to "play the game with such a time-server as Phil La Follette," he realized that no other state, except perhaps Minnesota, offered better prospects for leading the third-party movement. Wisconsin *was* the revolution for the moment, and in his more reflective moments he admitted that La Follette's cautious approach was justified. The governor, for his part, continued to cultivate Bingham's friendship, claiming commitment to the third-party idea. Bingham hoped to avoid an overt break with the La Follettes but grew more and more convinced of "the necessity for disregarding the La Follettes if they won't come along."[13]

Many inquiries were addressed to the La Follettes about their plans regarding a national third party. "The answer is that Wisconsin Progressives are going to do nothing at present," Aldric Revell, a reporter working in the governor's office, wrote one inquirer. "We do not believe that our party should push itself forward. If the nation wants the Progressive party we shall not be found backwards. But to push ourselves and to seek to jump ahead of the wishes of the people of this country is antithetical to our ideals." A new party would come eventually, but not necessarily in 1936, Revell counseled. "It *must take years*—it cannot be done overnight."[14]

At the first birthday celebration of the Progressive party at Fond du Lac on 19 May 1935, Phil La Follette reiterated his belief that political realignment was coming soon, but he implied that an all-out effort in that direction in 1936 would be premature. The process had to be one of patiently creating movements state by state, not "the dramatic, flag-waving, ballyhooing method" of imposing a structure from the top. Wisconsin's responsibility was to do a good job at home in order to provide a model for other states.[15]

When the newspapers reported that La Follette had ruled out national action for 1936, he summoned reporters into his office to try to convince them that he was not trying to discourage third-party efforts. "I will do everything I can to promote it," he said, estimating that "at least ten states" were ready for third-party action already. But he refused to speculate further about 1936 or 1940 except to say that if the choice boiled down to Hoover or Roosevelt, he would strongly back the president.

Obviously the governor hoped that nothing would upset the friendly understanding he had established with the national administration.[16]

Sen. Gerald P. Nye delivered the same message to third-party promoters who gathered in Chicago on 5 and 6 July for a Farmer Labor Political Federation conference and bravely decided to go ahead with plans for a third-party ticket in the upcoming election. Nye warned them that such a move could throw the election to the reactionaries, to which one delegate responded, "How can you build without making a start?" The conference declared that the New Deal had defrauded the people in order to protect the profits of large corporations and financial interests. The new party would be based upon the principles of "production for use" and an "economy of abundance" and would hold a nominating convention the following year. Hoping to broaden their appeal, they renamed their organization the American Commonwealth Federation, although units in the Midwest were allowed to retain the familiar designation of Farmer Labor Political Federation.

Amlie continued as chairman of the reorganized structure and Bingham as secretary, leaving operations essentially unchanged. The dilemma they faced was easily stated: they needed proven vote getters to head their crusade, but successful politicians of the caliber of Olson, Nye, and the La Follettes had more to gain by cooperating with Roosevelt for the time being. One participant at the conference succinctly stated their predicament: "The elimination of Roosevelt is a necessary condition for a third party." The irony, as Robert Morss Lovett remarked, was that the "chief obstacle to the formation of a national third party is the success that its natural leaders have achieved in several states." As long as they remained successful within the confines of the old party structure, they would be reluctant to venture into uncharted waters.[17]

Governor Olson sent a friendly message to the Chicago conference, but the La Follettes remained aloof. Senator La Follette was upset to see the big play that Evjue gave the meeting in the *Progressive* and asked Phil to complain about it. From conversations with several spectators, Bob concluded, "It was largely a group of crackpots who cannot possibly get anywhere in the formation of an important and new party movement." That attitude merely reinforced the feeling of Bingham, Selden Rodman, and other Federationists that they could not count on the La Follettes for help.[18]

Progressive doubts about the direction of the New Deal receded after

President Roosevelt moved off dead center in June 1935. His indecisiveness seemed to vanish after business unleashed new attacks on his administration and the Supreme Court invalidated the National Recovery Administration and other New Deal legislation on "Black Monday," 27 May 1935. Progressives heartily approved Roosevelt's swing to the left, which included his endorsement of the Wagner labor proposal. Also added to his must list of legislation were social security, banking reform, public-utility holding-company regulation, and a wealth tax. The *Madison Capital Times* commented, "The sudden decision of President Roosevelt to press for immediate enactment of liberal and labor legislation is regarded as a deterrent to demand for a national party in 1936."[19]

By July it became apparent that the La Follettes would back the president's reelection. Governor La Follette told *Milwaukee Journal* reporter Fred Kelly that the immediate organization of a national third party was unrealistic and that a "real leftist party" could not be established before 1940. The governor said he perceived in the electorate a great cleavage, which would leave middle-of-the-roaders completely isolated. Eventually everyone would have to decide whether he was a reactionary or a radical.[20]

But La Follette's radical tone and denigration of the moderate position did not prevent him from mapping out just such an intermediate path for himself. After returning from a trip to Madison, Leo Crowley informed presidential secretary Marvin McIntyre, "Governor La Follette promised very definitely that he would go along in 1936 and would take an active part in support of the President." When reporters interpreted his prediction of Roosevelt's reelection as an endorsement, La Follette emphasized that he was merely forecasting what would happen, not stating a position on the question. One political columnist observed, "The La Follettes are sailing between Scylla and Charybdis when they mention their apparent belief that President Roosevelt will be re-elected to succeed himself." On the one hand, they hoped to avoid a third-party movement; on the other, they wished to retain the good will of the third-party promoters and to maintain their own freedom of action.[21]

In July 1935 Roosevelt invited the La Follette brothers to Hyde Park "so we can plan the coming campaign." They were overnight guests during the first week in September. One of Governor La Follette's secretaries, A. W. Zeratsky, came along to explain how the president could use a letter campaign to rally support. "Z," as he was affectionately called by his friends, had applied his experience in the mail-order business to the mailing of letters from the governor's office addressed to school teachers, veterans, pensioners, and other special-interest groups. That March, La Follette had solicited the views of hundreds of Wisconsin clergymen about the relief situation. Roosevelt seemed intrigued by the idea and asked Zeratsky to prepare a similar letter for his signature. Unfortunately, Zeratsky's draft reproduced several passages from the one used earlier, and the press had a great deal of fun comparing the language used in the La Follette and Roosevelt efforts. That embarrassing fiasco brought a quick end to this presidential experiment.[22]

One evening late that fall Phil La Follette impulsively put a phone call through to the president, who, as La Follette later recalled the episode, was in quite a jovial mood.

"Hello, Mr. President, how are things with you?" the governor said.

"Just fine, and with you?"

"O. K. I haven't a thing on my mind. I just called to tell you that I think things are shaping up splendidly for next year. You are doing a grand job. And unless I miss my guess you are going to give the 'Old Guard' a real licking next year."

Chatting later with Bob La Follette and Harry Hopkins, the president laughed, "Say, I want to tell you a rare and remarkable experience I had not long ago. Phil called me on the phone. Believe it or not *he didn't want anything!* He just called to tell me things were going fine and wanted to say 'Hello.' I nearly fell off my chair!"[23]

Phil La Follette's decision to go with Roosevelt for 1936 resulted largely from simple political calculation. Although he continued to hold serious reservations about some New Deal policies, he muted his disagreements and portrayed Roosevelt as "the poor man's friend." He also stressed the difficulties of launching a new party and asserted that the only realistic alternatives this time lay within the Republican and Democratic parties. By the end of 1935 many Progressives were predicting Roosevelt's reelection.[24]

While the La Follettes carefully distanced themselves from Amlie and Bingham's Farmer Labor Political Federation, they recognized certain advantages in organizing such a group at the state level. Its dangers would probably be outweighed by the possibilities it would open for welding together all the left-wing groups in the state. The dismal results of the 1935 legislative session spotlighted the need for obtaining greater cooperation between the Socialists and other radical and liberal groups if better results were to be achieved during the next session. Different groups had their own motives for being interested in amalgamation. Labor and farm organizations wanted assistance in enacting their special bills and hoped to do better than the Farmer Labor Progressive League in imposing party discipline through control over platforms and candidates. Many Socialists were prepared to make concessions in return for support for their candidates in local elections. The Progressives were well aware that capturing several more seats in Milwaukee and along the shore of Lake Michigan could give them control of the next legislature. Those areas of high labor concentration seemed available if only the left-wingers could pool their resources.[25]

However, substantially different opinions and competing ambitions stood in the way of unity. Old-timers in the movement saw little reason to change their ways, while many radicals resented the way in which the La Follettes dominated the party. Mayor Daniel Hoan of Milwaukee had announced after the Progressive party's formation that Wisconsin's Socialists would waste no time on the La Follettes since they were merely trying to patch up an obsolete capitalistic system. But Socialist political difficulties and the enticing prospect of electoral gains from fusion with the Progressives put the Socialists into a more cooperative mood by the end of 1935.[26]

The animosities and divisions that normally separated Progressives from Socialists were temporarily cast aside as they sensed the opportunities available in united action. The Wisconsin State Federation of Labor initiated the process at its annual convention in July 1935 when it issued a call for a conference to be held later in the year. Thomas Duncan, who represented the Progressive party during preliminary discussions, vigorously pushed for harmony. At a meeting in October, he reluctantly assented to "production-for-use" language and also to the idea of an individual-membership, dues-paying, disciplined organization, although he realized that many Progressives, including his boss, rejected the notion. He believed it necessary, however, for the Progressives to be flexible if they expected to obtain cooperation from the Socialists and the State Federation of Labor. Even then the crucial question remained whether the Socialists would go along.[27]

On 30 November and 1 December 1935, representatives of the Progressive party, the Socialist party, the Farmer Labor Progressive League, the Wisconsin State Federation of Labor, the railroad brotherhoods, the Workers' Alliance, the Farm Holiday Association, the Farmers' Equity

Union, and the Wisconsin Cooperative Milk Pool convened in Milwaukee to create the Wisconsin Farmer-Labor Progressive Federation. Duncan played so visible a role in writing the platform and directing the meeting that many observers incorrectly assumed that he, rather than Henry Ohl and the labor unions, was the driving force. Duncan skillfully created a semblance of unity by suppressing obvious points of disagreement. The platform prompted minimal debate, since only its production-for-use phraseology distinguished it from the typical Progressive document. The Progressive party's executive committee had earlier rejected the right of a disciplined, dues-paying group to write platforms or endorse candidates, but those reservations were muffled at the Milwaukee meeting, and the Progressive delegates joined in the display of unity.[28]

The establishment of the Wisconsin FLPF heartened Bingham, who viewed it as a vehicle for checking the La Follettes' personal machine and stimulating the third-party movement. In fact, the federation's basic orientation was local, not national. Although the State Federation of Labor professed to want a national third party eventually, throughout 1936 it discouraged speculation about one. Very few Wisconsinites were thinking along those lines.[29]

Critical to the success of the unity movement was the participation of the Socialists, who held a referendum of party members in January to determine their position on the new federation. They found no encouragement in comments made by the governor, who told J. C. Ralston of the *Milwaukee Journal* that the federation possessed no power to write platforms or endorse candidates. That was exactly what it had been established to do, retorted Socialist organizer Andrew Biemiller, who said that Progressive party delegates who had attended the conference could confirm it. Moreover, Duncan had sat on the subcommittee that drafted the platform, including the controversial *production-for-use* phrase. How could the governor now suggest that the term was vague and open to misunderstanding, Biemiller wondered. La Follette's disparaging references to the Socialists and his apparent refusal to accept what his own party's delegates had agreed to would have to be straightened out, Biemiller told Duncan, or the federation would probably be rejected in the Socialist referendum. Despite their misgivings, at the urging of Mayor Hoan the Socialists voted, by a margin of five to one, to join the Farmer-Labor Progressive Federation and to withdraw their party from the ballot in return for having Socialist candidates in a number of slots on the Progressive ticket. The coalition, it was hoped, would add 50,000 votes to the Progressive totals the next time around, while the Socialists would benefit from Progressive votes in local contests. Representatives of the two parties planned to meet before elections to plan strategy.[30]

Duncan continued to play a leading role in the FLPF, but Governor La Follette never joined it or endorsed it. He benefited from Socialist votes and legislative support and endeavored to maintain left-wing unity, but he also tried to limit the FLPF's growth to the industrial counties in the eastern part of the state. He quietly advised Progressives to build up their own party organizations rather than worry about the FLPF; that coincided with the inclinations of most Progressives, especially old-timers and rural residents, but a sizable minority within the party favored the new organization. La Follette cited the same arguments that he had used against the Farmer Labor Progressive League. In a formal letter to the federation in June 1936, he rejected candidate endorsement and party discipline and warned that the concept of production-for-use was vague and open to misunderstanding.[31]

The governor's standoffishness created an awkward dilemma for the FLPF, since one of their cardinal rules required that only members of the organization could be endorsed for office. Yet to endorse somebody other than La Follette for governor would have seemed ridiculously counterproductive. After a lengthy debate, which included both condemnation and praise for the governor, the first state convention, held on 20 and 21 June 1936, decided to endorse no one for the top office. It did endorse every incumbent Progressive congressman except Madisonian Harry Sauthoff, one of the few Progressive officeholders besides the La Follettes not to sign up. At that convention, La Follette also was able through Duncan to get the offensive *production-for-use* phrase removed from the FLPF platform. In its place went an innocuous proposal for the formation of corporations that would operate like the Tennessee Valley Authority "to perform such functions of government as the welfare of the people makes necessary."[32]

The relationship between Phil La Follette and the farmer-labor groups in Wisconsin resembled the one between Franklin Roosevelt and radical, progressive, and third-party forces in the United States. Both leaders were simultaneously attracted to and repelled by groups to their left on the political spectrum. Roosevelt needed to appease the regular Democrats, and La Follette depended mainly on moderate Progressives; in each case the regular organization objected to flirtations by their leader with the left-wingers. Just as Roosevelt solicited Progressive support while hoping to defuse third-party efforts, so La Follette sought friendly relations with the farm and labor radicals while discouraging the expansion of the FLPF. Many Federation members considered the La Follettes to be ideologically weak and resented their aloof attitude; the Progressives similarly awaited more clear-cut signs of Roosevelt's friendship and solicitude. Despite all their talk about principles, platforms, and party discipline, the Wisconsin FLPF welcomed members almost as indiscriminately as the Progressives. When conservative or nonideological politicians such as Sol Levitan, a banker who served as state treasurer, and Theodore Dammann, the long-serving secretary of state, were heartily welcomed into the new organization, it became obvious that the terms of admission were not ideologically rigorous.[33]

The Farmer-Labor Progressive Federation disappointed those who hoped to construct a mass-membership organization. Many moderate and rural Progressives boycotted it. By the end of 1936 only slightly more than 5,000 members in 32 counties had signed up, and the original goal of 50,000 dues-paying members remained distant. In many counties there were only token units, composed mainly of officeholders who welcomed federation endorsement but cared little about stimulating membership. Schisms marred the relationship between the farmer-laborites and traditional Progressives in a number of counties. It gradually became apparent that the FLPF would never get far in converting the masses to a production-for-use program, so instead it evolved into a lobbying organization to back farm and labor measures in the legislature. Its removal of the Socialists from the ballot gave a sharp boost to the Progressives' electoral chances, but the long-held desire on the part of La Follette and others to unify all liberal elements in Milwaukee failed. Bickering and factionalism continued to characterize Milwaukee's Progressives.[34]

While he was trying to ready the party for the next election, Governor La Follette continued to devote much of his time to the problem of relief. He was upstaged in March when more than a hundred WPA strikers under the banner of the Workers' Alliance commandeered the assembly chamber in the state capitol and refused to budge until they were given higher wages, additional days off, and improved working conditions. The governor stated his sympathy for the plight of the strikers and wrote a personal check for thirty dollars to help them buy food, but he advised them to direct their protests at the real culprit—the federal government. Some of the strikers grumbled that if the La Follettes could make Ralph

Immell state works administrator, they surely had the power to secure a wage increase. When they received no satisfaction from the governor or new state WPA head Martin Torkelson, some of the strikers accused La Follette of being antilabor and called him "Foxy Phil, the wishy-washy liberal." They complained that his defeated works bill had become his "biggest alibi."

Public opinion quickly turned against the strikers. The State Federation of Labor supported the governor and denounced the strikers' actions. Many people, angered by seeing a gang of radicals lay siege to the capitol, called on the governor to oust them. After the *Capital Times* ran an editorial entitled "Anarchy or the State," strike leader Lyle Olson began calling Evjue "Hearst Number Two." La Follette waited a week and a half before finally ordering the capitol police to evict the men.[35]

The strike highlighted the expense of relief and intensified the controversy over it, both of which urged the governor to seek better remedies to the problem of unemployment. "It seems to me we must turn our backs upon the whole idea of getting something for nothing," he wrote a group of clergymen. "We must return again to the sound and wise policy that America owes no able-bodied person a living—but that we do owe every able-bodied person a real opportunity to earn his own living." Although the La Follette brothers were known for advocating generous relief spending, Phil La Follette's antipathy toward continued relief expenditures grew increasingly evident.[36]

The depression challenged many people's basic beliefs, and La Follette shared in the general ferment. Although his political outlook remained basically consistent, his prescription for recovery shifted from redistribution to expansion. By 1936 La Follette had begun to concentrate on the need to expand production and to downplay the argument for redistribution of wealth as a means of stimulating consumption. Careful listeners could have detected a shift in emphasis in his rhetoric as early as 1934, when La Follette stepped up his criticisms of New Deal agricultural restrictions and demanded the creation of constructive jobs in the place of continued relief. In an article for *Common Sense* in July 1934, he reiterated his long-held position that nothing was wrong with production: "The sooner we stop wasting our time and energy there, the sooner we shall get to our real difficulty—redistribution." Yet, on the hustings that fall he frequently repeated "the parable of the seed grain." Surplus money and credit were like "economic seed grain"; just as seed planted in the ground multiplies itself many times over, so economic seed grain when put to use would multiply wealth for everybody. La Follette sounded very much like conservatives who stressed the need for capital investment. He praised President Roosevelt's statement at Green Bay that the economic problem lay less in addition and subtraction than in multiplication. "If I interpret him rightly," La Follette said, "he meant that our task is to revive and increase our total national income." Earlier than most other politicians, he began to advocate explicitly the expansion of the country's productive capacity and output as the true solution to the depression.[37]

By early 1936 La Follette was making economic expansion the major theme of his speeches. Discerning listeners could have perceived in his messages subtle modifications that were carrying him in a more conservative direction. In rejecting any *"radical* sharing of wealth," he relied upon the same sort of rhetorical device he had used earlier in condemning Herbert Hoover's philosophy of *"rugged* individualism," except that now the criticism was directed at the left rather than at the right. La Follette also argued for strengthening "the vitality and character of the American people" by providing jobs for all and argued for the philosophy of "pay-as-you-go" in government expenditures. Balanced budgets not only made economic sense but also constituted "a moral responsibility." Those themes emerged frequently as La Follette crafted an image of himself that no longer emphasized his radicalism but rather focused on his moderation and common sense; he identified himself not with spending, planning, and relief, but with policies of economic growth. La Follette refused to cast his ideas in the simple terms of being pro-New Deal or anti-New Deal. Since he was committed to cooperating with Roosevelt's reelection plans, his options were limited, but within those boundaries he continued to search for reasonable, workable policies that would elicit popular support. Establishing a position that would satisfy liberals as well as third-party advocates, appeal to a broad spectrum of voters, and conform to the real problems facing the country remained his goal. If the results were sometimes disappointing, the handicaps under which he labored were many, and individuals who could serve as standards for comparison hardly merited higher judgments.[38]

"Roosevelt is *it* this year," even Alfred Bingham was ready to admit by May 1936. The formation a month earlier of Labor's Non-Partisan League to work for the reelection of the president had destroyed any realistic hopes for a third-party movement that year. Bingham still wanted to hold a conference that summer to build enthusiasm for the future, but even that hope was dashed when the La Follettes called a conference of Progressives to meet after the Democratic convention. He consoled himself with the hope that the American Commonwealth Federation could go along and "help steer the thing right." The October issue of *Common Sense* grudgingly counseled its readers to support Roosevelt for reelection and then to withdraw support "the day after election day."[39]

Both the Wisconsin Progressives and the Minnesota Farmer-Laborites had disappointed the third-party enthusiasts by going along with Roosevelt. Phil La Follette avoided potentially embarrassing questions about the future of the Progressive party when its second anniversary was celebrated in Milwaukee on 19 May—he and Isen were vacationing in Guatemala.[40]

The Roosevelt tide proved irresistible that year. Only a handful of Progressives, most prominently Walter Graunke of Marathon County, supported the presidential candidacy of Congressman William Lemke on the Union party ticket, whose major appeal in Wisconsin was to Catholic voters. Backing the Democrats appeared to be the only feasible alternative for the Progressives. The national administration had openly courted the La Follettes, to the continual frustration of state Democrats. While Progressives obtained some WPA posts and other slots, Postmaster General Farley saw to it that most patronage jobs did go to Democrats. A few party leaders, such as former state chairman Otto La Budde, argued the case for cooperating with the Progressives, but most of them, especially state legislators, remained hostile to reform and were openly critical of the New Deal. That made it all the more difficult for Roosevelt supporters such as Duffy and Broughton to obtain any help from the president. It was a vicious circle.[41]

Memories of Roosevelt's visit to Green Bay in 1934 haunted Democratic strategists, and they feared some kind of replay if the president entered the state again. In fact, Governor La Follette was working with Marvin McIntyre on a whistle-stop itinerary. Senator Duffy, who was kept in the dark about all this, meanwhile was counseling the president to avoid the state. Luckily for the Democrats, Roosevelt's decision to attend Secretary of War George Dern's funeral forced him to cancel his plans for visiting the state. Instead he took La Follette's advice and decided to invite him and several other midwestern governors to a conference in Des Moines to discuss drought problems in the area.[42]

Roosevelt's efforts to satisfy both Progressives and Democrats in Wisconsin clearly left the former group more satisfied. He used personal contacts and the discreet mediation of Leo Crowley to woo the La Follettes while relying on Farley's organization to keep the Democrats in line. Farley sympathized with Duffy's frustration. "I realize that you are up against certain difficulties," he wrote. "You certainly have been placed in many embarrassing positions, but I know that you will do the best you can under the circumstances."[43]

There was never a real possibility during the 1930s that the Progressives would amalgamate with the Democrats, for the Progressives treasured their independence too much and esteemed the Democrats too little. Nor were state Democrats willing to do in 1936 what their Minnesota colleagues did in withdrawing their senatorial and gubernatorial candidates from the race in favor of Farmer-Labor candidates. The only important party switch in Wisconsin occurred when Progressive State Sen. John E. Cashman, a strong spokesman for dairy interests from Brown County, obtained the Democratic congressional nomination in the Eighth District. He retained his Progressive ties, however, and remained in the state senate after losing his bid for the House of Representatives.[44]

Roosevelt's fraternization with the La Follettes and other independent liberals reflected his desire to break free of traditional party loyalties and to lay the groundwork for a truly liberal political coalition. The power of inertia was not easily overcome, however. Until the liberal forces could be brought together, Democratic party organizations had to be placated. Playing such a double game could not possibly satisfy either group. William Rubin, reflecting Democratic disgruntlement, complained that every time Phil La Follette headed for Washington, the papers splashed the news all over their columns, allowing the Progressives to gain publicity and take credit for every federal program in the state. As a result, Democratic regulars in Wisconsin grew even more antagonistic toward their president. The irony of Roosevelt's alliance with the La Follettes was that it resulted in setting back chances for liberalizing the Democratic party in the state. Yet, until the Democrats did become more liberal, the Progressives would never consider cooperating with them. Rather than receding under Roosevelt's tutelage, animosities dividing the two groups reinforced each group's intransigence.[45]

Most Wisconsin Democratic party leaders, in fact, felt much more comfortable in siding with conservative Republicans. A long string of temporary alliances between the two groups had established a basis for unity in opposition to La Follette Progressivism, and the battle over the works bill during the 1935 legislative session had welded together the anti-La Follette coalition in that body. By 1936, some party leaders were

openly advocating fusion in order to rid the state of La Follettism.
Earlier efforts to unite their forces during two special senate elections in
April 1935 had failed, but the fusionists continued to argue that their
approach would succeed if conservatives in each party would only give
it a chance.[46]

The election of 1936 marked fhe political apogee of both the New Deal
and the Wisconsin Progressive party. Phil La Follette later recalled it as
"perhaps the most pleasant year I was to have in public life. . . . We
were on—for once—a political plateau: we did not have to climb so
hard." La Follette was in high spirits when he and Bob visited the White
House on Phil's birthday, 8 May. He later conveyed to Roosevelt his
approval of the Democratic platform. Another potentially embarrassing
flap reminiscent of the Zeratsky letter to the clergy was avoided when
Bob La Follette pointed out that material he had supplied had been
taken from his father's 1924 platform. Harry Hopkins had planned to use
it in the peroration of the platform, but when Bob informed Samuel
Rosenman of its source, Democratic platform writers were put to work
rewriting the section. Roosevelt's acceptance speech impressed Phil La
Follette as "one of the best, if not the best thing" that he had done.[47]

President Roosevelt again decided to establish a special committee to
line up Progressive voters behind his candidacy and chose Bob La
Follette to head it. Phil La Follette contributed a list of national
third-party leaders and assisted Bob in organizing a conference that met
in Chicago on 11 September to establish the Progressive National
Committee. The meeting had a heavy Wisconsin flavor; about 20 of the
150 participants were from the state, including the La Follettes, Evjue,
Amlie, Elizabeth Brandeis, Herman Ekern, Gerald Boileau, Gardner
Withrow, Harry Sauthoff, and George Schneider. As he looked around
the gathering, New York's Fiorello La Guardia noticed many fellow
campaigners from the 1924 La Follette for President drive. The
delegates adopted a statement of principles that came largely from the
Wisconsin Progressive platform, including the six principles that had
originally been part of Phil La Follette's personal platform in 1934. Their
statement declared that political realignment could best be promoted
that year by maintaining liberal unity. Roosevelt was endorsed upon "a
strictly nonpartisan basis, with complete reservation of freedom of
action in the future, and not necessarily endorsing any political party."[48]

Phil La Follette finally openly endorsed the president, but not without qualifications. "It is clear our next president will be Roosevelt or Landon," he told the gathering. "With that choice, in my judgment, all liberal-minded people should support Roosevelt. That doesn't mean I'm satisfied with all phases of the New Deal." That evening, after the conference had adjourned, the president called to congratulate the La Follettes and several of their friends. The meeting, in his opinion, had been "grand." During the next several weeks, Bob La Follette made several radio broadcasts for the committee, but Frank P. Walsh ran its daily operations. Phil La Follette made a small financial contribution and allowed his name to be listed as a member of the speakers' bureau, but he devoted the remaining eight weeks before the election entirely to promoting his own chances and the candidacies of Progressives in Wisconsin.[49]

Throughout the 1936 campaign, La Follette's relationship with President Roosevelt grew increasingly close. On election eve the La Follettes wired Roosevelt, "We hope you know what a magnificent job you have done throughout this whole campaign. You brought it to a climax Saturday night with the greatest speech you ever made. Every Progressive in America is proud of you and will be at the polls tomorrow with his coat off to give the reactionaries the licking they so richly deserve for their rotten campaign. Affectionate Regards. Bob and Phil La Follette."[50]

It was Roosevelt's year, and the prospects of victory on his bandwagon brought a semblance of unity to liberals of varying persuasions. Just as the Roosevelt drive smothered Progressives' doubts and enticed them into the fold, so the La Follette allure in Wisconsin smoothed over divisions among left-wing elements and welded them into a unified force. How long this cooperative spirit would last remained to be seen.

The Progressive political machine was loosely organized, informal, and personal. It revolved largely around the personal leadership of the La Follettes and those close to them. Mainly dependent on dedicated volunteer workers, local Progressive clubs, which remained relatively dormant most of the time, came alive around election time in order to get out the vote. Their size and activity depended almost entirely on the local leadership, with each county possessing its own special character. While internal disputes occasionally led to requests for mediation from Madison, for the most part the local groups were on their own. Duncan spent many fruitless hours trying to straighten out the confused situation in Milwaukee, but La Follette tried to avoid entanglement in such situations. To one inquirer he wrote, "It has been my policy not to interfere with the running of the various local organizations throughout the state. I am interested only in keeping them active and helping them develop."[51]

The governor constantly stressed the importance of putting full slates of local candidates in the field in order to stimulate interest for the entire ticket. He also encouraged local organizations to develop extensive lists of voters for election time. Sporadic efforts emerged to establish a permanent Progressive headquarters in Madison and to form a speakers' bureau, but enthusiasm for both ideas waned between campaigns. La Follette attended as many fairs, picnics, meetings, and fund raisers as possible, and local Progressive clubs sometimes sponsored dances, bazaars, and card parties in order to raise money. In spite of all this, campaign funds were always meager.[52]

The governor sometimes drew pointed criticism from local leaders who complained about the weak or nonexistent Progressive organizations in some counties. They criticized him for lackadaisical leadership and for allowing local Progressive clubs to stagnate between elections. They wanted more literature to distribute and more patronage jobs to be available, and a few of them even requested paid organizers to manage Progressive campaign operations. The governor responded that there was no money to do those things and that his intervention from Madison would in most cases only complicate things for local groups "who do not like to have outsiders meddle in their affairs." Every two years he tried to visit every county on the election trail, and in every town he entered he discussed organizational matters with the local leaders.[53]

Dozens of disparate county and local organizations constituted the Progressive party; what held them together more than anything else was the personal leadership of Phil La Follette.The Progressive state organization actually consisted of the thousands of names, faces, and bits of information stored in the governor's memory and in the little black loose-leaf notebooks he carried with him. Through persuasion, conciliation, and sheer force of personality, he welded together the diverse interests within the Progressive coalition. One appreciative state leader commended La Follette for his "hard work, sacrifice and willingness to take the brunt of things upon your shoulders." He declared, "Folks have a genuine affection for you, Phil, and this fact crops out in every conference I have attended. They like you as a man." There was a Progressive State Central Committee, as required by law, and differing points of view competed for hearings in party councils, but throughout his tenure as governor, La Follette provided the Progressives with direction and symbolized their purposes.[54]

Despite his clear position as leader, though, Phil La Follette denied that he ran a "machine." It certainly was a different kind of machine than most of the better-known ones outside Wisconsin. It had little money to spend, relied almost entirely on volunteer help, usually rewarded the party faithful only with a sense of personal satisfaction, and was virtually untouched by corruption. But the Progressives organized their forces at election time, rewarded campaign workers with jobs when any were available, kept the party control within a small leadership group, and practiced the politics of self-interest and compromise that existed everywhere else. The Progressives were different in many ways, but they were not as unique as they liked to think.[55]

Their opponents liked to charge, outside observers often assumed, and the Progressives themselves sometimes complained that the La Follettes dictated party decisions. References were made to the "La Follette dynasty," the "Madison gang," and the "State of Wisfollette." Since the senator generally avoided local matters and left the responsibility in his brother's hands, the contention makes little sense in Bob's case. As for Phil La Follette, there is some evidence to support it. His active intervention in legislative matters, his visible presence in party councils and conventions, and his ability to set the agenda for Progressive issues and activities point to the central and dramatic role he played in the party while he remained in office. One could readily agree with those who said that Phil La Follette *was* the party. And yet he did not dictate slates of candidates, he could take only partial credit for writing party platforms, he had little money or patronage to distribute, and he exerted minimal control over local party activities. La Follette could not replace Secretary of State Theodore Dammann and State Treasurer Sol Levitan as his running mates with more liberal candidates, and when he did seem to be meddling in the nomination process, he invited the wrath of disappointed contestants.[56]

Perhaps the best measure of La Follette's dominance in the party was that throughout the decade no one ventured the slightest challenge to his leadership. People might sometimes complain about what was happening, but even in 1934 and 1938, when La Follette indicated a reluctance to run, no one stepped forward to test him. His failure to encourage the emergence of other leaders in the party gravely injured the party's chances after he left office. Although La Follette genuinely loved the party and was committed to its cause, his primary interest lay with his own personal advancement, which did not include the cultivation of alternative leadership.

The election of 1936 was a crossroads for Phil La Follette and the Wisconsin Progressives. Taking advantage of the new party machinery that had been established over the previous two years, benefiting from unprecedented unity among left-wing forces in the state, and basking in the glow of New Deal favor, they aimed for a victory that would not only guarantee the success of their programs in the state legislature but also establish the basis for a genuine national political realignment. Principles tested by experience guided their efforts, but portents for the future included the difficulties confronting third-party promoters, the consolidation of the New Deal coalition, and the growing importance of radio. For the present, though, the Progressives were riding high; concerns about the future could wait.

Once again, Phil La Follette mapped out an itinerary for 1936 that would take him into every part of the state. Starting out in Baraboo, he delivered more than two hundred speeches before winding up in the crucial urban centers of Kenosha, Racine, and Milwaukee. Gordon Sinykin, the governor's legal counsel and personal adviser, coordinated the campaign from the Madison headquarters. He provided suggestions for attracting large crowds and composed daily press releases so the papers would have fresh news about the governor's activities. He continually had to remind his boss to include the released statements in his speeches, a request La Follette frequently forgot to fulfill. Money, as always, was scarce, with most of it coming from small contributions, supplemented by larger gifts from Progressive candidates and other supporters, and a few donations from out-of-state admirers such as Paul M. Herzog, Kenneth Shumway, and David K. Niles. La Follette spent only about four thousand dollars for each of his campaigns for the governorship. Most legislative candidates spent no more than a few hundred dollars, and some reported spending nothing at all.[57]

Politics in the thirties was undergoing a transformation under pressure from national trends, especially the increasing use of the radio, but campaign practices still looked to the past more than to the future. Face-to-face contact remained the rule. Families would pack picnic baskets and drive for miles to hear the candidates square off. La Follette sparkled in that kind of personalized environment, where he could touch and talk directly to people. On the platform, shaking his fist, rolling up his sleeves, now calm, now animated, now reasonable, now ranting, he found his true metier. When Robert Morss Lovett, who was more used to Chicago-style politics, characterized the first Progressive birthday party in May 1935 as a throwback to an earlier, more primitive and intimate political era, he was describing the political milieu in which progressivism thrived. La Follette himself observed, "Since the early days of the Progressive movement in this state, the major share of our work has been done by reaching large numbers of people through word of mouth."[58]

Radio, however, was already beginning to recast the traditional political culture that had nurtured the progressive movement. Governor La Follette had quickly grasped the potentialities of the new medium and frequently used it, both for campaigning and for explaining his legislative programs to the people. He had successfully adapted his speaking style to fifteen-minute time slots by reading from a manuscript and trying to obtain the effect of talking directly to his listeners. He respected and envied President Roosevelt's marvelously effective radio "crooning," as he called it, and he voiced some concern about the implications of the new political methods encouraged by radio and advertising. A story in the *Progressive* pointed to the perils radio posed to the traditional personal style of Progressive campaigning. It had "completely changed the type and temper of public oratory," in the opinion of John Haynes Holmes, who predicted that mass meetings were on the way out and with them the whole paraphernalia of political campaigns.[59]

Three themes dominated La Follette's speeches during the campaign of 1936: the Wisconsin works bill, his pay-as-you-go philosophy, and the necessity for new laws to benefit farmers and workers. He emphasized his ability to obtain federal funds for the state, pointing out that Wisconsin surpassed every other state in expenditures on rural electrification. But he also argued that Wisconsin provided a favorable climate for business, citing a Chamber of Commerce pamphlet on the superior tax position enjoyed by Wisconsin residents.[60]

As elsewhere, the depression had polarized and sharpened ideological tendencies among the Wisconsin electorate. Winter Everett, a perceptive conservative political observer whose columns ran regularly in the *Wisconsin State Journal* and several other papers, detected more clear-cut cleavages along liberal and conservative lines than ever before in his memory. The bitter discord of the legislative session carried over into the following year's campaign. Progressives, who heard themselves being called leftists, radicals, wreckers, and communists, routinely addressed their opponents as reactionaries, "Hoovercrats," and spokesmen for privilege and special interests.[61]

Between the lines of the governor's strident rhetoric, however, some observers could detect a more conciliatory attitude toward business and conservative groups. Some of his ideas held considerable appeal for at least some conservatives, especially his insistence on ending relief and finding jobs for everyone. The *Waupaca County Post* editorialized, "To our mind it seems that conservative business leaders have learned a new attitude toward the governor. A La Follette is no longer regarded as a long-haired fanatical political demagogue or wild-eyed theorist."[62]

For Progressives the results were gratifying. They and the New Dealers rode to victory together in 1936 as Phil La Follette garnered 573,724 votes (47.6 percent of the major party vote) to 363,973 for Republican Alexander Wiley and 268,530 for Democrat Albert Lueck. All seven Progressive congressmen were reelected, and 48 assemblymen and 16 state senators were successful. In the presidential tally, Roosevelt obtained 802,984 votes to 380,828 for the Republican Landon, 60,297 for the Union party's William Lemke, and 10,626 for Socialist Norman Thomas. All around the state, most of those who voted for Landon also cast ballots for Wiley for governor, while only a small percentage of them gave their votes to La Follette. Those who voted for Roosevelt generally divided their votes between La Follette and Lueck. Progressives and New Dealers drew upon the same base of support.

Between 1932 and 1936 Roosevelt's share of the Wisconsin vote increased by only 1 percent, although in the heavily urban and industrialized counties of Milwaukee, Racine, and Kenosha it increased by an average of 4 percent, to 80 percent in Milwaukee, 71 percent in Kenosha, and 69 percent in Racine. Economic issues had become more salient during the early New Deal years, and the vote reflected it. Dramatic gains obtained by Phil La Follette and other Progressives between 1934 and 1936 resulted mainly from a falloff in the state Democratic vote and from the success of the Farmer-Labor Progressive Federation in uniting left-wing elements in the urban areas. While the Democratic percentage of the vote dropped from 40 to 22, the Republican increased from 19 to 30 and the Progressive from 41 to 48. The gains were not equally distributed, however. La Follette, who had trailed Albert Schmedeman by 32,643 votes in Milwaukee County in 1934, topped his nearest competitor, Lueck, in 1936 by 39,802. In two years he transformed a 4,270-vote deficit in Racine County to a 6,088-vote surplus and increased his plurality in Kenosha County from 601 to 7,373 votes. In those counties his percentage of the major party vote increased from 33 to 47, 33 to 47, and 42 to 56, respectively. In Dane County his percentage improved from 52 to 64, in Eau Claire County from 39 to 50, in Douglas County from 49 to 60, in La Crosse County from 43 to 59, and in Rock County from 29 to 39. Those counties included most of the largest cities in the state. Crucial to gains in areas along the lakeshore was the removal of the Socialists, who had obtained 44,589 votes in the gubernatorial contest in 1934. More important in inflating La Follette's overall totals, however, were his identification as a liberal in a liberal year and the influx of many voters who had voted Democratic in 1934. According to Michael Rogin and David L. Brye, the Progressive vote correlates strongly with the postwar Democratic vote, indicating that the Progressive party was important as a transitional vehicle for progressives and liberals who later formed the basis for a liberalized Democratic party in the forties and fifties.[63]

After the election, congratulatory messages poured in from all over the country, including telegrams from Fiorello La Guardia, Sidney Hillman, Donald Richberg, Felix Frankfurter, Alfred Bingham, and Harry Hopkins. La Follette elatedly wrote back to Hopkins, "Wisconsin did a good job. I think you will find that the President carried Wisconsin by a larger proportion than any other state." Somewhat disingenuously from one who had been a frequent critic of federal works programs, he added, "I hope you know how deeply we all appreciate the magnificent job you have done. In the face of a constant barrage from the front and snipers from the rear and flanks, you have gone ahead and done your job, kept your head and mouth closed excepting when you had a load for the enemy. Only those who have been close to you have any understanding of the difficulties you have had to work under." From the president came a complimentary note with a handwritten message scrawled on: "Let's keep up the good work."[64]

Victory was sweet, but already La Follette was looking ahead to the legislative session and beyond. The Progressives had demonstrated that their initial success had been no fluke, but if they were to extend their influence and consolidate their gains, they would have to make a better record in the legislature. Now was not the time to relax. Gordon Sinykin sent out a message from the governor's office as soon as the election was over: "It is a good idea to start working right now for the next campaign in 1938." For the moment, however, La Follette's primary task would be to translate the goals of the various groups within the Progressive coalition into effective legislation. The Socialists, and the farm and labor groups represented in the new Farmer-Labor Progressive Federation, would have to be satisfied. On the governor's success in unifying all of these diverse elements depended the Progressives' future and La Follette's own political career.[65]

Chapter 6

Wisconsin's "Little New Deal"

Entering his third term as governor, Phil La Follette faced new challenges and opportunities. Capitalizing on liberal trends that undergirded the development of a New Deal political coalition, the Progressives succeeded in capturing working control of both houses of the legislature. Governor La Follette seized the opportunity to push through a series of laws collectively constituting a "Little New Deal" for Wisconsin, but the tactics he used to force legislative action loosed a torrent of criticism. Having accomplished most of his goals in Wisconsin, La Follette began seriously to consider political realignment on a national scale and to reevaluate his own political future. Uncertain of how to proceed, through most of 1937 he voiced strong support for President Roosevelt and departed from many liberals in his wholehearted approval of the plan to increase the membership of the Supreme Court. The relationship between the two was never closer. That fall, however, as the economy went into a tailspin, the governor perceived growing vulnerability in the Roosevelt administration and decided to risk his political future on a third-party attempt to exploit that situation.

After the November 1936 elections, the La Follettes decided to take advantage of the period before inauguration day to take another trip to Europe. This tour would be just a pale version of the one four years earlier, since they had only a couple of weeks this time. In London, Isen stayed behind as Phil proceeded to Sweden and Norway, where he conferred with heads of government, politicians, and informed sources, including Prof. Gunnar Myrdal, to whom he took an immediate liking. The Progressives liked to cite Scandinavia as a model for the type of economic planning that they thought could work in the United States. Influential in their thinking was a book published in 1936, *Sweden: The Middle Way,* by political reporter Marquis Childs, a graduate of the University of Wisconsin and an acquaintance of the governor. Both La Follette brothers had spoken highly of the Swedish example. Not surprisingly, therefore, Phil discovered in Sweden and Norway evidence that

101

seemed to substantiate claims he had been making at home. He characterized their recovery programs as "a near duplication" of the Wisconsin works program. Sweden's budgetary system, he asserted, resembled proposals he had made in Wisconsin. Economics was not the only topic discussed, though; now even more than in 1933 war dominated people's thinking. Many Europeans already accepted its inevitability, La Follette observed.[1]

Back home a less pleasant task awaited the governor. In fact, he purposely shortened his European trip in order to be present for the showdown over the University of Wisconsin. The controversy would cost him much of the support and good will he had previously accumulated, and he later characterized it as "one of the most unpleasant, unsatisfying affairs in my public life."[2]

Like both of his parents, Phil La Follette was a graduate of the University of Wisconsin and felt a special attachment to it. His father had advocated a fusion of government and university through the Wisconsin Plan and from time to time had personally intervened in university affairs. Many of Phil La Follette's closest friends served on the faculty, and from 1926 to 1930 he had been a part-time law professor. It was widely assumed that Glenn Frank's appointment as president of the university had been dictated by the Progressives since Frank had established a reputation as a liberal journalist. In fact, the senior La Follette had favored Robert Morss Lovett, an English professor at the University of Chicago. After Dean Roscoe Pound of Harvard Law School turned down an offer, Frank, who was the editor of *Century* magazine, took it, largely as a result of the efforts of a friend, the noted Wisconsin author Zona Gale, who sat on the board of regents. The new president was a smooth and inspiring platform orator, a charming conversationalist, and a man of liberal instincts, but he possessed little talent for administration.[3]

Although Phil La Follette originally was receptive to the new president, he quickly concluded that the man was "shallow." During his first budget hearings as governor, he became convinced that Frank was mismanaging university affairs, but he hesitated to press the issue during the legislative sessions of 1931 and 1935 in the face of more insistent problems. In addition, Frank's ostentatious style of living, which included a liveried butler and chauffeured limousine, contrasted visibly with the deprivation caused by the depression, and it irritated the governor and many other Madisonians who considered it out of place in their town. The president's large salary and his reluctance to absorb a proportionately larger pay cut when salaries were slashed antagonized many faculty members and outside observers. Although many Progressives were comfortably well off, lavish displays generally did not appeal to them. To some Madisonians, the Franks epitomized an Eastern style of social climbing that was alien to the neighborly Midwest. A brief comment from the *Progressive* nicely reflects this attitude: "The Glenn Franks were recently in Chicago and their names were chronicled daily on the society pages with the uppity socialites of Chicago." Phil La Follette hobnobbed with wealthy businessmen and the social elite, too, but maintained a low profile doing so while managing at the same time to have reporters write about his subway rides and other common touches when he visited the city.[4]

La Follette obviously would have preferred to see Frank leave quietly but did not want to appear to have given the fatal push. Indirectly, he could influence the situation by his appointments to the board of regents and by his cautiously revealed sympathies. In January 1936, the governor was able to appoint five new Progressives to the board, which meant that eleven of the fifteen regents were his own nominees. The leader of the anti-Frank faction on the board was Harold Wilkie, a Progressive lawyer from Madison who took over as president of the board in June 1935. He and the governor basically agreed about what needed to be done, and he required no prompting to take the initiative in ousting Frank once the new regents were in place. La Follette voiced no objection when Wilkie informed him in February that he intended to move ahead on the matter. But as rumors proliferated that politically minded board members were ganging up on the university's president, La Follette responded by publicly denying reports that he wanted the job for himself and by urging Wilkie to postpone action until after the November elections.[5]

By the time the La Follettes returned from Europe, the stage was set. After conferring with the governor, Harold Wilkie and another Progressive regent, Clough Gates, privately informed Frank on 9 December that the next board meeting would take up the issue of terminating his contract. He responded by asking them to wait several weeks to allow him to find another job and resign gracefully so as not to injure his career. They agreed, but instead of bowing out, Frank actively rounded up support and took his case to the public. His sponsor, Zona Gale, tirelessly encouraged alumni to protest and spread the word to Eastern editors about the nefarious conspiracy in Madison to make a scapegoat of her friend. One result of her effort was an editorial in the *New York Herald*

Tribune praising Frank's liberalism and asserting that the regents wanted to fire him "for the simple reason that Governor La Follette wishes him ousted. The issue is wholly personal. It has no apparent basis in the educational record." "To her it is a holy crusade," one *Herald Tribune* staffer told the governor, "and you are the sultan of the infidels."[6]

Realizing that Frank would not quit without a fight, Wilkie on 16 December read a list of charges he had prepared criticizing the president's administration of the university. By 7 January, when the board voted by a margin of eight to seven against renewing his contract, the story had aroused national interest, and what La Follette had feared was occurring. The nature of the case was almost bound to make the governor look bad. Academic freedom was the battle cry of Frank's defenders; incompetent administration was the issue in the eyes of his critics. More objectionable to many Progressives were his lifestyle and his presumed political ambitions; his name had frequently surfaced as a Republican presidential possibility.[7]

Governor La Follette worried less about the Wisconsin reaction, which was largely predictable, than about the conclusions that out-of-staters would draw. Surprisingly few newspapers expressed much sympathy for Frank. Even the anti-La Follette *Milwaukee Journal* favored his removal, although it disapproved of "political pressures" in higher education. People whose main concern was Frank's competency generally supported La Follette, while those who worried more about academic freedom tended to be critical. Outsiders with little direct knowledge of the situation often judged La Follette in the worst light and assumed that politics was the real issue. One who did was Walter Lippmann, who perceived in the episode a clear violation of academic freedom and the unjustified intrusion of politics. Heywood Broun called the governor's actions "a great deal less than decently democratic" and found him guilty of "gross stupidity" for his part in Frank's removal.[8]

Other observers expressed greater sympathy for the governor's dilemma and gave him the benefit of the doubt. Academic freedom was not the issue at all, Ernest L. Meyer concluded; rather, President Frank had been ousted for administrative incompetence. That was the message that La Follette wanted to convey. He urged Arthur Sulzberger of the *New York Times* to dispatch a reporter to Madison to obtain a firsthand account of the facts; the governor also conceived the idea of a prestigious independent fact-finding committee that would investigate the case and presumably exonerate him. He invited Wisconsin Supreme Court justice

John D. Wickhem, University of Chicago professor Charles E. Merriam, and Harvard University president James Bryant Conant to evaluate the allegations on both sides and make a report. Conant expressed doubt that such a body could quickly resolve so tangled a situation but stated his willingness to study the state's system of governing higher education to determine whether the process had become too political. That was an obvious slap at La Follette and the Progressive regents, but the governor's readiness to launch such an independent investigation demonstrated how confident he was that an objective panel would vindicate his actions.[9]

Little likelihood existed, however, that the governor could talk himself out of the mess. Although it is impossible to be sure, most faculty members probably agreed that Frank should resign, but few dared to say so publicly. The governor refused to discuss the matter lest by talking about it he confirm his interest in the case. In truth, the anti-Frank regents, led by Harold Wilkie, were perfectly capable of acting on their own. People who wrote letters to the governor on the subject received copies of Wilkie's charges against Frank, but La Follette decided that his wisest course was to remain patient. When people compared Frank's record with that of his successor, they would approve the regents' decision and with it the governor's behavior.[10]

Other problems quickly intruded on Governor La Follette's attention. Once again he faced the persistent problems of unemployment and relief. The day after Glenn Frank's removal, La Follette went to Washington to see Roosevelt. In a White House meeting attended by Bob La Follette, Phil told the president of his intention to reintroduce his state works program. Roosevelt made no immediate commitment but suggested that they discuss the matter with Hopkins, who later promised Bob to send someone to Madison to work out a plan that could be submitted to the president.[11]

Meanwhile, Governor La Follette's goal was to procure increased federal relief funds for the state. WPA cuts were leading city mayors to press the governor for supplemental state subsidies. When La Follette talked with New York's governor, Herbert H. Lehman, during the inaugural festivities in Washington, both agreed on the need for increased federal aid. Upon La Follette's urging, Lehman invited several other governors to join forces in lobbying the White House on the issue. On 28 February, La Follette and Lehman met in Albany with Governors Henry

Horner of Illinois, Elmer Benson of Minnesota, Charles Hurley of Massachusetts, and Robert Quinn of Rhode Island. Afterward they requested a meeting with the president to air their concerns.[12]

Roosevelt invited them to appear on 6 March. At that session Roosevelt, Hopkins, and Morgenthau listened as the governors warned that they would not "squeeze" the taxpayers just so the federal government could balance its budget. On this issue Phil La Follette readily abandoned his pay-as-you-go rhetoric. The governors indicated that the relief burden was leading their states to the limits of their taxing capacity but that they were ready to cooperate in a more generous federal program. Lehman set up another meeting at the White House for 9 April, which was attended by himself, La Follette, Benson, and Quinn. After that session, when reporters asked La Follette if he felt any better about the situation, he replied, "Not particularly." Roosevelt's decision to cut WPA spending and to try to balance the federal budget contributed to the recession that fall. La Follette considered the president's $3 billion relief request in April to be entirely inadequate and was disappointed when the House of Representatives decisively rejected Wisconsin congressman Gerald Boileau's proposal to double the figure.[13]

La Follette visited the White House again in May and found the president in a "fine mood." This time the governor tried to be cordial but disinterested in the hope that Roosevelt would realize the necessity for taking stronger action on jobs. La Follette wanted to show that he did not feel wedded to the national administration. He got the impression on that trip that the president was considering him for a Supreme Court appointment in order to get him "out of the way." In early June he formally renewed his request for federal cooperation in a works program similar to the one he had proposed in 1935.[14]

La Follette clearly was not being very realistic, for much had changed during the preceding two years. The WPA bureaucracy was well in place, and much of the appropriation had already been spent. Even Governor La Follette did not appear to be very enthusiastic about the plan, which remained unacted upon when the legislature adjourned on 2 July.[15]

Despite the obstacles that stood in the way of federal action, La Follette thought that he deserved better treatment for his works plan. He believed that Roosevelt owed him something, especially for the vigorous support he was giving to the Court-packing plan. The La Follettes' vocal advocacy of that idea set them apart from most of their liberal colleagues. Taking a cue from Roosevelt, Phil La Follette introduced his own judicial retirement bill, which would pension state judges on half salary when they turned seventy. He emphasized, however, that his plan differed from the president's in that it conferred on the governor no power to appoint new judges. La Follette obtained no better results on the issue than did Roosevelt, experiencing his first major setback of the legislative session when the assembly defeated his bill by a vote of 55 to 35, as 26 Progressives voted against it.[16]

La Follette offered to testify before Congress for the president's plan, and in February he told a national radio audience that it represented a courageous action on the president's part and provided a "legal and Constitutional means of doing what needs to be done when it must be done." For the president to back down on the issue would be a great mistake, Phil wrote Bob in June. It would be "like our giving up in the midst of the Frank case." The analogy was apt. Both incidents were politically damaging, and partly in anticipation of this both had been deferred until after the 1936 elections. Roosevelt and La Follette were both criticized for operating secretly and deviously during the episodes. Both of them suffered the consequences of challenging venerated symbols in American society—the Supreme Court and the principle of academic freedom. Both cases were devoid of simple solutions, and in both cases the conservative forces were strengthened as a result.[17]

Governor La Follette's outspoken advocacy of the Court-reform bill at a time when most progressive voices were silent or critical prompted speculation that Roosevelt might name him to the Supreme Court. Sen. George Norris told the president that he thought the Wisconsin governor would make a good nominee. But after Justice Willis Van Devanter announced his impending retirement, Roosevelt considered naming Lloyd Garrison, dean of the University of Wisconsin Law School, and then opted instead for Sen. Hugo Black of Alabama, a liberal Democrat, whose confirmation by the Senate would be more certain. Both La Follettes enthusiastically approved the choice, and in a note to the president, Phil went further:

> Your choice of Hugo is perfect—from every point of view it is a Ten strike! *From the South—a Democrat—a member of the Senate—but one whose philosophy and convictions have been proved in the test of experience.* That's a real "natural"!—Have been out some since last seeing you—Iowa—Illinois & Wisconsin—both *industrial* and *agricultural* regions—Conditions generally are good—and sentiment toward you *excellent*—Only sore spots are WPA situation—and some feeling among farmers that they are not getting enough consideration—But any Washington talk about your having lost ground is "baloney." The folks are *with you.*[18]

As late as August and September, Phil La Follette continued to sing Roosevelt's praises. The Supreme Court fight, in which many progressives abandoned the president while conservatives coalesced against him, left the La Follettes closer to him than ever before. The governor remained disappointed with federal relief policies and retained doubts about Roosevelt's commitment to progressivism, but since he believed that people were still behind the president, La Follette was ready to suppress his own reservations and to reaffirm his own commitment. Several considerations constantly tugged La Follette in different directions: his commitment to political realignment, his expressed intent to work for a national third party, his friendly relationship with Roosevelt, his estimate of public opinion, and his own personal ambitions. Ambivalence and commitment remained constantly in tension, but up to this point the governor still believed that working with Roosevelt was the best available option.

Meanwhile, Governor La Follette finally possessed the working majority of legislators that had previously eluded him. Reversing its record during the previous session, the state legislature in 1937 enacted a series of laws collectively labeled Wisconsin's "Little New Deal." Having increased their membership in the assembly from forty-five to forty-eight, the Progressives again controlled that body. Paul Alfonsi, a high-school teacher from Pence who was associated with the radical wing of the Progressive party, obtained the speakership over the more conservative Victor Nehs, a moderate Progressive from Neillsville who had the backing of most of the Democrats and Republicans. As the roll was called, Alfonsi noted the results on his tally sheet and finally remarked loud enough that people around him could hear, "Well, it looks like I've got it." That prompted Assemblyman Charles Beggs to switch his vote from Nehs to Alfonsi, who consequently won by a vote of 50 to 49![19]

Alfonsi respresented two counties on the state's northern border, and generally the northern and western parts of the state had the heaviest representation of Progressives in the assembly. But the election had also tipped the balance for the Progressives in several districts in the southeastern part of the state, primarily as a result of the activities of the Farmer-Labor Progressive Federation. The assembly now included a Progressive from Kenosha County, two from Racine County, and seven from Milwaukee County (out of a total of twenty in that county). Before, there had been only one Progressive from Racine County and two from

Milwaukee County. Andrew Biemiller, a Milwaukee Socialist, as a Progressive floorleader would play a major role in pushing the governor's legislation through the assembly. In the upper house the Progressives had two of Milwaukee County's seven senators after having none earlier.[20]

With Progressives controlling the assembly, the fate of La Follette's proposals lay once again in the senate. With eight holdovers in addition to three reelected and five newly elected senators, the Progressives had increased their representation in the body from thirteen to sixteen, to one less than a majority. The narrow defeat of Walter Hunt of River Falls, who had been a fixture in the senate since 1924, thus was especially frustrating to his party colleagues. The Progressives were able during the session, however, to rely on the votes of Phil Nelson, a Douglas County Republican who had frequently cooperated with them during 1935, and Arthur Zimney, a Milwaukee Democrat. Both were rewarded with positions on the important Committee on Committees, and they became the only non-Progressive committee chairmen in the senate. In addition, the governor appointed Nelson to the Grain and Warehouse Commission in October, and Zimney's brother got a job in the Beverage Tax Department. Nelson ably helped Progressive floorleader E. Myrwyn Rowlands maneuver bills through the upper house. Less cohesiveness marked the Republican and Democratic opposition this time. Armed with friendly rulings from Lt. Gov. Henry Gunderson and Assembly Speaker Paul Alfonsi and firmly in control of every committee in both houses, the Progressives possessed the opportunity they had been waiting for to push through their proposals.[21]

Thomas Duncan announced before the legislature convened that the governor's three top priorities would be a new labor law, a state power program, and budget and tax legislation. First on the agenda was the reintroduction of the labor disputes bill that had been roadblocked two years earlier. Designed to complement the National Labor Relations Act, it was labor's rallying cry, and Governor La Follette considered its enactment essential if he were to retain credibility with the Farmer-Labor Progressive Federation. The FLPF counted twenty-seven of the forty-eight Progressive assemblymen and eight of the sixteen senators among its members. On 1 April, Phil Nelson and Arthur Zimney provided the crucial votes for passing the Wisconsin Labor Relations Act.[22]

Wisconsin was the second of five states to approve a "little Wagner Act" that year. La Follette, while recognizing the significance attached to the law by the labor movement, viewed it less as a device to promote labor union growth than as a method to promote industrial peace. Mediation would be the primary purpose of the new Labor Relations Board, La Follette told people, and a new spirit of cooperation between management and labor would result. "This law is founded on the proposition that there are few, if any, disputes which fair and reasonable men cannot adjust if they will only sit down around the table and work out their difficulties," he asserted.[23]

Peaceful adjustment of disputes was the governor's continual refrain. To translate this goal into action, he called in business and labor leaders to draw up rules of the game that would be agreeable to both sides. He was determined to make the law work and to make it a model for other states. His appointments of Edwin E. Witte, Voyta Wrabetz, and Father Francis J. Haas to the new labor board quickly won unanimous senate confirmation and stimulated much favorable comment. Witte's prominent role in formulating the Social Security Act was widely recognized. Less conspicuous, but equally solid, were the records of Wrabetz on the Wisconsin Industrial Commission and the Milwaukee priest on the National Labor Board. The governor also enlisted the aid of two university law professors, William Gorham Rice and Nathan Feinsinger, to write an informational booklet setting forth the purposes and main features of the new law.[24]

La Follette expected the labor act to serve several functions. It would cement his position with organized labor, but he also attached to it broader significance. At the senate hearings, Jack Handley, secretary of the State Federation of Labor, had testified, "This is a labor bill. If it is to be turned into a bill for the further protection of the employer we would rather not have the bill at all." But the governor viewed it as more than a labor bill. Outside labor circles he played down the benefits it would confer on unions, concentrating instead on the contribution it would make to industrial peace and harmony. In a letter to employers and union leaders he urged them to adopt "a spirit of 'give and take'—a willingness to work together for our common betterment and a respect for the other fellow's rights as well as insistence upon our own." The act, La Follette hoped, would appeal to a broad spectrum of moderate voters and enhance his reputation as a moderate and sensible leader.[25]

The legislature's second major accomplishment was the budget act. The Republican-Democratic coalition again adopted the tactics of delay and amendment, but the Progressives, now wielding effective control of the senate, were able to override the opposition. Since income tax revenues had risen by 35 percent, Governor La Follette avoided a difficult tax fight and easily won assent for renewing the emergency tax of 1935 in order to finance a $10 million budget increase.[26]

By far the toughest fight of the session occurred over La Follette's plan for public power. In March the governor established the Wisconsin Development Authority (WDA), an independent, nonstock, nonprofit corporation, and then requested $60,000 from the legislature to keep it operating for a year. Its purpose was to promote and construct public power facilities and to educate the public about them. Cheap public power had been a fundamental concern of the Progressives, but except for laws passed in 1931 facilitating municipal organization of power districts and providing for easier financing of municipal utilities, little had been accomplished. The WDA was designed to do for public power what the Wisconsin Finance Authority would have done for public works—bypass state constitutional restrictions on governmental participation in building projects. How far the governor expected the agency to go in developing a broad state power program is uncertain, but subsequent court decisions, inadequate funding, and Republican cutbacks in 1939 severely limited its effectiveness and prevented it from realizing La Follette's dream of a "little TVA" for Wisconsin.[27]

Besides promoting state and municipal power projects, the WDA was also designed to coordinate funds obtained from the Rural Electrification Administration. Two years earlier, after conservatives in the state senate had blocked the creation of an administrative apparatus to handle funds from the new federal agency, La Follette had obtained a special grant of $300,000 from the Works Progress Administration, part of which was used to staff a state coordinating body that was named Rural Electrification Coordination (REC). Under the able direction of John A. Becker and former state senator Orland Loomis, the REC vigorously promoted rural electric cooperatives. Wisconsin's allotments of almost $3.5 million through October 1936 put it at the top of the list in per capita expenditures. Federal officials extolled Wisconsin's achievement, and in March 1937 Olaf H. Johnson, executive secretary of the Rural Electrification Administration, declared that La Follette had done more for rural electrification than any other governor.[28]

With REC funds depleted by early 1937 and no more in sight, the governor argued that the WDA was necessary for continued state participation in the federal program. Opposition legislators retorted that if that were all the WDA was meant to do, the governor should have requested

funds specifically for that purpose. Many conservatives thought it constituted something larger and more sinister—a payoff to the Socialists.
Those conservatives saw it as a production-for-use scheme with radical
and dangerous implications. Or, as some of them put it, the idea was a
"smokescreen, a betrayal of solemn promises, hooey, hokum, baloney."
Andrew Biemiller, who guided the bill through the assembly, seemed to
buttress this interpretation when he said that the WDA would mean cheap
power for the masses. Responding to these concerns, La Follette tried to
reassure his conservative critics by denying any intention on his part of
undermining private business.[29]

Nevertheless, the bill excited considerable passion among both its
supporters and detractors. Heated debate sounded from both houses, and
the scene of the bill's final passage was marked by such acrimony and
pandemonium that, in the eyes of one reporter, it "would have needed no
brightening or imagination for Gilbert and Sullivan to have translated it
into an operetta." Three times the senate voted. Twice conservatives
walked out in order to prevent a quorum. After efforts to round up the
absentees from nearby hotels and taverns failed, the Progressives finally
forced them to return by threatening to act upon a teacher tenure bill in
their absence. The vote for the WDA was 17 to 15, after which Democrats
and Republicans loosed stinging attacks on the governor and his colleagues for using dictatorial tactics.[30]

The rancorous debate over the WDA fueled the flames of confusion and
dissension in the legislature. Governor La Follette had dared to hope at
the start of the session that things would run smoothly, and for a while
they did. The temporary mood of harmony prompted one observer to
report that "the leaders of the opposing factions are getting along more
peaceably than they ever have before." At a legislative dinner the
governor applauded the prevailing spirit of good feeling and even went so
far as to suggest that critical opposition often resulted in better legislation.[31]

Such good will quickly dissipated, however, and the familiar sounds of
denunciation and recrimination soon began to reverberate through legislative halls. More worrisome to the governor was increasing evidence of
discord within the Progressive party itself. Their previous role of embat-
tled minority had at least carried with it a strong inclination toward unity
within the ranks. Taking over control in the legislature seemed to encourage intraparty squabbles, which never were far from the surface anyway.
After expeditiously acting on the Labor Relations Act, the legislature

slowed its pace and appeared to be headed for the same kind of stalemate that had characterized the long 1935 session. The governor's impatience grew apace, and he called in many legislators to state his displeasure. An editorial in the *Wausau Record-Herald* recognized the irony of the situation when it suggested, "There have been many occasions, no doubt, when Governor Philip La Follette mourned, secretly, of course, that he did not have a Republican-Democratic majority in the senate upon which he could place the blame for the legislative dilly-dallying." Power carried with it responsibility, much to the Progressives' discomfort.[32]

Ideological disparities, personal disagreements, and urban-rural conflicts all contributed to Progressive disunity. Long-standing strains between moderates and radicals within the movement had grown increasingly apparent since the establishment of the Farmer-Labor Progressive Federation. Its members, including Paul Alfonsi and Andrew Biemiller, were especially strong in the assembly and were determined to exert their influence. Other prominent FLPF assemblymen were John Grobschmidt of Milwaukee, David Sigman, a member of the executive board of the State Federation of Labor and a brother of Samuel Sigman, and Emil Costello, who became the leader of the Congress of Industrial Organizations in Wisconsin.

Especially disruptive of Progressive unity was the tendency of public antagonism toward growing union power to spill over among the Progressives, who historically had derived their greatest strength from rural areas. Although leaders like the La Follettes worked to bridge the chasm between traditional rural ways and modern realities, their efforts were not always successful. Wisconsin's labor movement enjoyed one of the nation's fastest growth rates, and especially in rural areas and in nonunion communities the unions' appearance frequently stirred apprehension. Farmers resisted the unionization of farm co-op employees, and townspeople who listened to news reports about sit-down strikes and labor violence elsewhere often blamed the unions. Compounding the problem, labor's own ranks were split, especially after the State Federation of Labor expelled CIO organizer Emil Costello from its executive board in March 1937. At the American Federation of Labor's national convention that year, Wisconsin and Minnesota were named as the states that had suffered most from labor's internal warfare. During the year, far more strikes were recorded in Wisconsin than ever before, although their frequency declined during the latter half of the year. As state organizer Henry Rutz toured the state trying to gain members for the Farmer-Labor

Progressive Federation, he observed considerable antagonism toward labor unions in farm areas. Governor La Follette recognized the dangerous implications of the situation for the Progressive party and often urged unity within labor's ranks. While continuing to cultivate the friendship of State Federation of Labor leaders, he conferred frequently with representatives of the CIO and spoke to several United Auto Workers meetings, including the national convention, which was held in Milwaukee that year. If his conciliatory efforts accomplished anything, though, it was not immediately apparent.[33]

For a while the Progressives seemed ready to expend more energy attacking each other than working for their legislative programs. The *Capital Times* reported the feuds within the party and itself contributed to them when it condemned "illiberal" party members, who, in the opinion of editor Evjue, deserved to be purged since they were nothing but "fakirs, camp-followers, two-timers, imposters, and barnacles on the movement." On the other side, more conservatively inclined Progressives accused some of their colleagues of being communists. Andrew Biemiller's socialized medicine bills created a barrage of abuse. Assemblyman Joseph Barber, a Marathon surgeon, called them "a lot of junk." Rural representatives grumbled that organized labor was "getting all the gravy" from the La Follette administration. Assemblyman Theodore Swanson, a farmer from Pierce County, said that when farmers desired legislation, they would draft it themselves "without the aid of the city of Milwaukee representatives."[34]

Personal rivalries and animosities compounded the Progressives' internal squabbles. The governor's office did not escape criticism. One Progressive assemblyman complained, "When the East Wing cracks the whip, we've got to change something we've done the day before." But rather than challenging the governor directly, frustrated party members often aimed their barbs at Duncan. The activities of this clever political operator—plotting strategy, roaming capitol corridors, and passing messages to his floorleaders—caused resentment among many Progressives. Why should they listen to this Socialist from a big city? How could the governor place so much faith in him?[35]

How long La Follette would be able to smooth over the rifts in the party became increasingly questionable. The Progressives' one-vote working majority in the senate was slimmer but actually safer than the larger advantage they enjoyed in the assembly, where factional feuds threatened to split the party. The governor therefore supported Sen. Herman Severson's motion that the legislature adjourn *sine die* on 2 July. Although many FLPF spokesmen vociferously objected, on 25 June the assembly concurred with the senate's action.

Federationists were fighting mad and blamed the governor for sending them home with important business still pending in both houses. But La Follette saw a chance to kill controversial bills that were exacerbating conflict and to provide a cooling-off period during which the Progressive legislators would come to realize the necessity of working together. He wrote Bob that the adjournment motion had been opposed by "a good many of the so-called leaders," some of whom "were interested in keeping the session on—to keep open consideration of their 'pet' bills—some of which were 'shake-downs.' With adjournment there will be killed some 200–300 bills that should be shoved away but which would have kept them here until September." During a special session of the legislature, he hoped, party members would submerge their differences and work together.[36]

During late August and early September, Governor La Follette conferred with legislators, farm spokesmen, union officials, businessmen, and others to ascertain subjects they wanted considered during a special session. Although the FLPF demanded consideration of a long list of proposals, the governor included in his call for a special session only the topics of supplemental relief funds, highway safety, and taxation. He promised to expand the agenda if the legislature acted quickly in these areas.[37]

The governor's hopes for a speedy, harmonious proceeding quickly evaporated. Senator Severson had earlier expressed the conservative view that a special session was unnecessary and that further relief was undesirable since farmers already were having trouble finding hired help. FLPF leaders, on the other hand, echoed the complaints of municipal and county officials that the governor's relief recommendations were completely inadequate. After Progressives in both houses added amendments to the relief bill that the governor found unsatisfactory, he intervened and persuaded them to unite behind a measure that essentially embodied his original proposal. The vote switchers were pilloried by Democrats and Republicans for giving in when the governor pushed them. Meanwhile, La Follette agreed to expand the subjects that could be considered by the legislators when they consented to special procedural rules that were designed to expedite debate: they were to meet six days a week, eight hours a day; they would waive all rules pertaining to public hearings and rules permitting delays; and they would adjourn on 16 October.[38]

Progressive legislators also agreed to caucus on every bill, accept the will of the majority, reduce debate to a minimum, and vote as a unit. As a result, during the next week and a half the legislature passed eleven bills—everything La Follette had requested—in an atmosphere of noisy and bitter partisanship. Sessions, which sometimes ran into the early morning hours, were marked by disorder, shouting, and furious exchanges of personal insults. Cries of "dictator," "fascism," and "reds" wafted through the chambers as Republicans and Democrats unsuccessfully sought to delay action with requests for additional hearings and debate. The governor met daily with his party's legislators to establish strategy. With Duncan calling signals from the sidelines, the Progressives ground inexorably forward, cutting off debate, shortening or dispensing with hearings, and voting on bills before there was even time to read them.

In the upper house, Lt. Gov. Henry Gunderson sometimes refused to recognize opposition senators and hammered so hard on his gavel that it splintered. In the assembly, Speaker Paul Alfonsi declined to entertain appeals against his rulings and shepherded legislation through. Progressive legislators who were accused of drinking on the floor retorted that they were not alone in doing it. Bathed in elements of farce and comedy, the scene provided ready campaign material for the opposition. As scheduled, on 16 October the session closed amid scenes of opposition legislators raising their arms Hitler fashion, shouting "Heil!," and walking out of the chambers. Gaping spectators listened to angry boos reverberate through the halls.[39]

Governor La Follette was not surprised by public reaction to his actions. He had been called a dictator and worse before, and he figured that while some people would disagree with his actions no matter what happened, most would observe the results and discount opposition rhetoric. La Follette's belief in action and results carried him dangerously close to the position that ends can justify means. Earlier that year while arguing for Roosevelt's Court bill, he had reminded people that "the most loyal servant of the Constitution in history" had taken the "terrifying responsibility of violating its letter in order to preserve its spirit." America in 1937 was not at war, but La Follette, with a well-deserved reputation as a liberal, a friend of labor, and an adherent of civil liberties, regarded his sincerity and devotion to democratic ideals as unassailable. "Democracy must be made to work," he said over and over again. If democratic governments failed to act, they could not survive. La Follette's reading of the European situation led him to conclude that only bold and decisive action, even if it violated normal procedural rules, would guarantee the longtime survival of democracy.[40]

By applying to himself a different standard of judgment than he used with others, La Follette showed a hubris that afflicted him throughout his political career. Few people he met matched him in intelligence, ability, and drive. Ambition flowered as the years passed, bringing visions of broader stages on which to act. Even the White House seemed attainable. From his boyhood, La Follette had collected autographed pictures of great men. He admired strong leaders and sought to be one himself. But failure in the legislature would block the paths leading from Madison to new leadership opportunities.

By clamping down on the legislature, the governor achieved more results in ten days than had been registered during the previous three years. After the session concluded, he used the radio to explain his actions and respond to criticism. Explaining that people were tired of legislative procrastination, he said, *"We have acted. We have acted wisely, and for the common good, but above all, we have acted."* The test of democratic government, he asserted, was its ability to function effectively, and Wisconsin had met the test. Important measures had been enacted to provide relief, liberalize old-age pensions, extend codes of fair competition, tax chain stores, extend farm-mortgage-moratorium legislation, and assist municipal participation in the federal housing program. Farmers were given a Wisconsin Agricultural Authority, which would promote Wisconsin farm products. Businessmen received a Department of Commerce to back research, provide advice, and promote Wisconsin's businesses. The economy resembled a three-legged stool, La Follette suggested; agriculture, labor, and business were equally important supports, and business deserved to have its own agency. "It is no wonder that many of our businessmen have felt that government was not sufficiently concerned with their problems," La Follette said, paving the way for a noticeable improvement in relations with businessmen.[41]

The special session's most significant accomplishment, in the governor's estimation, was the Governmental Reorganization Act, which authorized him, with the advice and approval of a special committee of legislators and state officials, to revamp the machinery of state government. Both houses of the legislature were given veto power over any proposed changes. Reorganization strongly appealed to La Follette because it presumably would increase governmental efficiency and effectiveness and it would concentrate greater authority in executive hands. The act, he asserted, went "to the very root of the problem of how to preserve democratic government and democratic principles in the face of changed conditions."[42]

La Follette had pushed through a "little New Deal" for Wisconsin, but at a heavy cost. A hornets' nest of dissension had been created both inside and outside the party. Evjue, who had turned cooler toward La Follette during the year, characterized the special session as a week in which "democratic processes were abandoned and an executive dictatorship was in the saddle." He thought that "there was too much that smacked of Hitler and Mussolini" in the proceedings. But La Follette now could cite a formidable record of legislative accomplishment as proof that the Progressives had something positive to offer to the rest of the country. With that in mind, he could begin seriously to consider the prospects for entering a wider stage of politics.[43]

Governor La Follette's thoughts frequently ranged beyond the borders of the state even while he was constructing his legislative edifice. Isen La Follette noted in her diary, "Phil is in one of those germinative moods when he is trying to see his way ahead; there is no way of hurrying the process—just have to wait until he works it through." He peppered his speeches with references to political realignment and national third-party possibilities. Privately he concluded that only if the Progressives expanded their political base could they hope to extend their influence into the national sphere. Obtaining harmony among farm and labor constituencies was especially crucial. But in addition to farm and labor groups and other traditional sources of support, the broad middle range of the electorate had to be shown how they stood to benefit from governmental action.[44]

Departing from his earlier emphasis on the irreconcilable conflict separating Progressives from their enemies, Governor La Follette shifted gears during 1937, accentuating harmony and cooperation. What had been only a faint glimmer during the campaign of 1936 now emerged clearly in his speeches. Especially indicative of his new train of thought was his carefully prepared address to the Harvard Business School Alumni Association on 18 June, copies of which he distributed widely. He reiterated those ideas in somewhat different form in a session at the Department of Contemporary Thought at Northwestern University on 22

July. In those speeches La Follette sought to introduce mediating principles that he believed could resolve many of the conflicts surrounding public issues. The effort of reconciliation reflected the contradictions that permeated his own thinking: commitment to both change and tradition, democracy and leadership, public action and private responsibility; adherence to balanced budgets and demands for increased federal spending; opposition to government interference and support for strong, effective government; reliance on experts and distrust of intellectuals; and, perhaps most importantly, devotion to individualism and faith in collective action. Such inconsistencies, long dormant in La Follette's thinking, were seldom directly confronted and were concealed in his rhetoric.[45]

At Harvard, La Follette continued to advocate collective action to provide "some common method of reaching common decisions," but clearly overriding that goal was the need to stimulate and maintain individual initiative and responsibility. Without abandoning his previous view on government intervention, by shifting his emphasis La Follette now seemed mainly concerned about the burdensome effects of government spending and bureaucracy. Profound social and industrial changes had rendered Hoover's type of "rugged" individualism obsolete, La Follette contended, but new methods of invigorating private enterprise and strengthening individual opportunity had to be found. Equality of opportunity had as its corollary the equality of responsibility. Clearly, the governor was seeking to graft onto his traditional liberalism concepts that would appeal to middle-class conservatives and in the process expand the base of Progressivism.

To strengthen his appeal, La Follette tried to project an image of moderation, experience, practicality, and frugality. The programs he continually cited as examples of his approach to collective action were the Wisconsin Workmen's Compensation Law of 1911, the Unemployment Compensation Law of 1932, and the Labor Relations Act of 1937. All were designed to stimulate individual initiative and responsibility while simultaneously affording opportunities for group cooperation, the governor asserted. Government should act like an umpire, enforcing the rules of the game without intruding too much in social and economic affairs. These "groping efforts" did not delineate in detail exactly what government should do but provided a framework for thinking about what role government should play. La Follette preferred at this time to talk about processes and to postpone details until later. Rather than fixing policy prematurely, he advised, people should "look to those leaders in all groups who in governing themselves give evidence of ability to create new instruments of government in which all may have faith and confidence; who, in the confusion and heat of passing conflict, keep clear minds and build bridges of good will across to future cooperation that will raise the national standard of life."[46]

In effect, the governor was asking his listeners to trust him since his record of leadership in Wisconsin had qualified him to instruct people in other states. Throughout the year La Follette continued to emphasize the need for cooperation and moderation in his effort to win over business groups, middle-of-the-roaders, and conservatives. His desire to mediate conflict, achieve consensus, and promote harmony found succinct expression in the title he gave to his speech at Harvard—"Orderly Progress." In it he criticized extremists of the left and the right and urged his listeners to join in a united front to achieve orderly progress. In the Golden Rule, he suggested, one could discover correct economic policy. That did not mean, however, that people should be given "something for nothing." Rather, by insuring equal opportunity for all, the enlightened application of the profit motive would guarantee progress. "Harness the profit motive for something besides selfish purpose," La Follette urged.[47]

The governor's shift in tone did not go unnoticed. Political columnist Winter Everett suggested that the governor was attempting to attune himself to the increasing conservatism of the electorate. The *Milwaukee Journal* found his emphasis on "equality of responsibility" to be both novel and reassuring. One newspaper reported that his Harvard and Northwestern speeches had won him approval as "a sane and sensible talker." Less charitably, someone else cynically placed La Follette among the politicians who possess "an uncanny ability to sense the trend of public opinion almost before the public senses the change itself. . . . Crafty in the knowledge of human nature, Governor La Follette trims his sails accordingly. . . . Now, if you have been keeping your ear to the ground of late, you are aware of the subtle change coming over the governor." The dualistic frame of reference—pitting progressive against conservative, the people against the interests, white against black—was set aside for an approach that sought to reconcile conflicting tendencies in American life.[48]

La Follette's shifting rhetorical stance derived not only from his assessment of public opinion but also from calculations about how best to promote political realignment and his own career. Even during his first term in Madison, many people believed that his ultimate goal was the presidency, and such speculation increased as time went on. La Follette, as was his habit, remained closemouthed on the subject. One major impediment constituted a unique advantage when considered in a different light. His position outside the major parties would be an obstacle to capturing either's presidential nomination; on the other hand, that position did provide the option of running either as a Republican or as a Democrat or on an independent ticket. During 1937 one of the latter two options appeared most logical, since the La Follettes, while remaining critical of some aspects of the New Deal, continued to cement their alliance with the Roosevelt administration more firmly than ever. The president's admiration for Bob La Follette had never been higher, and rumors were floating about that he was considering Phil for the Supreme Court or some Cabinet position, perhaps as a replacement for Secretary of Labor Frances Perkins.[49]

Governor La Follette continued to promote the idea of political realignment. Whether it would emerge through the Democratic party, the Republican party, or a new party was unclear, he told *New York Times* reporter Francis Brown, but he expressed certainty that such a transformation was coming. At the birthday celebration of the Progressive party on 19 May, he predicted that a national third party was "close at hand." A skeptical editorialist in the *Wisconsin State Journal* cynically remarked that such predictions were standard fare from the La Follettes, who continually talked about a national third party while never doing anything about it.[50]

In July the La Follette brothers joined Sen. Alben Barkley for a weekend cruise on the president's yacht. "They talked mostly politics," Isen La Follette later recorded in her diary. Governor La Follette informed the president that he intended to travel around the country in the coming months promoting political realignment. Roosevelt sounded pleased with the idea. "You fellows out West can do things I can't do," he remarked. "My hands are tied. I have the reactionary South on my hands and I cannot go into my own state, New York, and make the same appeal that you can make out West." La Follette gained the impression that Roosevelt was giving him carte blanche to proceed. That may have influenced his observation that Roosevelt had "grown and developed" during the preceding months. He concluded that the president had abandoned hope, for the immediate future at least, of liberalizing the Democratic party but that he genuinely desired eventual political realignment.[51]

The outing set people to speculating once again about the special relationship existing between Roosevelt and the La Follettes. Senator La Follette was working more closely than ever with Democratic majority leader Barkley in pushing administration measures through the Senate. Harold Ickes heard in August that Leo Crowley had it "straight from the White House" that Bob La Follette was the president's first choice to be his successor. In a book published in November, former presidential staffer Stanley High confirmed this view, and the following spring, in a meeting with Roosevelt concerning possible presidential candidates, Harry Hopkins jotted down in regard to the senator, "Fine—later—Secretary of State soon."[52]

Back in Madison, Phil La Follette called the New Deal the "greatest human experiment in history." James Farley, while visiting Wisconsin, heaped praise on both Senator La Follette and Senator Duffy and refused to speculate about how the administration might react if Phil La Follette challenged Duffy for the Senate in 1938. Into September, when the special legislative session of the legislature curtailed his speaking schedule, Governor La Follette continued to lavish praise on the Roosevelt administration. "Conditions have already improved in the last few years," he told one audience, "and I am not saying this as a partisan of the national administration, but we must admit that much of the improvement is due to the wisdom and courage of the present administration in Washington." The governor stated his support for New Deal spending and redistribution programs. Although he admitted that in some areas, especially on crop reduction policies, the administration was vulnerable, La Follette argued that overall the results had been quite good. He wrote to a friend in September, "My general impression after being in Wisconsin, Illinois, Iowa, and Nebraska is that all the talk about the President having lost ground is a lot of bologna. So far as the rank and file of people are concerned he still represents their best bet for constructive progress and improvement in their lot."[53]

In early October, Governor La Follette turned down Roosevelt's invitation to accompany him aboard the presidential train as it journeyed through Wisconsin on its way to Chicago, where the president delivered a major speech on foreign policy. La Follette did drive to Milwaukee on the morning of 5 October and chatted for a few minutes with an aide, who informed him that the president was still sleeping as the train made a routine early morning stop.[54]

As he had indicated, La Follette spoke out frequently on the subject of political realignment during August, September, and October. On 31 July he urged a group of progressives to form a new party in Iowa. He visited Senator Norris at the Nebraskan's summer cottage in Waupaca, Wisconsin, and later spoke at several Labor Day rallies in Nebraska. "Hardly a political article is written these days that doesn't mention the La Follettes in one way or another," one reporter observed. Many people believed that old party lines were crumbling, and the possibilities for the future seemed wide open. Some people predicted a merging of the La Follette forces with those of John L. Lewis of the CIO. A meeting between the governor and Mayor La Guardia in New York set tongues wagging. And in September when Governors Henry Horner of Illinois and Nelson Kraschel of Iowa went fishing with La Follette in Wisconsin's north woods, few people believed that fish were the real object of their attention.[55]

Yet as long as Roosevelt remained in the White House, third-party talk seemed fanciful. Phil La Follette could tell people, "We consider ourselves free agents, so far as the New Deal is concerned," but such statements carried a hollow ring. There had been a lot of talk, but as Max Lerner noted, "Like third-term talk, third-party talk is about one-quarter based on probabilities, one-quarter irresistible speculation, and the remaining half propaganda."[56]

Lerner was right. Phil La Follette had frequently discussed the idea of a new national party, but he had done practically nothing about it. Now the time had come to decide. The conclusion of the special session in October gave him the opportunity to consider carefully the available alternatives. He and Isen decided to take a United Fruit Company cruise in the Caribbean, where he could completely relax and forget his responsibilities for a while. She recorded in her diary, "The minute Phil steps on a ship his cares seem to be visibly rolling off his shoulders and it is a constant joy to see his utter satisfaction." As they traveled from Havana to Jamaica and Costa Rica, the governor soaked up the sun and worked on a stack of books that he had been waiting to get to. But aboard ship he developed a high fever and had to be hospitalized at Colon, Panama, where he spent a week and a half too ill to do anything. It was on this trip that La Follette finally decided to go ahead with a major effort to launch a third party. By the time he touched shore in New York on 21 November, he had almost made up his mind that he was going to push forward.[57]

La Follette did not make his decision in a vacuum. Crucial in his thinking was the economic downturn that began that fall. President Roosevelt also appeared vulnerable on the labor and relief issues, and foreign policy was starting to occupy many people's minds. La Follette's reservations about the New Deal had never vanished. Now it began to appear that public disillusionment with the New Deal could work to the advantage of a third party. La Follette believed that there was little more he could accomplish by remaining in Wisconsin and assumed that Roosevelt would not try for a third term. In his view, the Democratic party remained under the domination of conservative forces, a situation Roosevelt had been unable to alter. Thus, it appeared not impossible that by 1944, or even by 1940, people would be ready to look for an alternative to the old parties. No one could predict the future with certainty, but the dangers of inaction seemed no less formidable than those of action. La Follette had been ruled by his customary prudence and restrained by his recognition of Roosevelt's hold on public opinion, but now his gambling spirit took over and he decided on a bold play.

Since he was still weak from the flu, La Follette cancelled most of his December appointments and used the time to formulate his plans. He counted on minimal help from party politicians, who would be unwilling to risk a long-shot venture. He received some assistance from David K. Niles, a veteran of the 1924 La Follette presidential campaign and an aide to Harry Hopkins, in drawing up a list of prominent liberals who might be willing to discuss the possibilities of third-party action. One of the names mentioned was Felix Frankfurter of Harvard Law School, whose lack of enthusiasm helped persuade La Follette to forget about the list and to concentrate instead upon less established leaders who would have less to lose. He believed that only after a successful start would major figures be willing to join the bandwagon. He expected the press to distort the Progressive message, intellectuals to hold back, and other third-party leaders to resent it as a challenge to their own leadership. Compensations existed, however. La Follette probably figured that the absence of other prominent leaders would allow him mostly free reign. It would be a very personal venture.[58]

Fundamental to Governor La Follette's strategy was his assumption that traditional progressivism was losing its appeal, making it necessary to adapt to new political realities. Old battlecries were losing their capacity to inspire people. The electoral base of the movement—farmers, workers, and small businessmen—would have to be broadened.[59]

Calling up memories of his father and reciting the litany of Progressive principles no longer sufficed, La Follette believed. A new generation of voters was responding to new appeals, a fact expertly exploited by President Roosevelt. Whatever consensus had existed on Progressive principles was now forgotten as they splintered over ideological, factional, sectional, and personal disputes. Principles remained a favorite catchword for Progressives, but the contents of those principles, as one party member told Phil La Follette in 1937, elicited no broad agreement. Economic ideas ranged from laissez-faire to socialism. Uniformity existed on only a few general ideas—"that government should be honest; that the people should be kept informed and interested in matters of their government; and that taxation should be levied in accordance with ability to pay."[60]

The very notion that absolute principles existed was losing its meaning for many Progressives, a trend that reflected a broader American cultural transition. In *The Symbols of Government* and *The Folklore of Capitalism,* published in 1935 and 1937, Yale Law School professor Thurman Arnold dissected the mythology, folklore, and social rituals that paraded as fundamental principles in the public imagination. Most human action is symbolic, Arnold contended. "The words, ceremonies, theories, and principles and other symbols which man uses make him believe in the reality of his dreams and thus give purpose to his life," he wrote. The detached observer realizes that while rational or moral principles are useless for explanation or prediction, they are absolutely essential for maintenance of social control. Thus a troubling paradox arises: "Social institutions require faith and dreams to give them morale. They need to escape from these faiths and dreams in order to progress. The hierarchy of governing institutions must pretend to symmetry, moral beauty, and logic in order to maintain prestige and power. To actually govern, they must constantly violate those principles in hidden and covert ways." When people confront contradictions between myth and reality, they react in one of two ways, Arnold suggested. "The first is ceremony, drums and oratory. The second is reason and dialectic. The conflict must be made to disappear under a thick blanket of incense of some sort or other."[61]

Among the reviewers of *The Symbols of Government* was La Follette's friend Stuart Chase. He praised Arnold's analysis of the process by which people approach political and economic reality through high-level abstractions. Chase himself was an insightful student of words and language. A first-rate popularizer of ideas, he was writing a book about the rhetorical and semantic theories of Alfred Korzybski, I. A. Richards, and other pioneers in the field. In August 1937, when he sent La Follette a five-page outline of his forthcoming book *The Tyranny of Words,* the governor replied enthusiastically, "It looks fascinating! This question of misunderstanding through words and phrases is one of my pets." La Follette could have added that as a successful politician he used rhetoric as a tool to shape attitudes and win support. It was less important to him as a device to convey meaning than as a means of propaganda.[62]

As one of the most skillful practitioners of language in politics, La Follette frequently contemplated the process of language and often expressed his distaste for "mere words." Unattended by action, words were useless. He told Louis Adamic that the country had been flooded with too many "words and speeches, ballyhoo and blah, ideas and resolutions, theories and writings of all sorts, which for the most part have not clarified but only confused matters."[63]

Intellectually, La Follette wanted words used to clarify issues and convey specific meaning, but as a politician he recognized that words were also weapons to be used to command assent and support. He never abandoned reason and dialectic as rhetorical techniques, but in attempting to launch a new party he would lean heavily, in the words of Thurman Arnold, upon "ceremony, drums and oratory."

Chapter 7

The National Progressives of America
and Political Defeat

Phil La Follette's decision to gamble his political future on the prospects of a national third party carried considerable risk, but it also reflected the deliberate and mature calculations of a politician whose previous record had earned for him a place among the most successful and innovative governors in the nation. La Follette's ambition to play a role on the national stage developed within the context of his leadership of Wisconsin Progressivism, his persistent advocacy of national political realignment, and his ambivalent attitude toward Franklin Roosevelt and the New Deal. The dominant political reality of the 1930s was President Roosevelt's success in capturing, co-opting, and monopolizing left-wing support and in setting the agenda for liberal reform. For liberal Democrats, progressive Republicans, independents, radical third-party groups, Socialists, and Communists, the decision whether to stand with or against Roosevelt was the most important, and perhaps the only, decision they had to make.

Phil La Follette enjoyed an especially close relationship with the president but also probably had more contradictory attitudes about him than did most other politicians. Until the economic downturn called the "Roosevelt Recession" arrived in the fall of 1937, though, La Follette generally focused on the positive accomplishments of the New Deal. La Follette's crucial decision in starting his third party in 1938 was what stance he should take toward Roosevelt and the New Deal. His major blunder was to try to have it both ways, attempting to win over the alienated and disaffected and also liberal Roosevelt backers. His effort to broaden the base of Progressivism only confused people, however, leaving them uncertain about his intentions and motives. The failure of his new party was followed by a resounding defeat for the Progressives in the fall elections, and many observers both inside and outside the movement linked those depressing results at least in part to La Follette's abortive attempt to launch a new national party.

Even before Governor La Follette unveiled his plans for going into other states, some Progressives were noticing in the conduct of party affairs some interesting changes, especially the governor's growing reliance on Ralph Immell. The bluff, affable adjutant general, whose acquaintance with La Follette dated back to college days, had contacts all over the state as a result of his official duties. Lingering suspicions that he harbored political ambitions of his own intensified at the end of 1937 when thousands of Christmas cards, some of which were embellished with the picture of Robert M. La Follette, Sr., were sent from his office. The cards had been printed by the Minneapolis firm of Ward and Bigelow, leading to speculation that Charles W. Ward, a millionaire Minnesota businessman and close associate of the late governor Floyd Olson, might be looking for another politician to sponsor. Disturbed by what he observed, William T. Evjue ran a story in the *Capital Times* alleging that people in the governor's office were grooming Immell as a candidate who could appeal to conservatives, war veterans, and groups usually arrayed against the Progressives.[1]

Evjue perceived his influence in the party diminishing as Immell's enlarged, and he began to speak out against "new voices" in the party who were urging "new trends instead of the ways that have been followed during the past generation." He told the East Side Progressive Club of Madison that some people wanted to lead the Progressives away from their old moorings and believed that "the Progressive ship should sail out into more modern waters and anchor in a more modern setting." Evjue saw no need for the party to organize itself upon a broader base and warned that if time-tested principles were sacrificed to political expediency, the movement would alienate its traditional supporters. For Evjue, Progressive principles were as valid as they had been when Wisconsin's Chief Justice Edward G. Ryan had delineated them at the 1873 University Law School commencement. "The issue [*sic*] raised by Chief Justice Ryan, 'wealth or man,' by La Follette, 'the encroachment of the powerful few upon the rights of the many,' and by Franklin D. Roosevelt, 'the economic royalists,' are essentially the same," Evjue asserted.[2]

Franklin Roosevelt was Evjue's new hero, the legitimate successor to Old Bob La Follette's legacy. Phil La Follette himself may have been the person most responsible for the Madison editor's starry-eyed admiration for the president, whose phone call thanking Evjue for support during the 1936 campaign had overwhelmed him. Thrilled that "an obscure editor back in the hinter land" had been "singled out by the President of the United States for such honor and recognition," Evjue pledged his continued support. What he did not realize was that Phil La Follette had suggested that Roosevelt make the call.[3]

Evjue was not alone in criticizing new trends within the party. Also disturbed were Farmer-Labor Progressive Federation members who looked askance at Ralph Immell's military background and at his role as head of the National Guard during the milk strikes of 1934. In radical eyes, Immell offered nothing for farmers and workers, was fuzzy on issues, and hobnobbed too much with the rich. He could hardly claim to be a Progressive at all. Kenneth Hones, the president of the Wisconsin Farmers' Equity Union, promised to resist an Immell candidacy, and other FLPF leaders spread the word to local units about the threat.[4]

Governor La Follette attempted to remain aloof from these intramural squabbles as he turned his attention to national politics. Focusing on economic abundance, he warned against share-the-wealth movements that diverted people's attention from the real problem of expanding production. La Follette had been moving his attention from redistribution to expansion for four years, and by now the transition was virtually complete. Jettisoning redistribution as a goal, he focused on stimulating productive expansion as the remedy for the nation's economic problem.[5]

The theme was perfectly suited to the "Roosevelt Recession." Economic stagnation, labor conflict, and growing public disillusionment with relief all rendered the national administration vulnerable. Liberals criticized Roosevelt's vacillation on domestic policy, while growing international tensions spurred concern that Roosevelt might resort to arms spending to stimulate the economy. The Progressive congressional delegation heartily endorsed the Ludlow amendment for a national war referendum and denounced the president's billion-dollar naval construction bill. Senator La Follette demanded a clarification of United States foreign policy, and Evjue wrote, "President Roosevelt's attitude on foreign relations and his attitude on war and militarism is the side of President Roosevelt and his administration that this newspaper likes the least." Governor La Follette warned that arms spending would not end the depression but that it would increase the likelihood of war.[6]

The governor avoided any clean break with Roosevelt, but his disagreements with the president on both economic and foreign policy were mounting, and, even more importantly, he calculated that public dissatisfaction with the administration would increase receptivity to his third-party message. How far he would be willing to travel along his separate course, however, remained in doubt. Criticism could be tolerated, even flirtation with the third-party melange, but eventually the issue would narrow down to the simple question: was he for Roosevelt or against him? That was the question the president had asked when running for reelection, and that remained the crucial issue in 1938. La Follette's dilemma was between his desire to capitalize on Roosevelt's unpopularity and his simultaneous wish to maintain future cooperation. Keeping one's options open is a desirable goal in politics as in life, but at some point decisions have to be made, and Phil La Follette was not yet prepared to choose.

La Follette's decision to establish a national third party was essentially a personal one, geared to his own ambitions and estimate of political conditions. The Progressives had always made democracy one of their fundamental precepts, and without at least the appearance of broad consultation and support, the governor risked being tabbed as a power-hungry opportunist. In order to avoid that charge and also to sound out the attitudes and estimates of a wide assortment of individuals, La Follette held a series of meetings during March and April concerning his and the party's political futures. Several times weekly he assembled in his office groups of forty or fifty people —legislators, mayors, businessmen, farm and union leaders, doctors, lawyers, women, students, and party members. During sessions that sometimes lasted several hours, La Follette discussed the need for stimulating production and business investment and criticized the New Deal's lack of success in that area. He suggested that while the European dictators had committed deplorable excesses, they had proved what determination could accomplish and in the process had demonstrated the powerful effects of pageantry and symbolism. Those same techniques could be appropriated for democratic ends, La Follette asserted, and then unveiled a symbol that he and his wife had designed—a blue cross surrounded by a red circle upon a white field. It was meant to represent several things, the governor said—the ballot, the multiplication of wealth, cooperation among social groups, and the concurrent need for economic and political action. La Follette invited comments and questions from his listeners, but many who attended the meetings inferred that he really was not very interested in hearing negative or derogatory comments about his plans and that his mind was already made up.[7]

The governor was warned that people would misinterpret his new "mark." "My uneasiness centers around the *flag* idea," his good friend, philosophy professor Max Otto, wrote. *"If this symbolic flag can be made to seem* an attempt to substitute a new flag for the old one, you'll be taking something on: something which I believe can't be put over, and, I believe *shouldn't* be put over. . . . So if I were on the other side, that's what I'd go after."* Otto believed the cross-in-circle would simply confuse the issue, but La Follette had anticipated such objections and decided that the risk was worth running. He was intrigued by the uses of pageantry and symbolism in European countries and wanted to see if he could make them work for more positive ends.[8]

La Follette's meetings attracted only minor attention until mid-April, when he announced a series of radio talks in which he would discuss his views on the political situation. For four successive evenings beginning on 19 April, the fifteen-minute radio broadcasts elucidated the governor's criticisms of the New Deal's relief and recovery programs. Taking up his central theme of economic expansion, La Follette argued that only in a prosperous nation could freedom flourish, while economic depression bred dictatorship. The mistake of the New Deal had been opting for temporary "WPA-type jobs" rather than concentrating on the generation of economic expansion and productive jobs. Roosevelt, "the great humanitarian," had in the end little more to offer people than had Hoover, "the great engineer," La Follette asserted. Yet despite the general anti–New Deal tenor of his remarks, they also contained references to the president's "brilliant" leadership and to the "lasting debt of gratitude" owed him by the public. La Follette's decision to focus on the New Deal's failures left him in an uncomfortable position, and the ambivalence discernible in his remarks reflected this.[9]

During the last radio speech, Governor La Follette informed his listeners that he would lay out his future plans at a rally to be held in Madison on Thursday, 28 April. By remaining relatively secluded and avoiding most reporters' questions, La Follette allowed speculation and interest to build. Eastern newspapers, tipped off that something was brewing, dispatched reporters to Madison, just as the governor had hoped they would. He would need all the publicity he could get.

Acting alone had its advantages, allowing La Follette to call his own shots and to avoid the dissension usually associated with third-party groups. But the personal nature of his enterprise invited caution, and potential supporters hung back, watching developments before getting involved. No one knew what to expect. Bob La Follette possessed even less enthusiasm for this venture than he had for the Wisconsin Progressive party four years earlier. His perfunctory support for a national third party had never required action before. Now he was ready to go along with his brother but feared the possible repercussions on the Progressive movement and wished Phil would abandon the project. Unable to attend the rally because of a crucial vote on a naval arms bill, he told reporters before departing Madison, "A national third party is inevitable and now is the time to form one. Phil and I are back of this jointly as we have been in the past in Wisconsin and national affairs."[10]

The governor emerged from seclusion long enough to tell reporters that his recent statements marked "no new break" with the president. Conveniently disregarding the strong support he had given Roosevelt throughout most of 1937, he said that he had been criticizing the New Deal relief and farm policies for a long time. He denied that he was either to the left or to the right of Roosevelt but indicated that in some areas he would "cut more deeply and more drastically than the President has proposed." The New Deal, he believed, was being used too much "like a policeman" to try to regulate the details of people's lives. He agreed with the president on the need for strong government, but Roosevelt believed in government by regulation whereas La Follette believed in government by "direction and leadership."[11]

Such explanations hardly clarified things for people who wanted yes-or-no answers. The governor's aides indicated that their boss was planning "no clean break" with the national administration and expected to continue on friendly terms with it. Some Washington analysts believed that the president would welcome a "bolt from the left" that might push the Democrats in a more liberal direction. Veteran political reporter Thomas L. Stokes wrote, "President Roosevelt is watching these developments with relish. It has been his ambition to create a New Deal party from the ranks of Democrats and of Progressive Republicans who flocked to his standard in 1932 and 1936." In a press conference that week, when asked whether in light of Governor La Follette's activities he perceived a need for further organization among political liberals, Roosevelt replied, "The more liberal forces for liberal policies of the country the better." Undersecretary of State Adolf Berle was planning to go out to Madison, but Roosevelt said that he would not be representing the administration.

Berle, the only prominent out-of-state liberal to attend the meeting, told reporters in Madison that he was acting as an official observer for Mayor Fiorello La Guardia.[12]

Governor La Follette had anticipated the reluctance of national political figures, but he depended heavily on maintaining a solid front among his own Wisconsin Progressives. Especially important in this regard would be Evjue, whose criticism of La Follette's handling of the legislature marked a widening rift between the two that could only hurt the party. La Follette sought out his old friend more than once, but Evjue completely rejected his argument that the president was confused and discouraged and that the Progressives should be ready to pick up the pieces when public disillusionment inevitably set in. Instead of trumpeting the governor's cause, Evjue ran a front-page editorial on the day of the rally, "Which Way Progressives?," giving notice that "if repudiation of President Roosevelt is to be a requisite for joining this new venture, the *Capital Times* is frank in saying it will not go along." Admitting that his paper had sometimes been critical of the president's actions, Evjue argued that to desert him now "would only be another addition to the historic confusion and division of forces which have always been the curse of the liberal movement in the United States."[13]

Evjue did not even attend the rally that evening. Only one Progressive congressman, Tom Amlie, returned from Washington for the event, but hundreds of Progressive leaders from around the state showed up. In spite of the cold, rainy weather, five thousand spectators jammed into the stock pavilion on the University of Wisconsin campus, and several thousand others milled around outside listening to loudspeakers that had been set up for the overflow. They were treated to a production that had been carefully planned by the governor. Before the meeting began, a color guard and a drum-and-bugle corps circled the hall several times. A military band blared away with patriotic songs, and the crowd joined in singing "America the Beautiful," "The Battle Hymn of the Republic," and a campus ditty, "If You Want to Be a Badger." University athletes garbed in bright-red letter sweaters ushered people to their seats, while national guardsmen helped direct traffic outside. Every corner of the pavilion was festooned with American flags, and behind the podium hung a huge blue banner sewn by Isen La Follette, which was decorated with the cross-in-circle symbol.[14]

After a warm-up address by Judge Alvin C. Reis, Governor La Follette briskly stepped to the podium and began his long-awaited speech. It combined an odd mixture of traditional Progressive ideas, mystical allusions, religious imagery, and not-too-subtle appeals to conservative voters. Most of the ideas were familiar: the end of the frontier and its implications for American society, the need for productive expansion, the repudiation of fascism, communism, and socialism. The governor especially emphasized the need for increased capital investment. In enunciating six basic principles that would guide the new movement, he led off with a method for accelerating the flow of capital: "The ownership and control of money and credit, without qualification or reservation, must be under public and not private control."[15]

His second fundamental principle was the "absolute right" of each person "to earn his living by the sweat of his brow," an obvious appeal to critics of federal jobs programs and "relief chislers." Thirdly, he called for enlarging executive power while providing guarantees against its abuse. Fourthly, farmers and workers were entitled to economic security based on a "decent annual income" geared to the "contribution they were making." Fifthly, "We flatly oppose every form of coddling or spoon-feeding the American people—whether it be farmers or workers—whether it be business or industry." Everybody deserved the opportunity to help himself; after that, "he can sink or swim," La Follette said. Finally, in some of the strangest language he had ever uttered, he pronounced the Western Hemisphere a preserve that had been "set aside by our Creator for the ultimate destiny of man. Here a vast continent was kept virgin for centuries. Here it was ordained that man should work out the final act in the great drama of life."

The enunciation of these six principles culminated the governor's year-long attempt to redirect the Progressive party toward the broad middle of the political spectrum. Political divisions no longer cut between Republicans and Democrats, workers and farmers, or capital and labor, La Follette asserted. Rather, the critical split lay between "the earners on one side and the collectors on the other." He still employed a dualistic frame of reference, but its substance departed significantly from what it had been earlier. The implication was that deserving workers (with sweaty brows) and investors (with legitimately earned surpluses) were worthy and that relief recipients and businesses dependent on special privileges were not. His intent during much of the speech remained so vague, however, that he left many of his listeners completely baffled. La

Follette was attempting to forge an improbable consensus from elements that were not clearly defined, but he confidently predicted that "as certain as the sun rises, we are launching *the* party of our time."

President Roosevelt's brilliant leadership had failed to uproot conservative domination of his party, La Follette asserted. A national Progressive party would succeed by pointing its program in the right direction and then constantly improving it. The fundamental requirements were the repudiation of the idea of scarcity and the promotion of expansion. American freedom was rooted in abundance, and free people had to be productively employed. If anyone inferred that he was preaching an overly materialistic philosophy, La Follette portrayed his new movement in quasi-religious terms: as religion offers salvation and certainty to lost sinners, his party would provide a sense of direction to people with none.

The new organization—to be called the National Progressives of America—would enlist fighters ("In our fight we want no conscripts —only volunteers enrolled for the duration of the war"), pioneers ("The time has come when a new trail must be blazed"), and teachers (who would "take the fundamental teachings of the past and apply them to the modern world"). Most of all they would be evangelists ("Reduced to simplest truth, free from obscuring verbiage, our faith goes forth to conquer. In its best sense this new crusade is a religious cause"). Toward the end of his speech La Follette grew more histrionic, with hair tousled and arms waving, voice pitched high, by turns mystical and down to earth. "For the first time in history we enter a new age knowing what we do and where we go. . . . Truth has lost many a battle but never a war. The spirit of our people, marching under a common banner in freedom's cause cannot fail. . . . In the spirit of that great Crusader, James: 'Be Ye Doers of the Word, and Not Hearers Only.' "

After talking for an hour and forty minutes, La Follette concluded by suggesting that the cross-in-circle encompassed his purposes more eloquently than any words could. "What we believe in and what we propose is so clear, and so fundamental it can be told without words. It is expressed by a symbol." But La Follette's own language belied that contention. Desiring to extend his appeal to as wide an audience as possible and realizing that specific policies would inevitably antagonize many of them, he wanted to define his goals in terms as general as possible. Yet, in order to compensate for the vagueness of his message, he insisted all the more fervently that his intent was clear and obvious. The meaning might have been clear to him; it eluded most of his listeners.

For several days the National Progressives of America was front-page news. That the governor had· erred in his choice of symbolism quickly became apparent. Having disregarded numerous friendly warnings that his symbol would be misinterpreted, La Follette remained confident of his ability to explain its meaning. He wanted to appeal to people emotionally, and such symbolism, he hoped, could be useful in uniting people behind his cause. Unfortunately for him, many observers immediately likened the cross-in-circle to a "circumcised swastika." That, combined with several points in his speech, convinced many that La Follette had taken a sharp turn to the right. They found his actions disturbing and wondered just what he had in mind.

Intensifying the concern of liberals was the enthusiastic reception conferred upon the La Follette departure by some conservatives. *Common Sense* reprovingly remarked, "Never has a La Follette pronouncement been so welcomed by the conservatives of the country." Many former critics of La Follettism seemed intrigued by La Follette's message. Walter Lippmann, whose columns had taken the governor to task during the Glenn Frank flap and the Supreme Court controversy, now suggested that perhaps for the first time since Woodrow Wilson a potential progressive candidate for the presidency wished to use governmental power "not to supplant, but to liberate, private initiative." Lippmann judged the NPA philosophy to be wholly consistent with traditional progressivism but sharply divergent from New Deal ideas and practices. He applauded La Follette's unwillingness to court special interests with promises of governmental favors and asserted that the governor was the first important progressive in a decade to understand that the central economic problem of the time was not distribution but productive expansion.[16]

Dorothy Thompson, like Lippmann, changed her mind about Governor La Follette. She too had been critical of him during the Glenn Frank affair, but a lengthy interview in Madison impressed her with his rejection of class consciousness, his criticism of federal relief programs, his emphasis on capital formation, and his focus on production rather than distribution. Although she wished that he would discard the banners and emotionalism for concrete solutions, she was delighted to hear someone "cut loose on the social work, settlement house, and benevolent feudal landlord mentality that has dominated the New Deal ad nauseum."[17]

Other less discriminating journalists printed overly glib or superficial observations. Frank R. Kent, who especially liked La Follette's reference to "coddling and spoon-feeding," attributed liberal suspicions of the NPA to the governor's excess of common sense and absence of demagoguery. The *Wall Street Journal of Commerce* regretted that neither major party possessed the courage to opt for so conservative an economic program. The *New York Herald Tribune* praised La Follette's social philosophy as one which "enters and freshens the atmosphere of New Deal dialectic like a breeze of pure ozone." William Randolph Hearst personally phoned La Follette to register his agreement with the speech's "American point of view."[18]

Although some conservative spokesmen considered La Follette's move refreshing, many remained skeptical or hostile, albeit for varying reasons. The *Boston Herald* termed the NPA "a Midwestern tricked-up version of the share-the-wealth movement of Huey Long." The *Baltimore Sun,* however, was baffled. "If the La Follettes know what they are talking about, they will contribute very greatly to the mental comfort of many citizens by putting their thought into words that have meaning."[19]

Conservative enthusiasm for the La Follette venture deepened liberal misgivings about it. Especially unforgivable, in their view, was the NPA's potential for dividing liberal forces in 1940 and opening the door for a conservative victory. One wisecracking New Dealer suggested that the cross-in-circle could more aptly be called the "double-cross." Roosevelt's vulnerability, from which La Follette hoped to profit, drew most liberals even more closely to him, since he remained the best chance to promote their cause.

Even the editors of *Common Sense* had concluded that the moment had passed for a third party and that any new political alignment would have to be structured around the New Deal. With the New Dealers bewildered and stumbling, Progressives should provide them with direction, the magazine counseled. La Follette's belated push for a new party angered Alfred Bingham, whose patience had run out for the governor, whom he characterized as "an arrogant, ignorant, Fascist-minded little demagogue." Bingham complained to Tom Amlie, "This announcement of the National Progressives is only the last of a long series of snubs and insults which I have taken from him since I started being interested in the movement."[20]

Congressman Amlie, who had long admired La Follette's dedication and political savvy, was one of the few left-wing politicians to have anything to do with the NPA. He especially liked the governor's emphasis on economic expansion, a goal Amlie was promoting through his industrial expansion bill. While admitting that La Follette had made some mistakes, Amlie persuaded Bingham to tone down a scathing editorial the latter had prepared for publication in *Common Sense*. "Certainly it would be a great mistake if the liberals were to join with Heywood Broun and others who are attacking the whole project," Amlie believed.[21]

The obstreperous Broun was merely the most outspoken of La Follette's left-wing censurers. He jumped on the governor's references to "coddling and spoon-feeding," his mystical nationalism, his subordination of distribution to production, and his failure to identify with the labor movement. The influential columnist granted that one might infer too much from one speech, especially since it was all "pretty vague and oratorical." Generally, however, the message was thoroughly reactionary, containing little to which Herbert Hoover would not add his amen. "This is no thunder on the left," Broun concluded, "but mere heat lightning well to the right of Roosevelt and the New Deal."[22]

What Broun thundered dogmatically against, others perceived as worrisome. The *New Republic* called La Follette's speech "a mixture of commendable enthusiasm, indisputable truths and practical vagueness." It wondered where the Wisconsinite was heading but hoped he would nudge the New Deal further to the left. The *Nation* was more critical, concerned about La Follette's enthusiasm for fascistlike propaganda techniques. Like many others, the magazine's editors found the signals confusing. Whether intentionally or not, they observed, La Follette had "succeeded in giving the slip to the professional direction-finders, and has doubled back on his trail so many times as to leave the hounds baffled." The magazine found it impossible to determine whether the new organization was to the left or to the right of the New Deal and whether it was progressive or conservative.[23]

Liberal critics of the NPA feared that it would divide their forces and undercut the New Deal. Worried about the fascistlike symbolism, they disliked La Follette's negative references to relief and the New Deal, wondered what attitude he would take toward the labor movement, asked for specifics on how the vaguely stated principles would be implemented, and regretted that the governor had felt it necessary to launch his organization in such secrecy without soliciting advice and aid from prominent national progressives and liberals. It was too much of a one-man show.

Some liberals, especially those who were well acquainted with La Follette, had no fears about his intentions. Oswald Garrison Villard attributed no "machiavellian subtlety" to him and welcomed the new venture. David Cushman Coyle wrote, "Hot dog. Your platform seems swell to me." Ernest L. Meyer, a college classmate who had sometimes been critical of the governor in the past, rejected Broun's notion that La Follette possessed fascistic tendencies: "Heywood knows as well as I do that all parties, from conservatives to Communists, have a hint of mystical excitation and are one and all built around slogans and banners." Overtones of mysticism and piety appealed to Lutheran Wisconsin, where orators tended to "lean a bit heavily on the Lord." Give Phil some air and fighting room, Meyer counseled. He saw the governor as a politician and an opportunist, essentially a man of action, who had become impatient with debate and delays. He was a dreamer, but more than that a doer, who based his visions on the things he had planted and seen thrive in his own backyard. Meyer was neither sure about nor worried about how the specifics would be worked out. "On the basis of his Wisconsin record," he wrote, "I trust Phil."[24]

Practicing politicians in liberal and progressive ranks were skeptical or hostile about the NPA. Liberal Democrats rallied firmly behind President Roosevelt. Political independents generally kept their distance. Reporting on political responses to La Follette's move, Raymond Clapper remarked that one thing that the NPA had clearly demonstrated was the "loyalty which Roosevelt's followers bear toward him." Thomas L. Stokes reported that when La Follette carried his message into Iowa, a chorus of applause arose every time he mentioned the president's name, a fact that led the governor immediately to soften his criticisms. Clapper concluded, "It seemed to be evident that he had misjudged the extent of the rebellion against Roosevelt and was compelled to fall a little more into step with him."[25]

La Follette had failed to consult any of the nation's leading progressives, and none of them volunteered any aid. Mayor La Guardia, after listening to Adolf Berle's report, announced that he would not support a new party at that time. Senator Norris said he would join no effort that might harm the president's effectiveness and that any move should wait until after the president decided against running for another term. Gov-

ernor Benson and his fellow Minnesota Farmer-Laborites were awaiting further developments. Gov. Frank Murphy of Michigan said that
while the NPA looked appealing, he and other liberal Democrats
believed that their own party should serve as the nucleus for a progressive party in the United States. Senator Wheeler predicted that only if
the Democrats nominated a reactionary in 1940 would a liberal third
party stand a chance. The Communist party denounced the NPA, and
the Socialist party caustically dismissed it as "the personal party of a
man intensely ambitious to be President" and warned about its "fascistic tendencies."[26]

The Wisconsin Progressives in Congress spoke favorably about the
new party whenever they did mention it. Gerald Boileau predicted that
it could become the most important political development of the
twentieth century. But except for Amlie, they remained mostly quiet
on the subject. Among national spokesmen of the left, a Socialist,
Upton Sinclair, was the only enthusiastic proponent of the NPA.
Favorable assessments came mostly from conservatives, such as Sen.
William King of Utah and former president Herbert Hoover, who
seemed pleased that the new organization might serve as a wedge to
return Republicans to public office.[27]

That conservatives might exploit the new organization troubled
Secretary of the Interior Harold Ickes, who considered La Follette to
be overly ambitious. At a discussion of the recent events in Madison in
a Cabinet meeting on 29 April, several of those present surmised that
the governor might harbor fascist tendencies. President Roosevelt
seemed unconcerned. On a weekend cruise on the Potomac he informed Ickes that unless La Follette went too far, his actions might
result in uniting liberal Democrats for 1940. Ickes inferred that the La
Follettes had not consulted Roosevelt and that their intentions were as
puzzling to him as to others. After Governor La Follette carried his
show into Iowa, Roosevelt seemed less certain that he would not "go
too far."[28]

The president made no public comment on the new movement but
privately expressed considerable interest in it. In a jocular tone, he
wrote to Amb. William Phillips:

> Do you know that Phil La Follette started his Third Party with a huge
> meeting in Wisconsin, the chief feature of which was the dedication of a
> new emblem—a twenty foot wide banner with a red circle and a blue cross
> on it? While the crowd present was carried away with the enthusiasm of the

moment, most of the country seem to think this was a feeble imitation of the Swastika. All that remains is for some major party to adopt a new form of arm salute. I have suggested the raising of both arms above the head, followed by a bow from the waist. At least this will be good for people's figures!

Roosevelt took the NPA as a direct personal challenge. The somewhat distorted version of the rally he had obtained from the media and personal accounts—that La Follette had stood alone on the speaker's platform and that photographers had been required to take pictures from below in order to make him look larger—reinforced Roosevelt's doubts about the governor's motives and stability. Roosevelt's former brain truster, Rexford Tugwell, wrote La Follette, "I have followed your recent activities with, to say the least, great interest. I realize that this sounds as though I were being cagey. As a matter of fact I am merely puzzled."[29]

The president had never been as close to Phil as he was to Bob; perhaps he distrusted anyone as politically motivated as himself. Tugwell later wrote that Roosevelt had cast a wary eye on Phil La Follette from the start. Each circled the other warily, exchanging favors while trying to fathom the other's intentions. Roosevelt told Secretary Ickes that he considered Bob to be "much more substantial" than Phil and that he was willing to make a deal with the La Follettes, bringing Bob into the Cabinet as secretary of state, thereby affording Phil the opportunity to move into the Senate, and this "would take care of both of them." How serious the president was about this idea is hard to say.[30]

When Roosevelt invited the senator along on a weekend cruise in the presidential yacht, Bob quickly accepted the opportunity to demonstrate that he bore the president no animosity and harbored no conflicting personal ambitions. The public never learned what they discussed that weekend, but the press interpreted the meeting as an indication that Roosevelt bore no animosity toward the La Follettes.[31]

On the ultimate objective of political realignment they seemed to substantially agree. Roosevelt's method was to liberalize the Democratic party, while Phil La Follette had finally staked his hopes on a third party. His own national ambitions and his increasingly negative assessment of the New Deal and Roosevelt's leadership lay at the heart of his decision. Bob La Follette, a sincere advocate of political realignment, possessed no stomach for a third-party drive but felt obligated to go along with his brother. His lack of enthusiasm for the effort upset Phil, whose insensitivity to Bob's reasons in turn aggravated the older brother. But the two maintained their customary united front for the public and refused to discuss their disagreements with the press.[32]

Although liberalizing the Democratic party constituted one of President Roosevelt's fondest desires, he had continually avoided an open break with the conservatives in his own party. Even before coming to Washington, Roosevelt had expressed his desire for a liberal party made up of progressive Republicans and liberal Democrats. He thought of himself as a progressive Democrat and told Tugwell while still in Albany: "We'll have eight years in Washington. By that time there may not be a Democratic party, but there will be a Progressive one." Although as president he did cooperate with several progressive Republicans during election campaigns, he also tried to maintain peace within the regular Democratic machinery and relied heavily on party chairman James Farley to build up the organization. Campaigning for reelection in 1936, he seldom mentioned his own party by name and invited support from liberal, progressive, and independent voters. He predicted to Ickes a political realignment within the next four years, and through the Progressive National Committee he hoped to insure continued progressive support for himself and to head off any significant third-party moves.[33]

The Court reform fight of 1937, which precipitated the development of a conservative coalition in Congress, convinced Roosevelt more than ever that conservative Democrats were major impediments to his goals. Responding to entreaties of Hopkins and others, he began devoting serious attention to the idea of "purging" recalcitrant Democrats from the party. Hints of this were circulating before the appearance of La Follette's NPA, but the move could only have strengthened Roosevelt's resolve to liberalize the party. Later Isen La Follette recorded in her diary that they had heard on good authority that Roosevelt himself had indicated that the NPA was really responsible for the "purge," but no convincing evidence exists that it was his only or most important consideration.[34]

Considerable irony therefore attended Phil La Follette's hostility to Roosevelt's decision to attempt, at considerable risk, to defeat conservative Democratic congressmen. Having opted for the third-party route toward realignment, La Follette could only reassert his contention that realignment through either of the old parties would be impossible. He predicted that Roosevelt's purge would fail and took grim satisfaction when it did, proving, he asserted, that he had been right about the futility of trying to reform the Democratic party from within.

Roosevelt's failure was no greater than La Follette's, however. Both honestly desired political realignment; neither possessed a distinct notion of what that would entail. Both liked to talk about realignment; neither did much about it until 1938. Both gained reputations for radicalism; neither strayed far from the political mainstream. Both realized that true realignment would require long, patient efforts at the grass roots; neither worked hard to achieve this. James MacGregor Burns has concluded that while Roosevelt hoped for a more liberal Democratic party, he was "unable to take the necessary steps and unwilling to make the necessary sacrifices and commitments." The same could be said of Phil La Follette with regard to a third party before 1938. Roosevelt and La Follette were preeminently practical politicians. Not till the time of maximum opportunity had already passed did either strike out to sunder the bonds of normal politics.[35]

As a Progressive critic of the New Deal, La Follette operated as an outsider; as governor, he acted as an insider. The different roles demanded different attributes. The first allied the governor with radical critics of the New Deal, third-party organizers, and congressional spokesmen who felt free to oppose any aspect of administration policy. Possessing no responsibility for the New Deal, he was free to explore many different political options. In his administrative role, La Follette had to balance the budget, cut spending, promote efficiency, reassure businessmen, provide relief, satisfy farmers, laborers, and other interest groups, cooperate with the legislature, run the bureaucracy, lead his party, and appeal to public opinion. All of those requirements imposed significant constraints on his behavior.

The alternatives La Follette could offer to the New Deal were further limited by the nature of his Progressive ideology. The depression raised questions hardly considered by his father and the previous generation of progressives. Phil La Follette helped modernize progressivism by directing its attention toward the problems of unemployment and relief, identifying more closely with the labor movement, and placing greater reliance on government planning and federal spending. Though still made up mostly of farmers and rural residents, his constituency was more urban. Nevertheless, Phil La Follette did not question the fundamental values of liberal capitalism, which meshed with his style of modern progressivism. He thought that equality of opportunity, individual initiative and responsibility, market mechanisms, business competition, and government regulation to guarantee free access to the marketplace would guarantee continued progress and freedom.

Although for a time while it was faddish he welcomed the radical label, La Follette's words and actions hardly fit that designation. His brand of progressivism deviated only slightly from the New Deal version and perhaps found its most typical expression in his willingness as a state governor to spend more federal money than was being offered to him. When it came to state funds, however, the governor adhered to strict orthodoxy, following a pay-as-you-go policy. His radicalism remained more a matter of personal style than of political substance. In comparison to the hidebound conservatism of some other politicians, he did appear innovative, though, and during the thirties La Follette's Wisconsin became one of the most innovative states in the Union.

Having gone as far as he thought he could in Wisconsin, Phil La Follette would have preferred to leave office following his third term and briefly considered resigning in order to devote his time to promoting the National Progressives of America. After the stock pavilion rally he immediately set out to carry his message to other states. To his disappointment, he soon discovered that political realignment was easier to discuss than to achieve. With obstacles everywhere he turned, even now he was not free to operate as boldly as he wished.[36]

La Follette learned the same lesson that Roosevelt did—just how difficult it is to revamp state and local party structures, which normally are more attuned to local concerns than to external direction. Deeply rooted inertia and resistance to change had discouraged La Follette and Roosevelt earlier; even now they hedged their bets by retaining some of their traditional political ties. Neither of them possessed a clearly articulated vision of what he hoped to accomplish.[37]

Governor La Follette predicted that the NPA would field independent candidates for Congress in ten states in 1938 and that it would endorse other candidates who were sympathetic to its goals and principles. Starting with a nucleus in the Midwest the new organization would reach out to other states. Michigan and Illinois possessed independent groups that might sign on. Indiana was less promising, but La Follette had several contacts in the Hoosier State. Nebraska was a special case because of Senator Norris, who the governor hoped would be friendly. Both of the Dakotas had potential. Most important were Iowa and Minnesota, whose cooperation was essential for the success of La Follette's scheme.[38]

The day after the stock pavilion rally, Governor La Follette traveled to Des Moines, where he delivered a slightly different version of his speech over national radio. He hoped to make an NPA affiliate out of the Iowa Farmer-Labor party, which had polled over thirty thousand votes in the 1936 election, and whose leaders had been in communication with him. His frustrating experience in the state, however, graphically illustrates some of the pitfalls standing in the way of a new national party. Internal dissension racked the Farmer-Labor leadership, and one party mainstay observed, "Very few, if any, of the self-styled and professed leaders of the Farm Labor movement in Iowa have any conception of the ills of our economic system and are practically utterly devoid of ability to think out an instructive forward-looking program for the economic and political future of the country." Delegates to a convention in July split over the question of whether to retain the name of *Farmer-Labor* or to adopt the *Progressive* label. La Follette preferred the latter but refused to get involved in such questions or in the selection of candidates, which he said were matters for local determination. He dispatched as his personal representative Gordon Sinykin, who helped write the party's platform, which drew largely upon the NPA statement of principles. In August, the Iowa Farmer-Labor party became the first state group to announce its support for the NPA.

La Follette's efforts in Iowa were complicated by his relations with the state's Democrats. Governor Nels Kraschel, who had been all smiles after the previous fall's fishing expedition with the governor, worried about the impact the National Progressives might have on the Democrats' reelection chances. However, his request that La Follette keep hands off fell on deaf ears. Complicating matters was the decision by a faction of Farmer-Laborites only six weeks before the election to establish a separate Progressive party. Thus, by the time the La Follette brothers managed to squeeze appearances in Iowa into their campaign schedules that fall, not only were they alienating New Deal Democrats, but they were also speaking to a divided coterie of third-party adherents. Yet Iowa constituted the showplace of the NPA outside Wisconsin.[39]

Strangely enough, significantly enough, what ability La Follette commanded to influence the situation in Iowa derived not so much from the strength of the third-party movement there as from its weakness, which rendered it more amenable to outside direction. In states having vigorous third-party organizations, the National Progressives generated scant response. Friendly wariness characterized relations between Wisconsin's Progressives and Minnesota's Farmer-Laborites. Phil La Follette had had good relations with, although he was not close to, Governor Olson, and this cordiality carried over to Olson's successor, Elmer Benson. But La Follette's failure to consult them before launching his new organization offended the Minnesotans, who had no desire to be the tail on La Follette's kite. Also, Governor Benson expected President Roosevelt's new spending program to restore economic growth. He and his colleagues adopted a wait-and-see attitude toward the NPA. In May, Benson and La Follette and several dozen aides and associates conferred at a barbeque at Charles Ward's farm in Hudson, Wisconsin. La Follette asserted that early response to his summons had greatly exceeded his expectations, and he appealed to the Minnesotans for assistance. Benson politely declined. His high regard for La Follette had not diminished, but he did not consider the NPA program to be radical enough, he objected to its symbolism and its overdependence on La Follette's personal leadership, and he refused to undercut President Roosevelt. La Follette could expect little help from his neighbors to the northwest.[40]

In states where strong third parties already existed, La Follette indicated, those groups would not be asked to abandon their party labels. American Labor party officials in New York nevertheless wasted no time in rebuffing his overtures. Executive Secretary Alex Rose commented that an organization whose central philosophy was the derogation of the New Deal did not deserve to be called a third party but merely reinforced the Republican opposition. La Follette's friends in New York wielded little political influence. Mayor Fiorello La Guardia said that a third party at that time was undesirable, and reporters noted La Follette's failure to visit the mayor when the Wisconsin governor passed through New York City in early June.[41]

Except for the South, which remained oblivious to his call for political realignment, the East was most foreign to La Follette's experience. Anxious to test the political waters there, he accepted an invitation to address the Young Republicans of Vermont, which resulted in his spending the first half of June in New England and New York. After a visit to Dartmouth College, where he spoke to a group of students, La Follette and his wife proceeded to Rutland, Vermont, where he shared the stage with Gov. George Aiken, a Republican whom he praised for his liberal record. They stopped over in Boston, and then Roy E. Larsen of *Time* magazine took them by yacht to Nantucket, where they spent a relaxing week with Isen's relatives. Another ride on Larsen's yacht took them to New York City, where La Follette visited publisher Roy Howard, some *New York Herald Tribune* executives, and several other contacts that Bill Benton had made for him.[42]

William Benton had earned a fortune in the advertising business with his partner Chester Bowles and then had retired to become a vice-president of the University of Chicago. He was interested in getting into politics and after meeting Phil La Follette the previous New Year's had kept in contact and gone to several meetings with him. The governor benefited from Benton's numerous contacts in the East, such as Larsen and Howard. Others he contacted included advertising executive Bruce Barton and *Time-Life* publisher Henry Luce, whose *Life* magazine ran a big story on the La Follettes in May. La Follette's conversations with prominent businessmen and newspaper publishers reinforced the impression of many that he had "gone conservative." In fact, the only difference now was that such acquaintances were garnering more publicity. He had established a close relationship with Alex Gumberg, a Russian émigré businessman, and with Gumberg's associates at the Atlas Corporation, Boyd Hatch and Floyd B. Odlum. For La Follette, private association with financiers and businessmen easily coincided with public criticism of their failures.[43]

Back home in Madison, the governor reported that people in the East were "enthusiastically open-minded" about a new party and predicted that in a year's time NPA groups would emerge all over the country. Little warranted such optimism. Only in Massachusetts, where Harry Hopkins's assistant, David K. Niles, expressed interest in the new movement, did the NPA develop a semblance of an organization. The Vermont Young Republicans were unlikely allies, and La Follette advised them not to rush things. "From every possible angle it would be a grave mistake for you or anyone in your group to make any move prior to the election this year," he counseled. He did hope that the group might swing into action after the election to begin making plans for 1940. "Anything that Bob or I can do to be of help we will do most gladly," he added.[44]

In fact, he could do little of a practical nature to help them, for encouragement was about all he had to offer. There were no funds to print literature, no speaker's bureau to spread the message, no local leaders to operate organizations, no platform to delineate a position. Local leadership and organization were prerequisites for national success, but they were unlikely to develop in the absence of a going national party in the first place. The dilemma had frustrated earlier third-party attempts, and La Follette, who clearly recognized the problem, was again powerless to resolve it.

To make things worse, the few local affiliates that did sprout up often turned out to be more embarrassing than helpful. La Follette did not wish to alienate such groups but hesitated to certify them until learning something about their make-up. Third parties, as he well knew, attract a large share of kooks and visionaries. When the head of Pennsylvania's Pathfinder party announced after a meeting with La Follette that efforts were afoot to create a new "middle-of-the-road" party, the governor let it be known that neither the Pathfinder head nor anyone else had been authorized to speak for the National Progressives in that state. La Follette received a letter warning him that two men who were organizing a group in the state of Washington could not be trusted. After learning further details, he had Immell, the NPA director, inform them that they were not authorized to represent the NPA in the state. They avowed their dedication and sincerity, but Immell replied, "We are not in any great haste for the time being, since we are thinking in terms of years, rather than months." In due time, he promised, he and the governor would visit the state, meet their leaders, and map out their strategy. La Follette evidently was more impressed with the coterie of progressive Democrats from Texas who set up an NPA chapter, and they received a charter in the mail. He encouraged the leader of the group to visit him in Madison, but apparently the man could not afford to make the trip.[45]

If the meager results in those states were disappointing, the discord and bungling in other states were even more disconcerting. California, even more than Iowa, demonstrated the capacity the NPA possessed for undermining liberal unity. Professor Paul Douglas had brought Raymond Haight, the leader of the California Progressive party, to Phil La Follette's attention in 1937. During Haight's visit to Madison in November of that year, the governor had promised to return the visit soon. But when Haight claimed La Follette's backing for his gubernatorial candidacy, the governor backed off. California Democrats were protesting loudly, claiming that Democratic State Sen. Culbert Olson deserved the support of liberals and that a vote in the Progressive column would only aid the Republicans. When Herman Ekern scouted the situation in March 1938, he reported that Haight was running a purely personal organization composed of little-known people who alienated other progressives. All the while that Governor La Follette postponed his trip, he continued to receive suggestions that California would be "a good state to stay away from." Senator Olson traveled to Madison to argue against any endorsement of Haight while the Progressives continued to seek all-out support. Sensing a no-win situation, La Follette took advantage of the launching of his own reelection campaign as a good excuse for staying home. In the end no one knew for sure where the governor stood, but the California Progressives, despite their disappointment, pledged their support to the NPA.[46]

Except for the Midwest, the Far West presented the most fertile ground for third-party cultivators. The situations in Washington and California, however, posed sticky problems. In Oregon, which like Washington possessed an active Commonwealth Federation, the NPA generated no positive response. A small group of progressives from Utah journeyed to Madison and talked to Governor La Follette, but they did not get involved. In Idaho, where Ray McKaig had spearheaded the progressive movement since the heyday of Old Bob La Follette, it appeared possible that some sort of New Deal–NPA alliance might emerge. The loss of liberal New Deal Sen. James Pope in the Democratic primary in 1938 prompted some of his followers to approach Bob La Follette about the possibility of putting Pope's name on the Progressive ticket. But Phil La Follette replied that they could not dictate candidates from Madison or Washington and that a name had already been selected. In any case, it was a matter for the Idaho Progressives to settle among themselves. Although the Progressive nominee obviously had no chance of winning, he refused to step aside and thereby blocked a real opportunity for establishing links between the National Progressives and liberal Democrats in the state.[47]

Governor La Follette found it impossible to honor requests from other fledgling NPA units to visit their states. He sent Gordon Sinykin on several errands to Iowa and North Dakota. Ralph Immell also visited those states and made a speech in Virginia for the NPA. La Follette himself directed most of the organizational work with help from Sinykin, Immell, and several others.[48]

Their efforts were fruitless. New Dealers refused to do anything that might divide liberals and bring a conservative revival. They often conceded that La Follette probably meant well, but they wondered about his methods, disliked the trappings, and were irritated by his failure to consult them. Many liberals were frustrated with Roosevelt, but they saw nothing in La Follette to make them think that he had any better solutions. He was asking for blind faith. His point was that once the direction was set, details would iron themselves out. For those demanding blueprints he expressed only impatience. "Look at our record in Wisconsin," he told questioners. Getting specific too soon, he believed, would provide targets for criticism, allow others to steal his thunder, and give substance to allegations that he was personally dictating everything.

More than that, La Follette simply had no coherent alternative to offer to people. For all his criticism of the patchwork quality of New Deal programs, he had developed no comprehensive set of policies that were significantly different from what the Roosevelt administration was already doing. He thought of his works program as a total approach to the problem of economic recovery, but applied on a national scale it probably would have differed little from the federal works programs. Additional spending on railroad modernization and housing construction were hardly new ideas. His advocacy of governmental control of money and credit was intriguing but vague. Some commentators likened it to Father Coughlin's proposals, others termed it socialism, and others said that it simply referred to greater governmental incentives for investment. What merited greatest attention was his call for productive expansion, but that did not seem to make much impact on his audiences. Perhaps it was too obvious; after all, was not increased production what everyone wanted?

La Follette's vagueness was partly intentional and partly the result of his failure to formulate anything new. Elmer Davis later commented, "Those ideas of his—fascinating but misty, ideas that give you the feeling there is much more in his mind than even he can put into words—are not so much doctrines of political philosophy as visions of the artist. It might have been better for him if he had written a novel about them instead of trying to realize them in practice."[49]

To be successful a new party must possess an issue or issues that hold special appeal for specific blocs of voters. The NPA lacked both. Governor La Follette's effort to develop a broad following caused uncertainty in people's minds about what he really stood for. Being unable to pinpoint the new movement's ideology, people naturally tended to focus on its surface characteristics—the symbolism, trappings, and rhetoric—and those repelled, rather than attracted, most of them.

Other problems hampered the movement's growth. Skimpy financial resources and the difficulty of putting the Progressive name on ballots in various states hurt its chances. More of a deterrent in the long run were the normal inertia of voters and the tenacity of the country's two-party tradition. Some grounds for hope did exist, however. A Gallup poll in November 1937 revealed that 23 percent of Republicans agreed that the time had come to quit their party for an anti–New Deal coalition composed of both Democrats and Republicans. Discontent at the other end of the political spectrum was revealed in a January 1938 poll showing that 18 percent of those who responded were ready to join a farmer-labor party if one were on the ballot. Other evidence existed to show that many people were dissatisfied with the existing party lineup. Two weeks after the stock pavilion rally, 11 percent of the 64 percent of respondents who had heard about the NPA told interviewers that they were prepared to join it. Despite such hopeful signs, too many things were operating against the NPA. La Follette's best hope lay in the possibility that some dramatic trend or event would transform the political situation and the NPA would be there to take advantage of it.[50]

By early July the election campaign in Wisconsin demanded most of the governor's energies. A defeat in his home territory would severely cripple the NPA's chances in other states, and victory appeared questionable unless La Follette again took his place at the head of the ticket. He preferred not to run for an unprecedented fourth term, though, so that he could devote his energies to organizing the third party. However, his failure to encourage the development of other leadership in the ranks had prevented the emergence of any candidate of sufficient stature to replace him. As a consequence, party leaders of every stripe, including those like Evjue who disliked the NPA, pressured him to run again in order to unite the fractious Progressive forces and to boost the odds for other Progressives on the ballot in November. The party chieftains wanted the governor to forget about his national movement and to concentrate instead on the survival of the Progressive party in Wisconsin.[51]

Unity was essential, for long-standing cleavages were threatening to tear the Progressives asunder. The always tenuous farmer-labor coalition was disintegrating day by day. In rural areas farmers denounced strikes, labor violence, and the unionization of farm co-op workers. In Milwaukee and other urban areas the Socialists were growing more and more restless; dissatisfied with their treatment within the Farmer-Labor Progressive Federation, many were ready to pull out. Governor La Follette recognized those conflicts but was powerless to prevent them.

In late July, responding to demands from party leaders, La Follette decided to run for governor one more time. Herman Ekern, whom he had named as interim lieutenant governor two months earlier and who had the strong backing of William T. Evjue, announced his candidacy for the Senate the same day. Theodore Dammann, who had received the Farmer-Labor Progressive Federation's endorsement for governor, indicated his intention to run for a seventh term as secretary of state. That left the federation without an endorsed gubernatorial candidate for the second time in a row. Two days later Ralph Immell, who had been considering a Senate bid, decided against it, much to the relief of FLPF leaders. They were backing Tom Amlie for the position after their first choice, Milwaukee Mayor Daniel Hoan, refused to run. Some Federationists wanted to endorse somebody to challenge Governor La Follette, but the leadership, sympathetic as they were to the idea, realistically concluded that such a foolhardy move could completely destroy Progressive chances for victory in the fall. They decided instead to concentrate their energies on the Amlie-Ekern senatorial primary, which was shaping up as an intra-party battle between the congressman's leftist farmer-labor backers and the lieutenant governor's moderate or conservative supporters.[52]

The Amlie-Ekern contest symbolized the long-brewing split in the party between traditionalists and radicals. Ekern insured that it would become an ideological slugfest by taking direct aim at Amlie's industrial expansion bill, which the congressman had cosponsored in 1937 along with Maury Maverick of Texas, Jerry Voorhis of California, and Robert G. Allen of Pennsylvania. Accusations from conservative Republicans and Democrats that Amlie's ideas were un-American or even communistic could easily be shrugged off, but when fellow Progressives introduced similar criticisms in open debate, it was a far more serious matter. What had been muted in the past was now displayed for all to see—Progressives were arguing with each other over fundamental ideas. Ekern was correct in his belief that most party members had little use for the type of permanent economic planning advocated by Amlie, whose industrial expansion board would set production quotas, regulate sales, fix prices, and guarantee jobs for everyone.[53]

Ekern likened the board to the Russian five-year plans, and Evjue warned of the dangers it posed to free institutions, but Amlie countered that democracy and planning were compatible. The congressman, who had borrowed from the ideas of Department of Agriculture staffer Mordecai Ezekiel, wanted to go beyond the kinds of collective-bargaining protections, farmer cost-of-production guarantees, government works projects, and old-age assistance advocated by Ekern. He was backing the New Deal in Congress, he said, not because he liked it, but because it was better than nothing. Having given up on the third-party idea, he was now concentrating on pushing Roosevelt to the left and considered old-fashioned Progressives like Ekern to be hopelessly out of date. He took a swipe at those who clung to the principles enunciated by Old Bob La Follette when he joked that "a good definition of a conservative is a man who worships a dead radical."[54]

Ekern readily pleaded guilty to that charge. "I am an old-fashioned Progressive," he acknowledged. "I have been a follower of Old Bob for more than thirty years and I still believe in his principles. His philosophy was sound in all respects and is vastly preferable to the panaceas my opponent has been advocating." Antimonopoly was his main rallying cry. Realizing that Amlie's sympathetic response to Phil La Follette's NPA was unpopular with many of his fellow Federationists, Ekern pressed his opponent to state his position on the new organization. On specific programs for farmers, workers, and the unemployed they were generally agreed. On another level, more symbolic than anything, they were miles apart. "There is a very clear distinction in the principles we advocate," Ekern stated.[55]

The senatorial primary, more than any other episode during the decade, illustrated the gap that existed between left-wingers and moderates within the party. Ekern, a protégé of the senior La Follette, epitomized the Progressive tradition and remained loyal to its symbols and principles. Amlie represented the radical advocates of change within the party and spoke for the interests of workers, farmers, the poor, and the unemployed.

Each candidate claimed to be the true successor to the La Follette tradition. The old symbols were still invoked, and fighters were once again enlisted in the cause, but the cause itself now seemed uncertain. Evjue rebuked the FLPF for being "not satisfied with the kind of Progressivism typified by Governor La Follette." There was something ironic in the alacrity of the editor's defense of the man he had so recently censured for his actions with the legislature and the NPA. The governor himself remained formally neutral, but while remaining on friendly terms with Amlie, he probably preferred to see Ekern win the nomination.[56]

The parity of Amlie's and Ekern's supporters was reflected in the balloting on 20 September, which left the lieutenant governor ahead by 9,091 votes out of 150,679 cast in the Progressive column. Amlie immediately forwarded his congratulations to the winner and promised to work for the Progressive ticket in the general election.

With the discord of the primary out of the way, the party faced a more ominous prospect. The voting figures supplied evidence of an increasingly apparent trend throughout the Midwest—the resurgence of conservative Republicanism. Julius Heil, a Milwaukee business executive, captured the Republican nomination with only ten thousand votes less than Phil La Follette. Even more ominous was the success of candidates who were part of the Democratic-Republican coalition, which had been established for the specific purpose of dislodging La Follette and his Progressive colleagues from office. Democratic State Treasurer Robert K. Henry rang up 73,348 votes in the Republican primary and won the Democratic nomination with 64,363 votes, giving him a total slightly larger than the governor's. Moreover, coalition candidates Walter S. Goodland and John M. Smith captured both the Republican and Democratic nominations for lieutenant governor and state treasurer, respectively, and John E. Martin won the Republican contest for attorney general while running slightly behind on the Democratic ballot.[57]

Unassisted by top leaders in either party, the hastily constructed coalition had been spectacularly successful. Fed up with La Follettism and frustrated by the ability of Progressives to capture power while Democrats and Republicans split their votes, they had submerged party labels to purge state government. Coalition plans called for the candidates who won both the Republican and Democratic nominations to run in the general election as the nominee of the party that had given them the most votes in the primary. Since he had failed to sweep both contests, Robert K. Henry decided to withdraw from the November balloting and announced his support for the Republican Heil, calling on voters to "rid the state of the political adventurers grouped around the La Follette brothers." For four years Democrats and Republicans had complained that three-party politics resulted in minority rule, enabling the Progressives to govern without majority support. Now they had their chance to reverse the situation.[58]

Grimly the Progressives faced the challenge. Phil La Follette had been saying for years that no substantial differences separated Democrats from Republicans, and now it was literally true. Progressives, he said, should welcome the opportunity the situation presented for realigning the parties. The Progressive platform convention on 4 October showed unusual harmony as the delegates realized that unity alone would afford a chance for victory this time. Only twenty minutes were required by the platform committee to approve a lengthy document that Phil La Follette read to the assembled delegates. The absence of any mention of production for use, which had divided the convention two years earlier, indicated that the anti-FLPF forces were in control. And the absence of any reference to the National Progressives of America reflected the governor's willingness to subordinate national realignment to the demands of the state situation.[59]

Contrasted to the subdued efficiency that characterized the Progressive gathering, the mood among Republican platform writers was euphoric. They could already taste victory. The Democrats, left without a gubernatorial nominee after Robert Henry's withdrawal from the ticket, filled the slot with irascible State Sen. Harry Bolens. The voluble anti-New Dealer's lackadaisical campaign was intended only to pick up enough votes to keep the Democrats on the ballot at the next election and to afford the chance of Democratic patronage.[60]

Phil La Follette and the Progressives were on the defensive and knew it. Evidence of a conservative resurgence was abundant. The labor movement, rent by internal conflict, was generating fierce opposition. Farmers, disturbed by labor troubles and restive because of low prices for dairy products and other commodities, were moving back to the Republicans in wholesale numbers. The removal of Glenn Frank as president of the university reflected badly on the governor in the minds of many people. Many Catholics resented the sending of a letter of greetings to Spanish loyalists by a group of congressmen that included Bob La Follette and several Progressive congressmen. Adding to their problems was an automobile accident involving Thomas Duncan, who in March was convicted for manslaughter in the hit-and-run collision. The incident reflected adversely on the governor, but more importantly it deprived him of the counsel and assistance of a loyal and astute political aide. Duncan's ties with the Socialists and the labor movement had been especially helpful in placating the Farmer-Labor Progressive Federation and in maintaining Progressive harmony in Milwaukee. Now Governor La Follette would have to try to manage those situations on his own.

Trying to satisfy local Progressive units continued to plague the governor. In some counties bickering among contentious leaders hampered organizational efforts. La Follette's sporadic efforts to strengthen local party structures had borne little fruit. The much-publicized La Follette "machine" was a creaky mechanism, not the smoothly oiled apparatus sometimes depicted in the press. One county leader wrote to complain that his Progressive club had never received any assistance from Madison. Local issues, such as the controversial slot-machine question, frequently diverted attention from broader concerns. Also, few patronage jobs, sparse campaign coffers, and a generally antagonistic press made life difficult for the Progressives.[61]

A wealth of signals existed to indicate a significant shift in the public mood. The evident apathy and scanty turnout for the Progressive primary had been a warning, but party officials chose to believe that it simply reflected the lack of competition for nominations and that Progressives would turn out in full force for the general election. During the primary, incumbents Theodore Dammann, Sol Levitan, and Orland Loomis had run unopposed for renomination to their posts as secretary of state, treasurer, and attorney general. Some people took consolation in the thought that people might be staying home to listen to political speeches on the radio. "The thing that I have been worried about is the silence," commented one Progressive. "It doesn't seem as though you can get any political arguments started in the shops, poolrooms, stores or any meeting places. Everybody seems to be so quiet."[62]

From the party headquarters in Madison, campaign coordinator Gordon Sinykin reminded his boss not to slight Herbert Hoover: "It seems to me that one of the best and most vivid ways to attack the Republicans is to put the Hoover yoke on their necks." The governor needed no encouragement. Although he had adopted a new middle-of-the-road rhetorical style the previous year and had attempted to exploit dissatisfaction with President Roosevelt in launching the NPA, La Follette now reverted to the more familiar Progressive style. Polarization again became his strategy. The traditional dualism made so familiar by two generations of Progressives once more pitted forward-looking, practical builders against reactionary, selfish destroyers. The overt coalition of conservative Republicans and "Hoovercrats" in the Democratic party rendered the argument more plausible. "This deal has made the issue plain," La Follette asserted. "Shall we turn our government over to the Wisconsin reactionaries of the Hoover Republican crowd, which brought this nation to the brink of ruin in 1929, or shall we go forward as Progressives, carefully planning each step and then acting to deal with the fundamental problems confronting the people?"[63]

To bolster this line of argument, La Follette dropped his criticisms of Roosevelt and the New Deal and instead emphasized his ties with the administration. The turnabout made sense politically and demonstrated that the governor's wavering attitude was continuing six years after Roosevelt had introduced his New Deal. La Follette told listeners that despite their disagreements on various matters, he still recognized Roosevelt as "a truly brilliant leader and the most humanitarian President since Lincoln." He suggested that his ability simultaneously to criticize and to collaborate with Roosevelt was worth more to Democratic voters than the hypocritical lip service their own party's leaders paid to Roosevelt while they betrayed him at every opportunity. Besides trying to take advantage of his close relationship with the national administration, La Follette again made his traditional appeals to the interest groups that Progressives had habitually called upon. Specially tailored letters went out over his signature to veterans, teachers, WPA workers, and old-age pensioners. In one letter he wrote, *"Only the PROGRESSIVES have fought shoulder to shoulder with the President in his valiant effort to provide employment."*[64]

Employment remained the big issue for Governor La Follette, but his Wisconsin works plan, which had received top billing two years earlier, was scarcely mentioned this time. Instead of attacking a do-nothing legislature, La Follette was obliged to defend the accomplishments of the Progressive-dominated legislature of 1937. He sought to demonstrate that farmers, laborers, businessmen, teachers, pensioners, and the unemployed had all benefited from his leadership. Although in establishing the NPA he had criticized appeals to special-interest groups, the admonition was now forgotten. Self-righteously proclaiming their devotion to the general interest while simultaneously catering to demands of special interests had not previously embarrassed the Progressives, nor did it now. The new style of politics proclaimed by Phil La Follette in April was conveniently forgotten as the Progressives practiced politics as usual.[65]

Traditional rituals were reenacted. Beginning in Sauk City, as he had in three of his four previous campaigns, Governor La Follette retraced old routes, repeated familiar arguments, and aimed his appeal at the customary targets. The National Progressives of America was quietly shelved. Candidates ran not under the NPA banner but on the regular Progressive ticket, hopeful of repeating the formula that had proved so successful in 1934 and 1936. As a result, Governor La Follette, who had been disappointed to see such little response to the NPA from other states, did not even have an NPA designation on the ballot in his home state.

What was different this time was the conservatives' decision to pool their forces against La Follette. The predominant issue in the campaign was La Follette himself, and national questions received short shrift. Robert K. Henry's withdrawal from the gubernatorial race left the Democrats virtually invisible. With old Harry Bolens heading the ticket, one Democratic leader admitted that it was "reactionary from top to bottom." Many liberal Democrats were fed up with the governor's attacks on President Roosevelt and were voting against him. William B. Rubin was infuriated to observe once again the La Follettes' "usual stunt around election time" of claiming to be Roosevelt backers when they worked against him the rest of the time. The Milwaukee lawyer complained in a mournful letter to party chairman James Farley, "They are responsible for having divided the liberal forces and have thwarted every effort to unite the liberals under the banner of the Democratic party."[66]

Rubin was right about the La Follettes' adverse impact on the state's Democrats, but President Roosevelt himself shared the blame because of his cooperation with them. The Democrats, for their part, invited such treatment by their lukewarm support for the New Deal and fraternization with conservative Republicans. Anti–New Dealers dominated party councils, and in October 1938 William D. Carroll, one of the most outspoken anti-Roosevelt men in the state senate, took over as the new state chairman. Roosevelt's disdain for state party regulars reinforced their hostility. In 1938 he again steered clear of Wisconsin and responded to entreaties for an endorsement of Sen. F. Ryan Duffy with an ambiguous statement that could just as easily have been interpreted as a boost for Duffy's Progressive opponent, Herman Ekern. That was the extent of his activity for the Wisconsin Democrats. National Democratic party chairman James Farley of course went down the line for a straight party vote.[67]

On 8 November, what the Progressives had feared came to pass—a resounding defeat for them and their leader Phil La Follette, whose political career was over although he was only forty-one. In addition to the governorship, the Progressives lost every state office, their bid for a second U.S. Senate seat, and five of their seven congressional posts. They also saw their numbers reduced in the state senate from sixteen to eleven and in the assembly from forty-eight to thirty-two. The Republican party regained its historical dominance in state politics. The Progressives were victims of a national conservative resurgence; the NPA fared dismally wherever affiliated groups were active. In Iowa its 669 votes failed to qualify it for a permanent place on the ballot. The Progressive candidate in California did little better.[68]

Senator Duffy attributed his loss to Republican Alexander Wiley to the surge of anti-La Follette sentiment in the state. "There was a great resentment in the state against Phil La Follette," he wrote James Farley, "and many thousands of voters went into the booths and voted the straight Republican ticket." After having captured 41.2 percent of the three-party vote for governor in 1934 and 47.6 percent in 1936, La Follette dipped to 36.2 percent in 1938. Certainly widespread dissatisfaction with his leadership existed, but how much the Progressive defeat represented a reaction against him personally, how much it reflected a national conservative trend, and how much it resulted from the success of the Republican-Democratic coalition is difficult to assess. Voters responded to the situation in different ways. La Follette's totals dipped significantly in urban areas but less than they did elsewhere. Over the entire state his share of the major party vote declined 12 percent, while in Racine County the drop amounted to only 7 percent, in Milwaukee County 8 percent, and in Kenosha County 9 percent. That translated into a shift between 1936 and 1938 from a 39,906-vote surplus to a 30,701-vote deficit in Milwaukee County, from a 7,373-vote surplus to a 671-vote deficit in Kenosha County, and from a 6,088-vote surplus to a 3,914-vote deficit in Racine County. In other areas of traditional Democratic strength in eastern Wisconsin, the governor fared much worse, as was reflected in percentage drops of 14 in Manitowoc and Waukesha Counties, 16 in Jefferson County, 17 in Washington and Sheboygan Counties, and 27 in Kewaunee County. It was in the heavily German counties in the eastern part of the state that the Democratic-Republican coalition functioned most smoothly, and it was there that La Follette did most poorly. Dykstra and Reynolds estimate a 20 percent drop in the German-American vote for La Follette between 1936 and 1938, compared to only a 15 percent reduction in Scandinavian-American rural areas.[69]

In most of the German-Lutheran townships identified by David Brye, La Follette's vote totals fell by one-half to two-thirds of what they had been in 1936 (turnout declined on average by only 19 percent). The Democratic vote declined by 60 to 90 percent in many townships, as Democratic voters moved wholesale into the Republican column. In Lake Mills Township in Jefferson County in the southeastern part of the state, for example, La Follette's total declined from 292 to 125 and the Democrats' from 41 to 1, while the Republicans' increased from 63 to 131.

Except for the fact that the Democrat, Harry Bolens, did better than that in most townships, that was a typical story in German-Lutheran areas. In Norwegian areas the number of voters who switched from La Follette to the Republicans was smaller, but Democratic ballots were almost nonexistent. In Pigeon Township in Trempeleau County in the western part of the state, for example, La Follette dropped from 354 to 238, the Democrats from 35 to 3, and the Republicans increased from 77 to 86. Of the thirty-five townships identified as Norwegian by David Brye, only four gave more than 10 votes to Harry Bolens. The Progressives declined generally throughout the state, but they did worse in rural areas and among German-American voters than they did in cities and among traditionally supportive Scandinavian-Americans.[70]

Although approximately one-quarter of the people who had voted for Phil La Follette in 1936 shifted to the Republicans two years later, a hard core of Progressive support remained—something between one-third and two-fifths of the electorate. The party's chances for continued success were good if it could maintain its position and expand its appeal. Several factors contributed to the drift away from La Follette in 1938. The recession, which hurt Democrats and liberals elsewhere, worked against the Progressives, who were identified as the "ins" and therefore held responsible for economic troubles. Ironically, the depression had been La Follette's main point of criticism against Roosevelt, but now it worked against him. The governor perceived a feeling of "tired dejection" in people. It was a bad year for incumbents, especially liberals such as Governors Elmer Benson of Minnesota and Frank Murphy of Michigan, who also failed in their bids for reelection. La Follette considered one comment a good summary of the reasons for Republican gains in farm areas: "I guess you can't beat the price of cheese." At bottom, he believed, his loss resulted from a tide of anti–New Dealism.[71]

President Roosevelt's reaction to questions about the midterm elections was "I think they are all right." As a matter of fact, however, he had not anticipated the magnitude of liberal losses. At a Cabinet session, he blamed local issues for most of the results. Senator Duffy's defeat he diagnosed as a result of people's voting Republican to get rid of Phil La Follette. Searching for bright spots, he wrote his former navy boss, Josephus Daniels, "We have on the positive side eliminated Phil La Follette and the Farmer-Labor people in the Northwest as a standing Third Party threat. They must and will come to us *if* we remain definitely the liberal party." He seemed willing to cooperate with Phil La Follette, but only on his own terms, that is, within a liberalized Democratic party. Harold Ickes fully agreed with that point of view, observing, "How can you divide the liberal vote between two parties and expect to win indefinitely?"[72]

William T. Evjue spoke for many Progressives in assigning major responsibility for their defeat to the formation of the National Progressives of America. "The venture alienated thousands of Roosevelt liberals and left thousands of Progressives lukewarm," he observed. La Follette's effort to attract the middle class to his banner seemed, in Evjue's acerbic opinion, to have been based on the philosophy that "a stalwart in the bush was worth more than nine Progressives in the hand." He observed that the governor had begun seeing "more people who had never been identified with the Progressive movement" and that a "little coterie that was always hanging around the governor's office and a secretariat that never helped the governor much made it difficult for old time Progressives to see Phil." All of this, Evjue concluded, "was translated into indifference, resentment, and soreness WITHIN the Progressive movement which left his campaign without the customary spark for a Progressive battle."[73]

Evjue's reflections on the decline of the old crusading idealism and on the lethargy of many local organizations reinforced what many others had been saying. Phil La Follette was concerned, too. He tried to reassure people, urging them to "keep the faith" and predicting that the Progressives would bounce back just as they had done so many times in the past. Many friends wrote to wish him luck.[74]

La Follette's optimism is reflected in a letter from Isen to her sister-in-law Fola: "Now, as far as we are concerned I do hope that you aren't sweating blood over us, because we are swell! Phil foresaw this election so was not surprised. Also we find a second licking nothing so hard as the first one! I really mean that." She said that Phil was confident that establishing the NPA had been the right thing to do and that dissociating themselves from Roosevelt would leave them in fine shape for 1940. "We are certainly living in a wild period, when the old rules don't hold," Isen wrote. "I do want to get over to you, however, our own spirit of optimism. . . . It was well that we put up our flag last spring, as it is the only place we have to go."[75]

Phil La Follette was caught in the grip of events. Enthusiasm for a third party had peaked earlier, and most of its promoters were jumping ship.

The *Common Sense* group now was committed to nudging the New Deal leftward. Tom Amlie had concluded that Roosevelt offered the best chance for advancing his hopes for a better society. A group of liberals including Mayor Fiorello La Guardia, Gov. Frank Murphy, and Sen. Robert Bulkley met that fall and agreed that a third party was out of the question unless Roosevelt needed one in 1940.[76]

Unable to control the pace of change, La Follette decided to wait to see what the future would bring. Timing is of the essence in politics, and in 1938 it was working against the governor. Previously he had frequently benefited politically from hard times; now he became their victim. His luck had soured, but it had changed before and could do so again. Young as politicians go, La Follette had plenty of time to wait for people to change their minds. He told reporters that after people saw the reactionaries in power for a while, they would rush to join a new party, and when the time came, the Progressives would be waiting.[77]

Chapter 8

The Political Outsider

Few observers, least of all Phil La Follette himself, could have believed that when he returned to the status of private citizen on 2 January 1939 he had held his last political office. At age forty-one the former governor presumably could afford to wait for new opportunities to come his way. The National Progressives of America quickly faded from view, but far more damaging to La Follette's chances were the polarization and political upheaval subsequently wrought by the bitterly argued foreign policy debate, especially after war broke out in Europe in September 1939. The clash over war cut across domestic-policy issues and resulted in La Follette's association with an assortment of isolationists who represented all shades of political opinion. The unforeseen consequences of the debate were profound, for liberal internationalists in President Roosevelt's entourage by and large linked Phil La Follette and his colleagues in the America First movement with the conservatism and reaction that played a prominent role within that movement. With the central issue defined in the isolationists' minds as simply peace or war, old associations were sundered and new ones formed, and La Follette discovered his political options critically circumscribed as a result. Wartime service in the Pacific on Gen. Douglas MacArthur's staff reinforced his inclination to cooperate with conservative isolationists and Roosevelt haters. The chances for a political comeback after the war were sharply curtailed by the events surrounding the conflict, and La Follette gradually realized that his previous success as a Progressive leader was not translatable into influence within a significantly changed postwar milieu.

In sorting things out after his defeat in 1938, Phil and Isen decided once again that a European trip was what they needed. It would provide relaxation, a welcome respite from the rancor of politics, a firsthand view of the deepening crisis in Europe, and perhaps some new answers for America's problems. Leaving their children at home, they traveled for ten weeks through France, Italy, Germany, Belgium, Denmark, Sweden, and England. Along the way, taking advantage of contacts he had made on his earlier visit and armed with letters of introduction from some of his friends, the ex-governor was able to confer with many top government, business, and university officials.[1]

What he saw greatly disturbed him and challenged his isolationist assumptions. If La Follette were going to modify his views on foreign policy, this would have been the time. He learned firsthand about the machinations of Hitler and Mussolini and the threats they posed to world peace. But the former governor filtered his observations through his past experience and expectations and shaped his conclusions accordingly. Not surprisingly, he found evidence to support his previously held positions.

Upon his return, in speeches, congressional testimony, and several articles for the *Commentator* magazine, he conveyed his impressions of the European situation. Addressing New York's prestigious Economic Club on 18 April 1939, he called Nazism the gravest foreign danger America had ever faced. But the more important message he wanted to convey was that Germany provided a practical demonstration of his own ideas about putting people to work. While deploring the evils of Nazi rule and citing evidence of popular discontent, La Follette observed that many Germans who opposed the terror and repression nevertheless supported the regime because of its success in employment. Since the Nazi and fascist philosophies operated on the assumption that full employment and freedom were incompatible, he asserted, "Nothing would more certainly smash Hitler and Mussolini from within than our demonstration of the counterproposition that men *can* have work *and* be free."

The idea that America could transform the world by its moral example had long been a staple of isolationist thinking. In La Follette's view, providing the democracies with more tangible support in the form of military hardware and economic aid would likely only further entrench selfish and undemocratic elements, who had until then actually been encouraging the Nazis through policies of appeasement. Like other isolationists, he discovered almost as much to condemn in countries being threatened by outside aggression as in the potential aggressors. Considerable evidence existed, he contended, that the ruling elements in England and France had collaborated with Hitler in order to consolidate their own class positions. It would make no sense to him to get involved in another European war "just to pull British and French economic chestnuts out of the fire."

The ultimate threat of Nazism was ideological—"a return to Paganism—to the worship of the material and physical as the ultimate in life"—and the best thing Americans could do, La Follette said, was to "put their own house in order." That meant, first of all, putting everybody to work, which would be possible if a works bill of the kind he had proposed earlier were initiated. Beyond that the United States could furnish moral support to democratic elements in England and France as well as in Germany and Italy. To dramatically symbolize that commitment, La Follette suggested that President Roosevelt withdraw our ambassador to England, Joseph P. Kennedy, whom he characterized as an appeaser and a representative of wealth and privilege. "Nazism must be smashed," La Follette concluded, "but there is an excellent chance that it can be done without war." Starkly phrased, that defined the predicament isolationists shared with their fellow Americans during the next three years. They wanted Hitler smashed, but they hoped to avoid going to war themselves in order to accomplish it.[2]

After chatting briefly with President Roosevelt at the White House, La Follette penned a letter to his friend Robert Vansittart, then the chief diplomatic adviser to the British Foreign Secretary, expressing his apprehension that his fellow Americans might underestimate the strength and nature of the Hitler regime. La Follette's warnings about the menace of Hitlerism might have served as the basis for a reevaluation of his views on foreign policy, but in fact no such metamorphosis occurred. The grip of the past retained its hold, and La Follette never subjected his isolationist assumptions to critical examination.[3]

From Germany's invasion of Poland to Japan's attack on Pearl Harbor, Phil La Follette was one of the most vocal and active critics of the Roosevelt administration's conduct of foreign policy. Three weeks after the start of the German blitzkrieg, President Roosevelt asked Congress to revise the neutrality laws to allow belligerent nations to purchase ammunitions in the United States on a cash-and-carry basis. Phil La Follette hurried to Washington to join the isolationist resistance and promised to fight against repeal of the arms embargo "from hell to breakfast." He continually warned that aiding the Allies would inevitably carry the United States into the war. Much on his mind throughout this time was the abuse his father had endured two decades earlier as an accused friend of Germany during World War I. La Follette saw a direct parallel between the two situations and remained confident that he would win ultimate vindication just as his father had done.[4]

La Follette considered his approach more positive than the one his father had followed, however. Rather than simply arguing against war, he joined the isolationist chorus for a strong hemispheric defense and advocated the construction of a "ring of steel" around North and South America. If necessary, he believed, the United States might even have to violate the sovereignty of other nations in order to root out every trace of Nazism. At home the best defense against internal subversion was the restoration of economic expansion in opposition to the self-defeating scarcity and redistribution policies implemented by the British Labour Party, the French Popular Front, and the American New Deal. La Follette argued that the successful implementation of power abroad depended on a healthy economy and urged Progressives not to let their disagreements over foreign policy disrupt their efforts to achieve domestic reform. But foreign policy questions increasingly cut across domestic ones, blurring them in people's minds and reshaping political configurations.[5]

For a while during 1939 Phil La Follette still talked optimistically about organizing NPA units in every state, and he delivered several speeches around the country for the NPA. A neon cross-in-circle sign still flickered in the window of the Madison headquarters, and a few diehards continued to sport NPA lapel pins. He wrote his college chum Joe Farrington, "My best guess is that we shall get a conservative President in '40 and then a rather silent reaction setting in in '41 or '42. No one can now foretell which way that reaction will move. I hope that the Progressive forces will be well organized so that they can give it direction."[6]

Roosevelt's successful bid for a third term in 1940 killed that idea, and Phil La Follette did not even play much of a role in his brother's reelection campaign that year because he was afraid that he might hurt rather than help the senator's chances. Moreover, by then his antiwar activities were taking up much of his time. Although there was speculation that he might run again for governor, he did not seriously consider the idea. Three national radio broadcasts delivered prior to the Democratic and Republican conventions, in which he called for a national third party if the major parties failed to provide adequate candidates and platforms, attracted little notice. That fall La Follette did some campaigning for Progressive candidates in Wisconsin, but he ignored the presidential contest, which he considered to be a fixed fight between two liberal internationalists. He left the top column blank when he marked his ballot that year. Bob, who was as dissatisfied as Phil with the administration's foreign policies, nevertheless declared his support for a third term, and Roosevelt, without directly endorsing the senator, provided him substantial support in the form of Democratic campaigners who were dispatched to Wisconsin.[7]

The president's continuing solicitude for the La Follettes frustrated Democratic party regulars. At a rally in Madison when Secretary of Agriculture Henry Wallace expressed admiration for Senator La Follette, party leaders seated on the speaker's platform walked out. But many liberals within the party welcomed such cooperation and hoped that it would result in a combination of forces with the Progressives. They repudiated the deal that had been struck with the Republicans in 1938 and encouraged the Progressives to join the Democratic party. Former governor Francis E. McGovern, Mayor Hoan, and Robert Tehan were leaders in this effort.[8]

"Now they will have to come over to us," President Roosevelt had remarked after Phil La Follette and Elmer Benson were defeated. Largely because of the La Follettes, however, the Wisconsin Progressives were slow to follow the example of their Farmer-Labor associates in amalgamating with the Democrats. "I do not think there is the slightest danger of Progressives being absorbed by the Democrats," Phil La Follette reassured one inquirer. But William T. Evjue and others pressed for closer affiliation with the Democrats. Tom Amlie, who received a job in the Justice Department after congressional opposition forced the withdrawal of his nomination to the Interstate Commerce Commission, played a major role in leading Progressives into the Democratic party. Amlie's colleagues in the FLPF, such as Samuel and David Sigman, were other early converts. The exodus of liberals and left-wingers depleted Progressive ranks. Andrew Biemiller's wartime job in the Office of Production Management and subsequent election to Congress in 1944 as a Democrat symbolized the process. Phil La Follette treated the defectors as traitors to the cause and shunned their presence, being often more comfortable in the presence of Republicans and conservatives.[9]

President Roosevelt did not give up trying to woo the Progressives into the Democratic party. His helpfulness in 1940 to Bob La Follette's reelection campaign was part of that effort, but earlier he had told Henry Wallace that Phil La Follette "had not behaved himself any too well" and "would have to have a period of purification." In 1939, 1940, and 1942 liberal New Dealers Frank Murphy, Robert H. Jackson, and Thurman

Arnold participated as speakers at the annual memorial services for Old Bob La Follette. Some of Bob La Follette's closest friends in Washington were New Dealers who were only slightly acquainted with his brother, if at all. While Phil admired people like Jackson, Arnold, and William O. Douglas, more typically he expressed disgust for "those New Deal experts and intellectuals in Washington." Just as he was isolated physically from the New Deal coterie, his thinking also was far removed from theirs.[10]

Yet, even as late as the election campaign of 1940, Phil La Follette hesitated to sever his ties with the president. In May he cryptically wired the White House, "The time for action may be at hand; if I can be helpful inside or outside the trenches let me know." Next day he made a stab at humor, telling Roosevelt not to take "trenches" literally. He had been working on a resolution that would have created a national council to monitor presidential actions relating to national defense. Bob La Follette had no desire to submit the idea to Congress, and Roosevelt considered the proposal unconstitutional and emphatically rejected it, but Phil considered it a workable method of restraining the president's warmaking power.[11]

Phil La Follette played a major role during the summer of 1940 in the establishment of the America First Committee, which developed into the foremost organization in the isolationist effort to keep the United States out of war. In July he met in Chicago with his old friend Robert E. Wood, the chairman of Sears Roebuck, and during the next several months he worked with Wood and R. Douglas Stuart, a Yale law student, in rounding up support for a new antiwar organization. Among those he talked to were William Benton, Benton's former advertising partner Chester Bowles, labor leader A. F. Whitney, and journalist John T. Flynn. La Follette volunteered to do everything he could to help the committee, and between its formation in September 1940 and 7 December 1941 he spoke at America First rallies all over the country and sometimes even filled in for Wood at the Chicago headquarters when the general was out of town. "I just honestly can't thank you enough for the great job you're doing," Stuart wrote him.[12]

Although he contributed a great deal of time to the committee, La Follette never formally joined it. Like Stuart Chase, Norman Thomas, Charles A. Beard, and others, he felt uncomfortable among the kinds of right-wingers America First attracted. Certainly many of them viewed the organization as a vehicle for attacking not only President Roosevelt's foreign policies but his domestic ones as well. Listing Robert E. Wood, Burton K. Wheeler, Jay C. Hormel, Hugh Johnson, Kathryn Lewis, Hanford MacNider, Alice Roosevelt Longworth, and William R. Castle as illustrations of his point, Evjue charged, "There are always a number of dupes who lend their names to such committees, but really running the show will be found the chronic Roosevelt haters who organize outfits like the 'America First Committee' in order to spread their anti-Roosevelt venom." Phil La Follette's discomfort in the presence of conservatives who had been recent enemies was intensified by the efforts of liberals to use guilt by association to discredit people who cooperated with the America First Committee.[13]

While anti-Semites and pro-Nazis did attempt to exploit the organization for their own purposes, considerable energies were expended in trying to exclude them. Phil La Follette found it impossible to avoid every embarrassing circumstance, for America First attracted more extremists and kooks than did its interventionist counterparts. La Follette drew criticism for appearing on the same platforms with a Christian Fronter, with someone calling public ownership of utilities totalitarian, and with an assortment of other right-wingers. His refusal to criticize statements by Charles Lindbergh regarding the influence of Jews on American policymaking brought down the charge of anti-Semitism upon himself. Reason frequently succumbed to emotion and bombast, and La Follette contributed his share to the venomous atmosphere. Much malicious gossip circulated, with La Follette seen as a turncoat by many. Political columnist Robert S. Allen wrote his old boss Evjue that La Follette was closely associated with the right-wing group in Lake Geneva, Wisconsin, that published *Scribner's Commentator*. "Frankly, Bill, I think Phil is going completely bad," Allen wrote. "I have heard several very reliable stories about him lately that are shocking." The La Follettes' invitation to conservative Sen. D. Worth Clark of Idaho to speak at the 1941 memorial ceremony for their father seemed outrageous to Allen. "That's pure desecration and a man who would do a thing like that would stoop to anything," he grumbled.[14]

Enduring snubs from old friends and questions about his motives and intentions, Phil La Follette clung to the conviction that he would ultimately be vindicated. Unlike the situation during the thirties, the conflict no longer revolved around divisions between liberals and conservatives or between friends and enemies of the New Deal; rather, the poles were represented by the prowar party and the antiwar party, or, to put it another way, politics was divided between "those who are weak and those who are strong, those who believe in America and those who believe in hiding behind the British Empire."[15]

By the fall of 1941, Phil La Follette was ready to recast his hopes for a third party in the mold established by popular divisions over President Roosevelt's foreign policy. He was encouraged in August by the victory of a Republican isolationist over Thomas Amlie in a special election to fill the vacant First District congressional seat. He declared his readiness to join other liberals in an antiwar political movement and predicted that a new party could win the next election. "It may be that the Republican party can be reorganized with the ousting of the so-called 'old guard,' " he observed. "I don't care what name it has—Republican, Progressive, or something else—so long as the realignment is attained on a workable basis." On 1 November he gave the keynote speech at a Washington conference of America Firsters, who decided to support noninterventionist candidates in 1942 on a nonpartisan basis. The group denied any intent to work for a third party; opening a discussion of domestic issues would have undoubtedly generated conflict and dissent. Instead, La Follette declared, "We have only two planks in our platform: the Declaration of Independence and the Constitution. Our salute: 'I am an American.' "[16]

Nevertheless, La Follette hoped that something more permanent might emerge out of the antiwar coalition, and he told reporters that as old habits of thought became obsolete, voters agreed on foreign policy would remain together since those issues underlay domestic ones. That expectation was a thin reed on which to rest his personal political hopes.[17]

The war, when it came, was a distinct shock to most Americans. Like virtually everyone else, Phil La Follette had been focusing his attention on Europe, but it was Japanese actions half a world away that precipitated American entry into the war, immediately ending the foreign-policy debate in the United States. Despite his vociferous objections to war, La Follette had frequently reminded people that he was no pacifist and that if war came he would be found "in the front ranks." Apparently he did not discuss with his family and friends the idea of military service more than in passing, but five days after Pearl Harbor he volunteered for duty and, much to the consternation of his wife and family, quickly was offered a commission in the army.[18]

Phil La Follette had always wanted to be where the action was, and now it was no different. Politics during the war would be no more than a holding action in his view, and an extended vacation could purge him of the negative associations he had acquired during the foreign-policy fight. Having participated in the war effort, La Follette could expect to return home with a clean slate, ready to pick up the pieces. Always a man of action, he believed that it would be the people in the thick of the fight, not the stay-at-homers, who would govern postwar America.

Entering active duty as a captain on 28 March 1942, he was bored by his initial training assignment at Fort Myer, Virginia, but he enjoyed the camaraderie of the men, liked the long work hours, and welcomed the opportunity to forget about politics for a while. He scarcely saw a newspaper or listened to the radio, and he reported to Isen, "Have few if any opinions about the war, economics, sociology, etc. Am deliberately letting that part of my brain rest."[19]

After getting a transfer from the military police to public relations, La Follette was dispatched in August for assignment in the Pacific theater, winding up on the staff of Gen. Douglas MacArthur, a development that transformed his life. In short order the magisterial general assumed almost heroic proportions for the former Wisconsin governor, who, cut off from family and friends in a foreign environment, was susceptible to the great man's charisma. At their first meeting in November 1942, MacArthur graciously remarked that he had been a friend of the senior La Follette and that from long conversations with progressive reformer Frederic C. Howe he felt almost as if he knew Phil too. La Follette was flattered and, like many others on MacArthur's staff, developed a fierce loyalty to his chief. From his post in Port Moresby, New Guinea, he wrote Bob, "Am working like the dickens—really have a long day—but I enjoy it—the work is interesting and being thoroughly busy is what I like."[20]

La Follette had never been much of a letter writer when he was away from home, but now he and Isen communicated frequently, often daily. He eagerly devoured her long newsy letters about politics, friends, and life in Madison. He found it harder than ever to accept Bob's chumminess with President Roosevelt, and as time passed it became easier for Phil to forget how closely he had cooperated with the man who for Phil gradually was transformed into the personification of everything that was going wrong in America. He fretted about Bob's passivity and urged him to become more aggressive in criticizing the president's actions and to exert greater leadership back in Wisconsin.[21]

Phil's reproofs stung his brother, who protested that a vantage point in the Pacific made it difficult to perceive the complex factors that were operating in Washington. He would continue to object to administration actions when they merited it, but he reminded Phil that it was not easy for one senator "to be heard above the din and dust of war abroad and on the home front too." Following Phil's advice, he believed, would associate him too closely with Roosevelt's conservative critics, who were trying to foil the administration with petty issues.[22]

Separated by vast distances geographically and psychologically, the brothers grew resentful and suspicious. Hard feelings earlier repressed now emerged. Differences of temperament and ideas had not weakened their relationship before, when their complementary talents had often worked to good advantage. But now, with no common goals or interests to unite them, old hurts and annoyances surfaced. Neither had been very good at expressing deep emotions, although their letters were punctuated by frequent statements of sincere love and admiration for each other. Neither had learned to productively disagree with or criticize the other. Bob's disrelish in 1938 for the National Progressives of America was clear, but to avoid a large dispute he had unenthusiastically gone along. His lack of enthusiasm had deeply hurt Phil and Isen, who attributed it to his being ensconced in the Washington environment, which they thought isolated people from grass-roots sentiment.[23]

Phil's decision to enter the army brought out Bob's frustrations. He complained that Phil was walking out on him, unfairly leaving him with the burden of trying to manage state party affairs. Bob had let Phil run the party, but now Phil was taking a soft job in the army and leaving all the worry at a time when the party was slipping badly. Bob also opposed Phil's plan to turn the *Progressive* over to Morris Rubin and Gordon Sinykin. Rubin, who had been a brilliant *Wisconsin State Journal* reporter before going to work for Phil, had taken over as editor of the weekly in June 1940 when the La Follettes reacquired control of the paper from Evjue. As Phil prepared to leave Madison, he proposed to turn it over to Rubin, but Bob wanted the family to retain its interest in the publication and got Fola and Mary La Follette to go along with him.[24]

Phil attributed his disagreements with Bob largely to differing temperaments. He was a doer, a leader, a pusher. His impatience and aggressiveness had gotten him into trouble at times, but they had also achieved results. Bob, on the other hand, had more of his mother's disposition; he was more cautious, restrained, and contemplative. While Phil tore along with the bit in his teeth, Bob held onto the reins. "I think as we have gotten older we have both tended to move in the direction our respective temperaments have demanded and therefore moved further apart in what we wanted most out of life," Phil remarked.[25]

Phil's wartime letters reveal another side of his personality, contrasting sharply with his public image of mastery, decisiveness, and even cockiness. Beneath the posture of assurance and strength existed a vulnerability few people were aware of. Belle Case and Robert M. La Follette, Sr., harbored high expectations for their children and had provided models almost impossible to equal. Phil welcomed life's challenges and impressed people with his brilliance and intensity. While Bob never enjoyed many of his political duties and found personal interaction with his constituents almost painful, Phil loved politicking, worked hard at it, and could not get enough of it. While Bob had seemed destined for a journalistic or business career, Phil had always been bent upon politics. But when their father died in 1925, only Bob was old enough to run for the vacant seat under the requirements of the Constitution. Phil had always considered himself their mother's favorite, but after her husband's death Belle Case La Follette seemed to put her elder son in Phil's place and to devote her energy to Bob's success. Phil, meanwhile, played a distinctly subordinate role. He never got over an incident when his mother brusquely dismissed as ridiculous the idea of his running for governor. Later on, of course, she changed her mind.[26]

Their differing relationships with President Roosevelt also drove a wedge between the brothers. Bob saw less of his old patron during the war and disagreed with him frequently, but he never developed Phil's strong antipathy toward him. The debate over intervention poisoned Phil's relationship with the president, and later, as he brooded in the Pacific, his thoughts often turned to the harm he thought his former friend had inflicted on American society. Compounding his frustration and that of many others was the way in which the decision to concentrate first on Hitler shortchanged the Pacific theater of manpower and materials. His desire to give the Pacific higher priority associated him with other former isolationists and America Firsters who were readier to carry the war against Japan than against Hitler. MacArthur came to symbolize for many people the antithesis of Roosevelt and New Deal liberalism.[27]

La Follette's work in the America First movement had involved him with a whole new group of allies and had cut him off from former friends. Now, in his new and isolated environment, he went further in severing his liberal roots. Without ever explicitly repudiating his Progressive ties, he found himself increasingly in agreement with people he formerly had opposed and alienated from people with whom he had earlier cooperated. The evolution was more inadvertent than planned as the intensity of old issues faded and new ones took their place. Unemployment, farm prices, union organization, and social security were replaced as issues by foreign policy, wartime planning, and executive authority. Everything was in flux, and Phil La Follette saw the war as a turning point that would usher in a whole new configuration in politics.

He was more surprised than he should have been at the loud outcry from outraged liberals when he wrote a letter lauding General MacArthur's leadership to Col. Robert R. McCormick, who printed it in his *Chicago Tribune* on 26 October 1943. La Follette had wanted to thank the reactionary publisher for his outspoken editorial support for the general, but Isen and their family friends could not understand why Phil had sent the letter to such an outspoken opponent of Progressivism, especially when he realized it might be made public. Liberals interpreted the letter as further evidence of La Follette's swing to the right. Evjue lashed out at his old friend by saying, "Phil La Follette has now completed the circle." Bob La Follette worried about his brother's judgment and urged him to exercise more discretion. Trying to make some sense of the episode, Isen remarked in her column in the *Progressive,* "We find ourselves these days in the unwelcome position of keeping the strangest company." For Phil La Follette all the hubbub was disconcerting, but he recognized that alignments were shifting. "It is perfectly true that I would not have chosen this particular way of being aligned with McCormick," he wrote his wife, "but on the essential issue one's 'friends' in this business are those that fight on the side in which you believe."[28]

La Follette readily put that principle into practice when he played a central role in an abortive effort to obtain the Republican presidential nomination for MacArthur in 1944. The general undoubtedly wanted the nomination and had his staff work for it, but he also wanted to avoid any appearance that he actually desired to be president. Although Phil La Follette was not part of the inner circle around the general, his political experience and contacts gave him a special role in the scenario. A major MacArthur booster in the states was La Follette's friend Gen. Robert E. Wood, who had known MacArthur for forty-four years. During the summer of 1943, while on a business trip to Australia, Wood talked several times with MacArthur and in meetings with La Follette and other staff members became convinced that although the general would not actively seek the presidency, he would accept a draft. Wood later contacted Sen. Arthur Vandenberg, and the two began planning a MacArthur campaign. La Follette told Isen that he might come home to "look the ground over" for MacArthur; but Bob warned him that such a trip would only provide ammunition for Phil's critics, who were just waiting to destroy him, and Morris Rubin and other friends also thought it very unwise. Taking their advice, La Follette abandoned the idea.[29]

Nevertheless, Phil La Follette's name was publicly linked to MacArthur's candidacy by Lansing Hoyt, a wealthy Milwaukee businessman who had been active earlier in Republican circles and America First. Now, with no authorization from the general's staff, he personally initiated a MacArthur for president boom in Wisconsin and indicated his desire to run Phil La Follette as a delegate candidate on a MacArthur slate in the presidential primary. The War Department ruled in January 1944 that La Follette's military status disqualified him, but three other Progressives were on the MacArthur ticket in Wisconsin. The primary in April, which knocked Wendell Willkie out of the race, also virtually eliminated MacArthur as a possibility since he was able to capture only three delegates, but the experience only whetted his appetite for politics. While Phil La Follette remained silent publicly, behind the scenes he worked actively to promote MacArthur.[30]

The former governor's captivation by MacArthur reflected both the general's magnetic personality and Phil's sense of isolation from the centers of power and from his own past. Cut off from old friends and political associates, skeptical of the continuing relevance of traditional Progressive ideas, and convinced that New Deal liberalism had run its course, La Follette cast about for something new. He could not be certain what would emerge out of the war, but he was convinced that it would present Americans with something different. "Of course I do not want to get tied up with some gang with whom I do not agree," he wrote Isen, "but one has to take a broad view of 'what we agree on' if he expects to have other people—and from many different and differing sections agree with him." Opposition to Franklin Roosevelt had become an obsession, and in Douglas MacArthur he found someone who he thought could cut Roosevelt down to size. As the antithesis of his prime nemesis, the general embodied for La Follette not only a way out for America but a way back into politics for himself.[31]

Though seemingly near hero-worship of his commander, Phil La Follette did not overlook MacArthur's flaws, including his haughty arrogance. In this case, however, fault was translated into virtue when directed against the president, and La Follette took great delight in the story told by an army colleague, Gen. Bonner Fellers, about an incident at the July 1944 strategy conference in Hawaii attended by Roosevelt, MacArthur, Adm. Chester Nimitz, and their aides. As La Follette later recalled it, during the sessions MacArthur was interrupted at one point in his presentation to be told about the high casualties in his campaign up the coast of New Guinea. Greatly aroused, he walked directly over to Roosevelt and, pointing his finger in the president's chest, said, "I do not know who has given you that kind of information, but whoever he was, he told you lies." La Follette relished the image of MacArthur doing what he had never been able to do.[32]

In addition to serving as a foil to Franklin Roosevelt, General MacArthur alone seemed capable of comparison with La Follette's father. Something about the man, he wrote in 1951, "kept reminding me of the characteristics of my father." It was not merely their directness and well-honed sense of drama, but "the way they both spelled 'honor' with a capital 'H'; that nothing was worthwhile without moral integrity." Personality rather than political views constituted MacArthur's primary appeal for the former governor, although he did like to think of the general as a progressive. What counted most were the leadership qualities and the stature MacArthur could give to the country on the world stage. La Follette emphasized leadership over ideology and deemphasized progressive principles just as he had done in launching the National Progressives of America in 1938. Then he had invited people to trust him; now he would ask them to trust MacArthur.[33]

In August 1944 La Follette acted as a personal go-between for the general and the president. MacArthur sent a letter concerning his Philippine invasion plans with Phil, who was to deliver it to the White House as the first stop on a month's leave in the states. The meeting with the president aroused in La Follette a feeling of déjà vu; in the midst of wartime mobilization the two men's differences were temporarily laid aside. Roosevelt warmly greeted La Follette, who had not seen him in five years and to whom he appeared old and shaky. After opening the letter, Roosevelt chatted for a moment and then, before his old friend and critic could leave, took La Follette's hand and said, "Phil, I want you to stay here with me. I need you badly." Unsure of how to take it, La Follette replied that he was scheduled to be in on the invasion of the Philippines and that he thought he should return. The president sighed, "God bless you, boy," and La Follette departed. After a brief stay with his family in Madison, he rejoined his unit.[34]

"The fates were certainly on my side when I got sent to the Southwest Pacific Area," La Follette wrote Isen. "General MacArthur is going to stand out like Grant, Sherman, or Lee." Casting his lot with MacArthur meant repudiating his political past by allying with conservatives and nationalists against New Deal liberals and friends of Roosevelt. Moreover, his fascination with the untapped potentialities of the Pacific region and his assignment of a secondary role to Europe reinforced his links to the America First group and other former isolationists. La Follette spoke rhapsodically about the Pacific region and attached an almost mystical importance to it. He thought he could detect "gigantic, creating impulses of nature" stirring in the area and described its unexplored territory and undeveloped markets as "hungry for opening up." Here was the last frontier. Having earlier assigned a special role for the Western Hemisphere, he expanded his "hemisphere idea" to include the Pacific. The inclination to attach unique importance to his own locale was nothing new for one who had continually portrayed Wisconsin as the pacesetting state in the Union.[35]

As American units continued their advances, La Follette looked forward to the day when he could return home to tell what he had learned. He intended to reestablish his law practice, and when the time came he would be ready for another round of politics, although he told his wife that he had no interest in running for office again. He was ready "to wade into the domestic and foreign problems we face and contribute my 'five cents worth mixed.' " Convinced that old maps were obsolete and that new approaches would have to be tried, he wanted to start clean and "ride events as they came." Identification with the Progressive tradition would constitute no asset under the new regime. His own openness to innovation would cause him to outperform his overly cautious brother, who, he remarked, "thinks he is adhering to principle because he follows the same course on a given subject that Dad did 40 years ago."[36]

The shape of politics had been recast during the previous decade, and Phil La Follette now found himself in opposition to most of the people he had earlier been allied with. Progressives had always battled against special privilege, but in his view, "The 'Special Privilege' group has changed in the past twenty years—and a lot of 'Progressive liberals' don't know it yet. They are still fighting the enemies of twenty-five years ago, and don't know that the entire game has shifted to another field." Now it was the New Dealers, labor unions, FLPF-type groups, the *Nation,* the *New Republic,* intellectuals by and large, and the Evjues and La Guardias, all of whom he had worked with in the past, who constituted the major spokesmen for vested interests. The "New-Deal-up-lift-save-the-world-give-'em-art bunch," he believed, was essentially a scheme to procure an easy way of life for a small minority at the expense of ordinary folks. "Democratic soft-thinkers," "phony liberals," and "sap-headed internationalists" provoked his ridicule. "Our kind of people can never be a part of the FDR crowd," he said. "The 'liberals' there will always hate us—largely because of their own consciences. We must be in opposition to FDR and what he stands for. Because it's wrong and has been corrupting."[37]

Yet, after all that, La Follette could not completely write off the man with whom he had worked so well for so long. Even now, the ambivalence remained. He envied Roosevelt's consummate political skills and granted his good intentions, but he thought that the president had finally let the situation get out of control. "Sure wouldn't want to be in his boots —actually or in terms of history," he wrote in March 1945. A month later Roosevelt was dead. In a reflective mood, La Follette recalled the man's tactical genius, his winning personality, and a radio voice that was a "gift of the Gods." "What those gifts could have done had they been harnessed to deep conviction and far-sighted vision," La Follette mused.[38]

After he returned to Madison in June 1945, it took a while for Phil La Follette to get reoriented. "I shall be intrigued when I get home," he had written from the Pacific, "to see if I can still make a speech, and especially whether I can meet the challenge of the times, tempo, and conditions." But there was little opportunity for an ex-governor who had repudiated his New Deal friends and who remained uncomfortable among conservative Republicans to find a niche where he could reestablish himself as a credible political force. He quickly accepted invitations to speak to service groups and civic organizations, where his primary message was the ideological menace of communism, the vast potential of the Pacific region, and the outstanding leadership of General MacArthur. In league with countless others, La Follette apotheosized the "American way of life" as a counterforce to the Soviet threat, and he reverted to the kind of consensual rhetoric he had developed during 1937 and used in 1938 when launching the National Progressives of America. "Here at home we are inclined to emphasize our differences: capital against labor; city worker against farmers; Republican against Democrat," La Follette observed. "From across the vast waters of the Pacific we saw America as a whole. We thought of what united us, rather than what divided us. We saw and appreciated that at home in America our fathers had built a new way of life that is unique on this earth."[39]

Liberalism in 1945 was in retreat, and Wisconsin Progressives were assessing their future. The Progressive party, which had been floundering since 1938, seemed obviously headed toward extinction. The victory of former Progressive attorney general Orland Loomis in the gubernatorial contest of 1942 had been more of a personal than a party victory, and his subsequent death before he was able to take office dealt a severe blow to Progressive hopes. Their inability to attract more than 6 percent of the vote in 1944 served notice to realists that the end was near. Since Bob La Follette faced reelection in 1946, the decision about the party's future took on special importance.[40]

Plans were made for a group of Progressive leaders to meet in Portage in March 1946 to decide the party's future. Phil La Follette had been quietly urging people to keep it alive, but not many people were listening. His brother's campaign managers feared that Phil's presence at the conference might resuscitate old feuds or stimulate a last-ditch effort to save the Progressive party and thereby harm Bob's reelection chances. When they asked Phil not to attend the meeting, he complied. At the senator's urging, the conference voted overwhelmingly to disband the party and to return to the Republican fold. He had previously rejected overtures from Democrats to run on their ticket. By then the drift back into the major parties was almost complete, with old-timers and conservatives generally going with the Republicans, and liberals and younger Progressives moving into the Democratic party. Urban dwellers along the lakeshore and labor union members played a crucial role in the revitalization of the Democratic party during the 1940s. A youthful cadre of liberal activists, many of whom had started as young Progressives, eventually captured control of the Democratic party from the conservative old guard and transformed it into a vehicle for liberalism in the state. Carl Thompson, whose unsuccessful runs for governor in 1948 and 1950 opened the way for future party victories, had as a university student during the thirties been a leader in the Young Progressive Club and had served as Governor La Follette's chauffeur. State Sen. Gaylord Nelson, who in 1958 became the first Democratic governor in a quarter century, was the son of a Polk County Progressive leader and made an unsuccessful first bid for the legislature as a Republican in 1946. Other Democratic party leaders included former Milwaukee mayor Daniel Hoan, who during the late 1930s had cooperated with the Progressives as he progressed from the Socialist party to the Democrats; James Doyle, a law partner of Phil La Follette; Horace Wilkie, a son of the regent who had led the fight against Glenn Frank; John Reynolds, the son of a Progressive attorney general; and David Rabinovitz, a former Progressive fund raiser. Ironically, it was people like those who carried on the progressive tradition in Wisconsin within the Democratic party, while Bob and Phil La Follette reverted to Republicanism.[41]

While Phil La Follette remained on good terms with some of the architects of postwar liberalism in Wisconsin, his friends came from different circles. The treatment he received from Bob's campaign managers reflected the general opinion liberals had of him after World War II. They worried that he would be a drag on his brother's reelection chances, so he agreed to keep a low profile during the summer and fall of 1946. Elsewhere, liberals were more inclined to associate the former governor with the "circumcised swastika," America First, and General MacArthur than with his previous record of liberal reform. They wondered where he had gone wrong—what had pushed him to the right. Was he really a fascist or merely an unprincipled opportunist? Reflecting on the anomalous situation she and her husband found themselves in during the late forties, Isen La Follette remarked, "I have a sense that we are somewhat of a social problem in many Madison circles these days, as we are neither fish nor fowl and no one feels quite free to express themselves."[42]

Phil La Follette was eager to return to politics, but how? He still hoped to make his influence felt, but he faced unfamiliar terrain, possessed little political leverage, and lacked access to the places where the important decisions were being made. Politics after the war bore only slight resemblance to what he had been familiar with. The prematurely gray La Follette symbolized, it appeared, an era that was separated from the time they were living in by the cleft of World War II. His and Bob's decision to steer clear of the Democrats isolated them from their natural allies. Some Republicans were ready to welcome the La Follettes back into their midst, but the state party chairman, Tom Coleman, vigorously opposed any accommodation with them, and other conservative leaders insisted upon barring them from any role in party affairs. Phil sometimes told people that he had sworn off politics, but few believed that he could easily turn his back on what had been the center of his existence for most of his life.

In 1947 he turned down an opportunity to become the first civilian governor of Bavaria under the allied military occupation, citing personal finances as the reason for his reluctance to take the post. While most of his old liberal friends shunned him, his relations with conservative Republicans and businessmen were not a satisfactory substitute. For one so gregarious and personable to feel cut off from others was frustrating. His law practice did not keep him busy enough, and he gradually developed a serious drinking problem. The burden of readjusting to civilian life was more difficult than he had anticipated. To escape he retreated frequently to his farm twenty miles outside Madison. Having no great purpose in life, cut off from former friends, a pariah in many people's eyes, La Follette could not seem to pull himself together.[43]

A major opportunity presented itself during the months preceding the 1948 Republican National Convention, when La Follette performed prominently in another effort to draft General MacArthur for the presidency. He was in close touch with his old friend Gen. Robert E. Wood, who had been the key figure in the MacArthur movement in 1944. Again the Wisconsin primary was crucial to the general's chances, and La Follette was responsible for organizing the state as well as running himself as a delegate candidate for MacArthur. The Wisconsin campaign was directed from La Follette's office in Madison, with most of the daily operations being managed by his law partner Gordon Sinykin and long-time conservative Republican leader William J. Campbell. They called upon many former Progressives to circulate petitions and round up support. La Follette found himself working for the most part, however, with old political opponents such as Campbell and former governor Fred R. Zimmerman. La Follette subordinated domestic issues to foreign policy, portraying the general as a leader who could stand up to the Russians and also prevent World War III. He enjoyed the personal contacts with people and savored favorable responses to his speeches. Although MacArthur's unexpectedly poor showing in April proved fatal to his candidacy, Phil La Follette was pleased as the head of his delegate slate to have polled more votes than any other of the general's at-large delegate candidates. Viewing the campaign as an opportunity to regain a foothold in politics, he happily told his wife that maybe he did not have "political halitosis after all."[44]

But his years of success as an insurgent now blocked his ascendancy in the major parties. The Democrats were being taken over by a group of young liberals intent on their own advancement, and the regular Republican leadership was bent on expunging every trace of La Folletism. The disintegration of the Progressive party and Phil La Follette's failure to use the 1948 MacArthur campaign as a vehicle for capturing control of the Republican party left him isolated politically. In 1952 he backed California's Gov. Earl Warren for the Republican nomination and later gave his support to Dwight Eisenhower. By then he realized that electoral politics were out of his grasp. In 1955 he and Isen moved to Long Island, New York, where he became president of Hazeltine Electronics Corporation after serving as the company's legal counsel. But his heart remained in Madison, and after a five-year absence he and Isen returned home. His name was mentioned as a Republican gubernatorial possibility in 1960, but though he was flattered by the idea, he said that leadership was a job for younger people.[45]

During the years that were left to him he continued his legal practice, but more and more of his time was spent at the State Historical Society of Wisconsin, where he pored through old letters and documents and worked on his memoirs. Age had mellowed him, and his sense of humor was still operative. Jokingly he told people that he might call his book "The Second Son," but beneath the humor festered the accumulated hurts of a younger brother who believed that he had been required to work harder and sacrifice more in life only to achieve a smaller measure of recognition. Acclaim had come early for both sons, but their lives out of politics carried a sense of deep tragedy. Although at first he had welcomed the release from public responsibilities resulting from his loss to Joseph R. McCarthy in the 1946 Republican primary election, Bob La Follette failed to find much satisfaction in his position as a private citizen. Discontented with his private life, troubled by chronic physical ailments, and subject to deep fits of depression, he took his own life in February 1953. His death may have played a role in Phil and Isen's decision to find a change of scenery outside Wisconsin.[46]

Phil La Follette was acutely aware that for some reason he had never been loved as much in Wisconsin as had his older brother. Whereas Bob inspired trust and affection, Phil elicited admiration and astonishment. He was the activist, pusher, administrator, leader, and party organizer. Assertive, imaginative, and willing to take risks, his ambition carried him far before his political career was prematurely terminated. His outspoken style of advocacy continually invited controversy. Obsessed with the problem of leadership, he doggedly pursued it, desirous finally even of the presidency. In the end he overreached himself, and because he had failed and because of the methods he had used in the pursuit, he found himself branded as overweeningly ambitious, unprincipled, and even fascistic. He was classified with John T. Flynn, Burton K. Wheeler, and other isolationist progressives who had taken a turn to the right.

Certainly he was no fascist. Then the question persists: did he possess some sort of fatal flaw guiding him toward failure? Was there some quality inherent in his character that explains his actions and subsequent ostracism? In fact, no such interpretation is necessary. La Follette suffered from the consequences of rhetorical excess and unfortunate choice of symbols and especially from bad timing. The symbolism and trappings of the National Progressives of America differed little from the kind of hoopla that had been used by the National Recovery Administration five years earlier. Some of La Follette's rhetoric was mystical and demagogic, and his strategy revolved around people trusting him to do the right thing as leader. But he was no little führer, and every politician is prone to ambiguity and overstatement.

More than anything else, Phil La Follette was guilty of being an isolationist and of campaigning against President Roosevelt's foreign policy during the period before Pearl Harbor. His active involvement in America First cut him off from his old liberal internationalist friends and involved him with a whole new group of associates, many of whom were conservative businessmen and Roosevelt haters. Once again the issue resolved itself simply into the question of whether one was for Roosevelt or against him. Now, with the dichotomy defined as a conflict between the war party and the peace party, La Follette's lingering ambivalence about the president was transformed into an unremitting antagonism. His stint in the Pacific further reinforced it.

Phil La Follette's shift to the right was neither unusual nor surprising. Several things explain it. La Follette came to believe by 1937 that Progressivism needed to broaden its base of support, to accommodate itself to new ideas, and to question the assumption that continually expanding government was a solution for most social and economic problems. After the recession of 1937 set in, he concluded that President Roosevelt was politically vulnerable and that he could somehow exploit the situation for his own benefit by positioning himself further away from the national administration. Later, the great debate over foreign policy cut him off altogether from Roosevelt and turned him into a thoroughgoing opponent of the man who had earlier befriended him. Finally, the people that La Follette associated with in America First and in the MacArthur entourage were generally much more conservative than the people he had worked with in the thirties. Conversely, his old liberal colleagues, most of whom supported Roosevelt's internationalism, were alienated by La Follette's ties to people such as Robert E. Wood, Col. Robert McCormick, Charles Lindbergh, and Gen. Douglas MacArthur. It was this matrix of friends and associates, rather than any pronounced shift in political philosophy, that condemned La Follette in the minds of many liberals. Ironically, liberals who proscribed La Follette for the friends that he kept would later loudly complain about Sen. Joseph McCarthy's practice of guilt by association. In fact, Phil La Follette had not changed so much. Rather it was the times, the issues, and his friends that had altered. Added to this were La Follette's personal difficulties with alcohol and melancholy after the war. It is not hard to understand why people could believe that he had gone off the deep end, but a better explanation for his behavior lies in the context of depression and war. His willingness to challenge President Roosevelt on both domestic and foreign policy left him a man without a political home. He did not want the Democrats, and the Republicans did not want him; he was caught in the squeeze of the two-party system. During the thirties he had enjoyed the unusual privilege of being the undisputed head of a successful third party. But few politicians are afforded that luxury, and after 1938 he was not either.

Phil La Follette's early political success and the ever-present memory of his parents drove him to aspire to the highest job in the land. Driven by powerful ambition and sustained by a penetrating intellect and high qualities of leadership, he was a credible candidate for that job. Many are called, however, but few are chosen. Luck, circumstances, and timing are crucial in politics. For Phil La Follette, the timing was all wrong. The late thirties and early forties were not propitious for an isolationist, third-party presidential candidate. Had La Follette followed other advice and run successfully for the U.S. Senate in 1938, he could have bided his time and might have used his position to launch a bid later on.

Phil La Follette was a politician who was willing to risk much in the pursuit of high ideals and high office. Rather than sitting idly by, he preferred to act and was willing to suffer the consequences and to admit that some of his choices were wrong. He mapped out a special path for himself, and he trusted to his own instincts.

On 18 August 1965, Philip Fox La Follette died in Madison General Hospital; his death was attributed to pneumonia and lung complications. His favorite words from Ecclesiasticus 37:13–14 could have served as his epitaph:

> But let the counsel of thine own heart stand:
> For there is none more faithful unto thee than it.
> For a man's mind is sometimes wont to bring him tidings,
> More than seven watchmen that sit above in a high tower.

Appendix

Voting Patterns and Wisconsin Progressivism

The historian, by focusing too exclusively on the leadership of individual actors, faces the danger of obscuring more fundamental, long-range forces that are operating. The drama of the moment can make us forget that in politics habit and tradition play crucial roles. Phil La Follette drew upon a rich tradition of political liberalism that encompassed not only the progressivism that had been led by his father in the state of Wisconsin but also a whole gamut of left-wing social movements that Phil and his colleagues identified with. La Follette himself frequently argued that Wisconsin progressivism was simply a modern manifestation of a centuries-old conflict between privilege and the public interest. But since behavior at the polls reflects sociocultural background as well as economic interests, the determinants of voting are not easily disentangled; however, several studies of Wisconsin politics help illuminate the patterns of twentieth-century change.

Utilizing county voting data to refute the idea that support for Sen. Joseph R. McCarthy derived from agrarian roots similar to those sustaining La Follette progressivism, Michael P. Rogin argues for a basic continuity from turn-of-the-century progressivism through the Progressive party of the 1930s to postwar liberalism embodied in a resurgent Democratic party. Although problems exist with his use of county voting data, the general argument is substantially correct. There was a basic continuity, although certainly accretions and defections occurred along the way. Rogin suggests that there existed both an ethnic and an economic basis for Wisconsin progressivism. Crucial to the movement's success was the support of relatively poor Scandinavian, especially Norwegian, farmers and rural dwellers in the northern and western parts of Wisconsin. To a large extent their support for progressivism was a dimension of their Republican voting habits. Rogin, along with others, shows that during and after World War I, Robert M. La Follette, Sr., and other progressives benefited greatly from an influx of German voters who

186

agreed with their isolationist position on the war. Gradually during the 1920s, many of those people drifted back into the Democratic party. During the 1930s, the progressives built upon their rural base and added the votes of working people and urban liberals who also supported the New Deal. By 1936 economic motives had become significantly more important in determining the way people voted.[1]

Robert R. Dykstra and David R. Reynolds, using more sophisticated statistical techniques and voting data from townships, villages, and small towns, demonstrate that, at least in rural areas, there was "nothing like a permanent left in Wisconsin" during the first four decades of the twentieth century. Their evidence reinforces Rogin's emphasis on the central importance of Scandinavian voters and the lesser and fluctuating impact of Germans in the progressive coalition. Actually, Rogin tries to demonstrate the existence not of a permanent left in Wisconsin, but of a reorientation in the 1930s that was generated by the Progressive party and that "resulted in a positive relation between the Republican vote of the La Follette period and the Democratic vote of today." For all their criticism of Rogin's methodology, Dykstra and Reynolds seem unwilling to challenge this fundamental insight. They write, "Insofar as Rogin's description of Wisconsin voter perambulations is correct, his success seems more a triumph of intuition than method." What Dykstra and Reynolds successfully demonstrate is that we must be careful not to see too neat a line of continuity between the La Follette progressives and the modern Democratic party. The historical story is in fact more complicated.[2]

In what is certainly the most extensive historical analysis of the determinants of Wisconsin voting patterns, David L. Brye isolates relatively homogeneous wards, townships, villages, and cities and describes their behavior during the first half of the twentieth century. His thesis is that ethnicity continued to play the predominant role in influencing people's votes throughout the period, although its importance began to decline by midcentury. He convincingly demonstrates the importance of ethnic background, but since he does not test economic or other factors with equal rigor, the question of the relative impact of ethnic, economic, and other personal characteristics on voting remains an open question. Nevertheless, Brye's book is valuable for the estimates he makes of the support that was given by various ethnic groups to the competing parties in Wisconsin. Like Rogin, Brye sees the Progressive party as a transitional link between early twentieth-century progressivism and postwar Democratic liberalism.[3]

During the 1930s Wisconsin continued to have a higher percentage of foreign-born in its population than did the United States as a whole. Of the white population, somewhat more than 13 percent were foreign-born. Of the native-born, about 40 percent were of foreign or mixed parentage, that is, having at least one parent born outside the United States. Out of a total population of 2,939,067 in 1930, 608,200, or 20.7 percent, were born in Germany or of German parentage. Next in order in foreign stock were the Poles, with 139,255, or 4.7 percent of the population. Norwegians numbered 135,953 (4.6 percent). The Norwegians, combined with 56,915 from Sweden and 40,923 from Denmark, constituted a total of 8 percent of the population. Other countries that contributed significantly to the state's population included Austria, Hungary, and Yugoslavia, 72,876 (combined total); Canada, 64,718; Great Britain, 64,651; Czechoslovakia, 59,150; and Ireland, 40,417.[4]

Another significant demographic variable in Wisconsin politics was the physical distribution of the population. Two-thirds of the state's residents were located in the southeast, separated from the rest of the state by a line running from Green Bay through Madison to the Illinois state line. By 1930, 53 percent of the population was classified as urban. Slightly more than one-quarter of the population lived in the Milwaukee metropolitan area. The city itself numbered 578,249 residents. Its closest competitors were Racine, 67,542; Madison, 57,899; Kenosha, 50,262; Oshkosh, 40,108; La Crosse, 39,614; Sheboygan, 39,251; and Superior, 36,113. Since progressivism had traditionally depended so heavily on the rural vote, accelerating industrialization and urbanization posed serious problems for it. More than 60 percent of the population increase of 306,939 that occurred during the 1920s took place in Milwaukee County, and most of the rest occurred in another half-dozen counties. Fifteen counties lost population between 1920 and 1930. The areas of greatest Progressive strength were falling behind the rest of the state in relative population. If the Progressives were to survive and prosper, they would have to appeal to urban dwellers. Phil La Follette clearly recognized this as he cultivated the friendship of the labor unions and the Socialist party during the 1930s. The development of Wisconsin progressivism as a more urban- and labor-oriented movement during the 1930s reflected not merely the ideological convictions of the La Follettes and their followers, but also a rational response to the demographic realities of the twentieth century.[5]

Norwegians and other Scandinavians, who were the most consistent supporters of progressivism, were concentrated in the northwestern part of the state. Calculating the 1934 senatorial vote, David L. Brye estimates that 79 percent of Norwegian rural residents cast their ballots for Bob La Follette. Other estimates of Progressive strength included: Danish rural, 72 percent; Finnish rural, 71 percent; Swiss Reformed rural, 69 percent; Swiss Reformed villages, 66 percent; Swedish rural, 67 percent; Norwegian city, 66 percent; Norwegian villages, 58 percent; German Lutheran rural, 68 percent; German Catholic rural, 64 percent; Milwaukee German wards, 49 percent; other German city wards, 52 percent; German Catholic villages, 54 percent; German Catholic cities, 48 percent; German Lutheran villages, 50 percent; German Lutheran cities, 42 percent; French Canadian wards, 60 percent; French Canadian villages, 45 percent; Bohemian villages, 42 percent; English villages, 43 percent; English rural, 30 percent; Dutch Reformed rural, 37 percent; Dutch Reformed villages, 32 percent; Austrian rural, 27 percent; Welsh villages, 27 percent; native-stock villages, 41 percent; native-stock cities, 25 percent; and native-stock wards, 17 percent. For the state as a whole in 1934, Bob La Follette captured 50 percent of the vote.[6]

Those who seek an explanation for Wisconsin progressivism in its programs and ideology alone will be disappointed. There is no single key that unlocks the meaning of the movement. The progressives were leftists, reformers, and social critics. On specifics they frequently disagreed among themselves. They were for the most part ordinary people, similar to their neighbors who voted for Democrats and conservative Republicans. On the campaign trail, Phil La Follette traveled from town to town, sitting in the backseat of a car swigging orange juice and thumbing through his little black books. Being close to the people, he knew their foibles and strengths, hopes and fears and desires. He could talk their language, and for many of them the words *conservative, liberal, reactionary,* and *radical* did not mean much. They wanted somebody who could talk sense and somebody they could believe in. After the Progressive party was created in 1934, it accommodated radicals, liberals, moderates, and even conservatives. During a period of rapid change, the meaning of such labels was slippery anyway. Phil La Follette preferred to speak in concrete terms about his programs, ideas, and accomplishments, and the meanings of the words could take care of themselves.

List of Abbreviations Used in the Notes

BCL——Belle Case La Follette

Family Papers (with appropriate box and series numbers)——La Follette Family Papers, Library of Congress, Washington, D.C.

FDR——Franklin D. Roosevelt

FDRL——Franklin D. Roosevelt Library, Hyde Park, New York

FDR Papers——Franklin D. Roosevelt Papers, Franklin D. Roosevelt Library, Hyde Park, New York

IBL——Isabel Bacon La Follette

OF——Official File, Franklin D. Roosevelt Papers

PFL——Philip F. La Follette

PFL Papers——Philip F. La Follette Papers, State Historical Society of Wisconsin, Madison

PPF——President's Personal File, Franklin D. Roosevelt Papers

Press Conference——Available in microfilm at the Franklin D. Roosevelt Library, Hyde Park, New York

RML——Robert M. La Follette, Jr.

SHSW——State Historical Society of Wisconsin, Madison

Notes

Chapter 1: Introduction

1. Louis Adamic, "Hello Phil," *Common Sense* 7 (May 1938): 16–19; Leonard Lyons, *Washington Post*, 22 April 1938.
2. *New York Times Magazine*, 8 May 1938.
3. PFL to BCL, 8 May 1921, Family Papers; PFL, *Adventure in Politics: The Memoirs of Philip La Follette*, ed. Donald Young (New York: Holt, Rinehart and Winston, 1970), p. 6.
4. Fola La Follette to BCL, 20 November 1930, box A39, Family Papers. On RML, see the excellent biography by Patrick J. Maney, *"Young Bob" La Follette: A Biography of Robert M. La Follette, Jr., 1895–1953* (Columbia: University of Missouri Press, 1978), and another by Roger T. Johnson, *Robert M. La Follette, Jr. and the Decline of the Progressive Party in Wisconsin* (Madison: SHSW, 1964).
5. *Progressive*, 12 July 1930.
6. Fred Risser, quoted in L. David Carley, "The Wisconsin Governor's Legislative Role: A Case Study in the Administrations of Philip Fox La Follette and Walter J. Kohler, Jr." (Ph.D. diss., University of Wisconsin, 1959), p. 139.
7. On La Follette's childhood, see PFL, *Adventure in Politics*, pp. 1–29, and BCL and Fola La Follette, *Robert M. La Follette, June 14, 1855 to June 18, 1925*, 2 vols. (New York: Macmillan, 1953); interview, Mary La Follette, 30 March 1973; *Progressive*, 11 July 1931; *New York Times*, 27 September 1931; Lyle W. Cooper, "Good News from Wisconsin," *New Republic*, 64 (15 October 1930): 228.
8. Brandeis quoted in BCL and Fola La Follette, *Robert M. La Follette*, p. 295; Harold Groves, "In and Out of the Ivory Tower," box 40, Harold Groves Papers, SHSW; IBL memoirs, box 165, PFL Papers.
9. IBL memoirs, box 165, PFL Papers; interview, Gordon Sinykin, 4 May 1973.

Chapter 2: The Depression, the Governor, and the Progressives

1. Frank A. Hanna, *Wisconsin During the Depression: Industrial Trends and Tax Burdens*, University of Wisconsin Bureau of Business and Economic Research Bulletin no. 5 (Madison, 1936), pp. 12, 20, 23; Joseph A. Pechman, "Income Produced by the Manufacturing Industries in Wisconsin, 1919–1936" (Master's thesis, University of Wisconsin, 1938), p. 21, tables 1–3; Francis F. Bowman, *Industrial Wisconsin* (Madison: Department of Commerce, 1939), pp. 82–83.
2. Pechman, "Income Produced by the Manufacturing Industries," appendix, table 4; University of Wisconsin, Department of Economics, *Economic Conditions in Wisconsin*, 1 (1 March 1932); Robert C. Nesbit, *Wisconsin: A History* (Madison: University of Wisconsin Press, 1973), pp. 476–77.
3. The concept of urban liberalism is developed by J. Joseph Huthmacher in "Urban Liberalism and the Age of Reform," *Mississippi Valley Historical Review* 49 (September 1962): 231–41, and *Senator Robert F. Wagner and the Rise of Urban Liberalism* (New York: Atheneum, 1968). On the transition from progressivism to liberalism, see also Otis L. Graham, *An Encore for Reform: The Old Progressives and the New Deal* (New York: Oxford University Press, 1967).

4. RML to PFL and IBL, 25 January, 12 February 1927, box A35, Family Papers.

5. RML to PFL, 3 December 1927, box A35, Family Papers.

6. PFL to RML, 3 December 1927, PFL to "Dear Ones," 4 December 1927, box A35, Family Papers. On the 1928 election, see Thomas J. Schlereth, "The Progressive-Democrat Alliance in the Wisconsin Presidential Election of 1928" (Master's thesis, University of Wisconsin, 1965).

7. *Progressive,* 7 December 1929; RML to PFL, 10 December 1929, box A38, Family Papers.

8. For an indication that something was amiss, see *Progressive,* 31 May 1930.

9. *Progressive,* 7 December 1929, 17 May 1930; Lyle W. Cooper, "Good News from Wisconsin," *New Republic* 64 (15 October 1930): 228.

10. PFL to "Dear Ones," 9 June 1930, box A39, Family Papers.

11. PFL pamphlet, "Announcement for Governor," 26 June 1930, box 1, PFL Papers.

12. PFL to Fola La Follette and George Middleton, 26 September 1930, box A39, Family Papers; *Progressive,* 13 September 1930.

13. James Donoghue, *How Wisconsin Voted, 1848–1972* (Madison: Bureau of Government, University of Wisconsin Extension Division, 1974), section III; *Wisconsin Blue Book, 1931,* pp. 462, 467.

14. Fola La Follette to BCL, 20 November [1930], box A39, Family Papers; *Progressive,* 29 November 1930.

15. Charles B. Perry to PFL, 26 November 1930, box 2, PFL Papers.

16. PFL to RML, 16 December 1930, box A39, Family Papers; Melvin A. Traylor to PFL, 20 December 1930, box 2, PFL Papers.

17. PFL, *Adventure in Politics: The Memoirs of Philip La Follette,* ed. Donald Young (New York: Holt, Rinehart and Winston, 1970), pp. 147–48; *Progressive,* 3 January 1931.

18. *Progressive,* 20 December 1930.

19. PFL to "Dear Ones," 20 December 1930, PFL to BCL, 21 December 1930, box A39, Family Papers.

20. PFL press release, 10 January 1931, box 4, PFL Papers; PFL to "Dear Ones," 20 December 1930, box A39, Family Papers.

21. On the wide acceptance of the purchasing-power thesis among progressives, see Theodore Rosenof, *Dogma, Depression, and the New Deal: The Debate of Political Leaders over Economic Recovery* (Port Washington, N.Y.: Kennikat, 1975), pp. 39–43.

22. The entire speech is reprinted in the *Wisconsin Senate Journal* (15 January 1931): 13–37.

23. RML to BCL and Mary La Follette, 16 April 1931, box A41, Family Papers; *Madison Capital Times,* 14 January 1931.

24. BCL to Fola La Follette and George Middleton, 17 January 1931, box A40, IBL to BCL, 13 April 1931, box A41, Family Papers.

25. In 1931 the other Progressive state officials were Lieutenant Governor Henry Huber, sixty-one; Secretary of State Theodore Dammann, sixty-one; Treasurer Sol Levitan, sixty-eight; and Attorney General John W. Reynolds, fifty-four. Among Progressive leaders in the state senate were President Pro Tem Herman J. Severson, fifty-five; Walter Hunt, sixty-two; and Walter Rush, fifty-nine. In the assembly were John Gamper, seventy, and J. D. Millar, sixty-one; *Superior Evening Telegram,* 7 April 1931.

26. "Proceedings of a Conference of Progressives," 11–12 March, 1931, box 18, PFL Papers; *Progressive,* 14 March 1931; RML to Fola La Follette, 18 April 1931, PFL to Fola La Follette, 10 March 1931, box A41, Family Papers; Patrick J. Maney, *"Young Bob" La Follette: A Biography of Robert M. La Follette, Jr., 1895–1953* (Columbia: University of Missouri Press, 1978), pp. 85–86; Ronald L. Feinman, *Twilight of Progressivism: The Western Republican Senators and the New Deal* (Baltimore: Johns Hopkins University Press, 1981), pp. 23–25.

27. *Wisconsin State Journal,* 13 March, 2 June 1931; Bernard Bellush, *Franklin D. Roosevelt as Governor of New York* (New York: Columbia University Press, 1955), pp. 128–42, 182–88, 204; Alfred B. Rollins, Jr., *Roosevelt and Howe* (New York: Knopf, 1962), pp. 282, 297–303.

28. *Madison Capital Times,* 14 November 1931.

29. *Wisconsin State Journal,* 17 February 1931; PFL to BCL, 7 February 1931, box A41, Family Papers.

30. *Wisconsin State Journal,* 4 April, 2, 19, 24, 26 June, 7 July 1931; L. B. Krueger, "Taxation of Chain Stores in Wisconsin," *The Wisconsin Public Employee* 4 (October 1935): 5, 16–17.

31. *Wisconsin State Journal,* 5, 13 May 1931.

32. *Wisconsin Senate Journal* (4 June 1931): 1475–92.

33. *Wisconsin State Journal,* 4, 8; 11 June 1931; *Milwaukee Sentinel,* 2, 16 June 1931.

34. *Wisconsin State Journal,* 5, 15 June 1931; *Milwaukee Journal,* 5, 15, 16 June 1931; *Milwaukee Sentinel,* 17 June, 12, 16 July 1931; Frederick I. Olson, "The Milwaukee Socialists, 1897–1941" (Ph.D. diss., Harvard University, 1952), pp. 438–53, 476–80.

35. *Wisconsin State Journal,* 30 January 1931.

36. *New York Times,* 27 September 1931.

37. PFL, *Adventure in Politics,* pp. 160–63; "A Great Message," *Nation* 133 (9 December 1931): 629; Charles A. Beard to Roy Nash, 9 December 1931, IBL scrapbook, vol. 15, PFL Papers; Beard to PFL, 7 March 1932, box 18, PFL Papers; *Wisconsin State Journal,* 25 November 1931; *Milwaukee Journal,* 31 December 1961. The entire speech is reprinted in *Wisconsin Senate Journal* (24 November 1931): 23–55.

38. *New York Times,* 27 September 1931.

39. *Wisconsin Senate Journal* (24 November 1931): 40.

40. Harold Groves, "In and Out of the Ivory Tower," p. 141, box 40, Harold Groves Papers, SHSW; Paul A. Raushenbush, "Starting Unemployment Compensation in Wisconsin," *Unemployment Insurance Review* 4 (April–May 1967): 17–24; Raushenbush, "Wisconsin's Unemployment Compensation Act," *American Labor Legislation Review* 22 (March 1932): 11–18; interview, Raushenbush and Elizabeth Brandeis, 10 May 1972; Daniel Nelson, *Unemployment Insurance: The American Experience, 1915–1935* (Madison: University of Wisconsin Press, 1969), pp. 104–28; Roy Lubove, *The Struggle for Social Security, 1900–1935* (Cambridge, Mass.: Harvard University Press, 1968), pp. 168–74.

41. John R. Commons, "The Groves Unemployment Reserves Law," *American Labor Legislation Review* 22 (March 1932): 8–10.

42. Paul A. Raushenbush, "The Wisconsin Idea: Unemployment Reserves," *Annals of the American Academy of Political and Social Science* 170 (November 1933): 65–75; Elizabeth Brandeis and Paul A. Raushenbush, "Wisconsin's Unemployment Reserves and Compensation Act," *Wisconsin Law Review* 7 (April 1932): 136–45; Arthur M. Schlesinger, Jr., *The Coming of the New Deal* (Boston: Houghton Mifflin, 1958), pp. 301–5; PFL and RML to FDR, 7 January 1935, box 32, Paul A. Raushenbush to RML, 7 June 1935, box 37, PFL Papers; FDR, *The Public Papers and Addresses of Franklin D. Roosevelt,* ed. Samuel I. Rosenman, 13 vols. (New York, 1935–1950), 4:43–49; "Defeat the Wagner-Lewis Bill!" *Nation* 140 (17 April 1935): 433; *Wisconsin State Journal,* 24 April, 23 June 1935; *Madison Capital Times,* 29 August 1936.

43. Frank Kuehl to PFL, 22 August 1932, press release, 23 August 1932, Frank Kuehl Papers, SHSW; *Madison Capital Times,* 27 April 1932; RML to PFL, 9 May 1932, box A42, Family Papers; Reeve Schley to PFL, 14 April 1932, box 19, PFL Papers; *Boston Herald,* 13 April 1932.

44. PFL to John J. Blaine, 30 January 1932, John Blaine Papers, SHSW.

45. IBL to Fola La Follette and George Middleton, 17 February 1932, box A42, Family Papers.

46. PFL, NBC radio speech, 14 March 1932, box 117, PFL Papers.

47. PFL to RML, 15 May 1932, box A42, Family Papers.

48. PFL to RML, 24, 25 May 1932, box A42, Family Papers; IBL memoirs, box 165, PFL Papers.

49. PFL to RML, 14 June 1932, box A42, Family Papers; RML to PFL, 24 June 1932, box 20, PFL Papers.

50. IBL to Fola La Follette, 31 May 1932, box A42, Family Papers.

51. PFL, *Adventure in Politics*, p. 162; RML to PFL, 15 May 1930, box A30, Family Papers. In 1930 Roosevelt inquired about the university's Experimental College because one of his sons was interested in it; see Elliott Roosevelt, *F. D. R.: His Personal Letters, 1928–1945*, 2 vols. (New York: Duell, Sloan, and Pearce, 1950), 1:101. When BCL died, Roosevelt sent condolences to the family, saying that he had known her "in the old days in Washington"; see FDR to PFL, 21 August 1931, PFL to FDR, 12 September 1931, box 99, FDR Papers (Private Correspondence, 1928–1932). In March 1932, PFL solicited Roosevelt's advice on possible appointments to the Wisconsin Grain and Warehouse Commission; see PFL to FDR, 21 March 1932, FDR to PFL, 28 March 1932, box 99, FDR Papers (Private Correspondence, 1928–1932).

52. Arthur Hitt to PFL, 5 June 1932, box 19, PFL Papers.

53. IBL to Fola La Follette and George Middleton, 14 May 1932, box A42, Family Papers; PFL, *Adventure in Politics*, pp. 179–80; PFL to FDR, 4 April 1932, box 19, PFL Papers.

54. *Madison Capital Times*, 15 June 1932; Blaine got thirteen votes, eleven from Wisconsin and two from North Dakota, according to *Official Report of the Proceedings of the Twentieth Republican National Convention* (New York: Tenny Press, n.d.), pp. 185–86.

55. *Madison Capital Times*, 27–29 June 1932; *Milwaukee Journal*, 27 June 1932.

56. PFL to RML, 15 May 1932, box A42, Family Papers.

57. *Madison Capital Times*, 8, 12 June, 10 September 1932; *Wisconsin State Journal*, 20 August 1932.

58. *Progressive*, 17 September 1932; *Wisconsin State Journal*, 20 July 1932; David E. Lilienthal, *The Journals of David E. Lilienthal*, 4 vols. (New York: Harper and Row, 1964–1969), 1:28–29.

59. *Wisconsin Blue Book, 1933*, pp. 515, 561–606; *Milwaukee Sentinel*, 22 September 1932; *New York Times*, 22 September 1932; *Madison Capital Times*, 21 September 1932.

60. *Milwaukee Journal*, 21 September 1932; *Madison Capital Times*, 21 September 1932; *Progressive*, 24 September 1932.

61. Oswald G. Villard to PFL, 22 September 1932, Maury Maverick to PFL, 22 September 1932, Morris L. Cooke to PFL, 3 October 1932, Felix Frankfurter to PFL, 19 October 1932, boxes 22–23, PFL Papers; "Political Paragraphs," *Nation* 135 (5 October 1932): 293–94; *Madison Capital Times*, 21 September, 4 October 1932.

62. Fola La Follette to Mary La Follette, 22 October 1932, box A42, Family Papers.

63. *Milwaukee Journal*, 4 October 1932; *Progressive*, 8 October 1932; *Wisconsin Blue Book, 1933*, pp. 479–85, 491–500.

64. *Progressive*, 22 October 1932; "How They Are Voting: II," *New Republic* 88 (7 October 1936): 249; Robert M. Hutchins to PFL, 26, [?] October 1932, box 23, PFL Papers.

65. *Madison Capital Times*, 7 October 1932; *Milwaukee Journal*, 30 September 1932; *Milwaukee Sentinel*, 1 October 1932.

66. Ronald L. Feinman, "The Progressive Republican Senate Bloc and the Presidential Election of 1932," *Mid-America* 59 (April–July 1977): 73–91; William E. Leuchtenberg, *Franklin D. Roosevelt and the New Deal, 1932–1940* (New York: Harper and Row, 1963), p. 12; *Madison Capital Times*, 18, 19 October 1932; *Progressive*, 29 October 1932; PFL speech, Springfield, Ill., 23 October 1932, box 117, PFL Papers.

67. *Wisconsin Blue Book, 1933*, pp. 540–41, 552–56; quoted in Alfred R. Schumann, *No Peddlers Allowed* (Appleton, Wis.: Nelson, 1948). p. 281.

68. Fola La Follette to Mary La Follette, 9 November 1932, box A42, Family Papers; FDR to PFL, 19 November 1932, Bronson Cutting to PFL, 10 November 1932, box 23, PFL Papers.

Chapter 3: A New State Party

1. Frank Freidel, *Franklin D. Roosevelt: Launching the New Deal* (Boston: Little, Brown, 1973), pp. 144–45; Ronald L. Feinman, *Twilight of Progressivism: The Western Republican Senators and the New Deal* (Baltimore: Johns Hopkins University Press, 1981), pp. 49–54; PFL to RML, 9 December 1932, box A42, Family Papers.

2. PFL to RML, 4 January 1933, John F. Sinclair to RML, 15 December 1932, box A43, Family Papers; PFL diary, 3–4 January 1933, RML to PFL and IBL, 9 January 1933, box 135, PFL Papers; Henry Morgenthau to RML, 9 January 1933, box 24, PFL Papers.

3. RML to PFL, 20 January 1933, box 24, PFL Papers.

4. RML to PFL, 24 January 1933, box 24, PFL Papers; Fola La Follette to "Dear Ones," 10 February 1933, box A42, Family Papers; *Progressive,* 25 March 1933.

5. RML to PFL and IBL, 7 February 1933, box 25, PFL Papers; RML to PFL, 21 February 1933, PFL to RML, 23 February 1933, box A43, Family Papers; *Progressive,* 25 March 1933; Freidel, *Launching the New Deal,* pp. 145, 150–51.

6. The following account of La Follette's European trip is drawn largely from PFL, *Adventure in Politics: The Memoirs of Philip La Follette,* ed. Donald Young (New York: Holt, Rinehart and Winston, 1970), pp. 184–203; PFL's sporadically kept diary, 2 January–9 February 1933, box 135, PFL Papers; PFL's letters to his family, box 135, PFL Papers, and box A43, Family Papers; PFL memoirs, box 124, IBL diary, "Journal of Our Trip," box 162, PFL Papers; IBL. "A Room of Our Own," *Progressive,* 25 February, 4, 18, 25 March, 8 April, 12 August 1933; PFL's articles in the *New York American,* 23, 30 April, 7, 14, 21, 28 May 1933.

7. PFL to Nicholas M. Butler, 25 November 1932; Butler to PFL, 29 November, 8 December 1932, box 23, PFL Papers.

8. *New York American,* 14 May 1933; PFL, *Adventure in Politics,* pp. 186–87.

9. PFL to "Dear Ones," 18 February 1933, box 135, PFL Papers.

10. *New York American,* 28 May 1933.

11. PFL to "Dear Ones," 5, 18 February 1933, box 135, PFL Papers.

12. PFL to D'Arcy Osborne, 3 December 1932, box 23, PFL Papers.

13. RML to PFL, 6 March 1933, box A43, Family Papers; RML to FDR, 6 March 1933, box C11, RML Papers.

14. PFL, "Notes on Interview with President Roosevelt," 20 March 1933, PFL Papers; PFL, *Adventure in Politics,* pp. 204–6.

15. PFL to RML, 5 February 1933, RML to PFL, June [?], box A43, Family Papers. RML recalled that Roosevelt had offered PFL eight different posts, according to the *New York Times,* 25 October 1934.

16. Glenn D. Roberts to PFL, 4 February 1933, box 25, PFL Papers.

17. PFL to Ralph Sucher and Mary La Follette, 8 July 1933, box 135, PFL Papers.

18. *Progressive,* 18 March, 14, 21, 28 October 1933; PFL radio speech, 20 May 1933, box 117, PFL Papers; RML to Felix Frankfurter, 4 April 1933, box 74, Felix Frankfurter Papers, Library of Congress.

19. *Progressive,* 22 July, 5, 12, 19, 26 August, 2, 9, 30 September, 16 December 1933; PFL to Herman Lissauer, 16 September 1933, box 26, PFL Papers; RML to FDR, 13 July 1933, PPF 1792, FDR Papers.

20. *Progressive,* 24 June, 8 July, 5 August, 4 October 1933.

21. IBL, "A Room of Our Own," *Progressive,* 8 July 1933.

22. On the LIPA, see Robert E. Kessler, "The League for Independent Political Action, 1929–1933" (Master's thesis, University of Wisconsin, 1969); Donald R. McCoy, *Angry Voices: Left-of-Center Politics in the New Deal Era* (Lawrence: Regents Press of Kansas, 1958), pp. 3–40; and T. L. Tarson, "The Production-for-Use Movement, 1932–1936: An Examination of Third Party Activity" (seminar paper, Yale University, 1953), SHSW.

23. Donald L. Miller, *The New American Radicalism: Alfred M. Bingham and Non-Marxian Insurgency in the New Deal Era* (Port Washington, N.Y.: Kennikat, 1979), pp. 34–38, 67; Kessler, "League for Independent Political Action," p. 57.

24. Howard Y. Williams to PFL, 31 May 1933, PFL to Williams, 2 June 1933, box 26, PFL Papers; Tom Amlie to Williams, 12 July 1933, Williams to Amlie, 14 July 1933, box 10, Thomas R. Amlie Papers, SHSW.

25. Alfred Bingham to PFL, 13 July, 3 August 1933, PFL to Bingham, 5 September 1933, box 26, PFL Papers; Bingham to Tom Amlie, 3 November 1933, box 11, Amlie Papers.

26. On Amlie, see Robert E. Long, "Thomas Amlie: A Political Biography" (Ph.D. diss., University of Wisconsin, 1969); Theodore Rosenof, "The Political Education of an American Radical: Thomas R. Amlie in the 1930's," *Wisconsin Magazine of History* 58 (Autumn 1974): 19–30; and Stuart L. Weiss, "Thomas Amlie and the New Deal," *Mid-America* 59 (January 1977): 19–38. Tom Amlie to Henry I. Noe, 15 February 1933, Amlie to FDR, 20 February 1933, Amlie to Ross Collins, 31 May 1933, box 10, Amlie Papers.

27. Howard Y. Williams to Tom Amlie, 23 May 1933, Amlie to Ross Collins, 30 June 1933, Amlie to Charles Dietz, 18 July 1933, John Dewey to Amlie, 1 July 1933, Amlie to Williams, 7 August 1933, box 10, Amlie Papers.

28. Tom Amlie to F. S. Schlink, 22 September 1933, box 10, Amlie Papers; Amlie to PFL, 6 September 1933, box 26, PFL Papers; Miller, *New American Radicalism,* pp. 84–87.

29. Tom Amlie to John Strachey, 6 November 1933, box 11, Amlie to E. J. Lawson, [?] December 1934, box 14, Amlie Papers.

30. Tom Amlie to Alfred Bingham, 12 September 1933, Amlie to Gerhard Sorenson, 13 September 1933, box 10, Amlie Papers.

31. Tom Amlie to Alfred Bingham, 29 September 1933, box 10, Amlie to Howard Y. Williams, 24 November 1933, box 11, Amlie Papers; IBL political diary, 21 June 1935, box 161, PFL Papers; interview, Tom Amlie, 27 February 1973.

32. Tom Amlie to Selden Rodman, 30 October 1933, box 11, Amlie Papers.

33. Tom Amlie to Floyd B. Olson, 7 April 1934, box 12, Amlie to Alfred Bingham, 7 November 1933, 15 March 1934, box 11, Amlie Papers; Orland Loomis to J. W. Carow, 6 October 1933, Carow to Loomis, 3 October 1933, box 5, Orland Loomis Papers, SHSW.

34. PFL to RML, 11 November 1928, box A36, BCL to RML, 8 August 1931, box A40, Family Papers; *Progressive,* 4 April, 1 August 1931.

35. PFL to RML, 17, 28 May, 1, 13 June 1933, RML to PFL, 29 May 1933, Rachel La Follette to RML, 7 November 1933, box A43, Family Papers; RML to John J. Blaine, 27 May 1933, RML Papers; PFL to IBL, 9 December 1933, box 26, PFL Papers; *Wisconsin State Journal,* 22 October, 4, 23 November, and 3 December 1933.

36. PFL to RML, 3 May 1933, RML to "Dear Ones," 8 May 1933, RML to PFL, 6 June 1933, box A43, Family Papers; PFL to Marvin McIntyre, 18 May 1933, McIntyre to PFL, 15 May 1933, PFL to RML, 17 May 1933, box 26, PFL Papers.

37. PFL to RML, 1 June 1933, box A43, Family Papers; Tom Amlie to Ross Collins, 30 June 1933, box 10, Amlie Papers; PFL to Ralph Sucher and Mary La Follette, box 135, 8 July 1933, PFL Papers; PFL to Alex Gumberg, 23 September 1933, box 26, PFL Papers.

38. *Chicago Tribune,* 22 September 1933; *Wisconsin State Journal,* 22 September 1933.

39. *Progressive,* 25 November 1933; *Wisconsin State Journal,* 16 November 1933; PFL speech, "Wanted—A New Machine," Chicago, November 1933, box 117, PFL Papers.

40. RML to PFL, 18 October 1933, box 26, PFL Papers; Russel B. Nye, *Midwestern Progressive Politics: A Historical Study of Its Origins and Development, 1870 to 1958* (New York: Harper and Row, 1959), p. 331. A list of those invited to the Chicago meeting can be found in box 26, PFL Papers.

41. Arthur M. Schlesinger, Jr., *The Coming of the New Deal* (Boston: Houghton, Mifflin, 1958), pp. 236–40; Harold L. Ickes, *The Secret Diary of Harold L. Ickes,* 3 vols. (New York: Simon and Schuster, 1953–1954), 1:110, 129; PFL to IBL, 9 December 1933, box 135, PFL Papers; RML to Fola La Follette and George Middleton, 11 December 1933, box A43, Family Papers; Clough Gates to PFL, 27 February 1934, box 26, PFL Papers.

42. Winter Everett, who provided astute although generally anti-La Follette coverage in his regular political column, asserted that both La Follettes were trying to suppress the third-party movement, as were most other Progressive leaders. "Around the Statehouse," *Wisconsin State Journal,* 7, 20, 22 November, 9, 15, 19, 20 December 1933; PFL to RML, 12 February 1934, box A43, Family Papers.

43. *Madison Capital Times,* 20 July, 23 November 1933, 25 February 1934; PFL to RML, 12, 24 February 1934, Theodore Dammann to John Hannan, 15 January 1934, box A43, Family Papers; *Oshkosh Daily Northwestern,* 16 December 1933.

44. RML to PFL, 29 January, 16 February 1934, box A43, Family Papers; *Madison Capital Times,* 25 February 1934; Patrick J. Maney, *"Young Bob" La Follette: A Biography of Robert M. La Follette, Jr., 1895–1953* (Columbia: University of Missouri Press, 1978), pp. 133–40.

45. Ickes, *Secret Diary,* 1: 149–50; RML to PFL, 27 February 1934, box A43, Family Papers.

46. RML to Rachel La Follette, 2 March 1934, PFL to RML, 21 February 1934, RML to Herman Ekern and others, 27 February 1934, Fola La Follette to George Middleton, 5 March 1934, box A43, Family Papers; Tom Amlie to Alfred Bingham, 21 May 1934, box 12, Amlie Papers. A list of those invited to the 2 March meeting can be found in box A43, Family Papers.

47. PFL, *Adventure in Politics,* pp. 207–9; Tom Duncan to PFL, 15 March 1933, box 25, RML to PFL, 19 October 1933, box A43, PFL Papers; *Madison Capital Times,* 25 February 1934; *Milwaukee Sentinel,* 3 January 1934.

48. Minutes of progressive organizational meeting held at Park Hotel, Madison, 3 March 1934, box 26, PFL Papers; *Milwaukee Journal,* 3–5 March 1934; *Madison Capital Times,* 3–5 March 1934.

49. Tom Amlie to Howard Y. Williams, 5 March 1934, Amlie to Alfred Bingham, 5 March 1934, Amlie to John P. Retzer, 7 March 1934, Bingham to Amlie, 12 March 1934, box 12, Amlie Papers.

50. PFL to Boyd Hatch, 21 March 1934, box 11, Alex Gumberg Papers, SHSW; PFL to RML, 31 March 1934, box A43, Family Papers.

51. PFL to RML, 10 April, 1 May 1934, box A43, Family Papers; minutes of third party committee meeting, Madison, 4 May 1934, box 12, Amlie Papers; *Madison Capital Times,* 12, 18 May 1934; *Milwaukee Journal,* 1, 5 May 1934.

52. PFL to RML, 14 May 1934, RML to PFL, 11 May 1934, box A43, Family Papers; Hubert Peavey to Tom Amlie, 15 March 1934, box 12, Amlie Papers; *Milwaukee Journal,* 13, 18 May 1934; *Oshkosh Daily Northwestern,* 18 May 1934.

53. Rexford Tugwell diary, 19 May 1934, box 14, Rexford Tugwell Papers, Roosevelt Library.

54. Minutes of Fond du Lac Progressive conference, 19 May 1934, box 27, PFL Papers; *Milwaukee Journal,* 20 May 1934.

55. Tom Amlie to PFL, 15 May 1934, Amlie to Alfred Bingham, 21 May 1934, Amlie to Aubrey Williams, 28 May 1934, Amlie to D. D. Alderdyce, 22 May 1934, Amlie to William Sommers, 23 May 1934, Amlie to Howard Y. Williams, 24 May 1934, box 12, Amlie Papers.

56. *Milwaukee Journal*, 22 May 1934; William Sommers to Tom Amlie, 21 May 1934, Sam Sigman to Amlie, 21 May 1934, Fred S. Gram to Howard Y. Williams, 20 May 1934, box 12, Amlie Papers.

57. Sam Sigman to Tom Amlie, 21 May 1934, Amlie to Howard Y. Williams, 29 May, 4 June 1934, Horace Fries to Amlie, 15 June 1934, box 12, Amlie Papers; Miller, *New American Radicalism*, p. 117.

58. Horace Fries to Tom Amlie, 17 June 1934, box 12, Amlie Papers; IBL memoirs, box 165, PFL Papers; *Milwaukee Journal*, 24 May 1934; *Wisconsin State Journal*, 24 June 1934.

59. PFL to IBL, 30 June 1934, box 135, PFL Papers; Sam Sigman to PFL, 2 July 1934, box 2, Samuel Sigman Papers, SHSW; Tom Amlie to William Sommers, 21 June 1934, Sigman to Amlie, 1 June 1934, box 12, Amlie Papers; *Milwaukee Journal*, 30 June, 1 July 1934; *Progressive*, 7 July 1934.

60. Sam Sigman to Walter Melchior, 13 August 1934, Sigman to Tom Amlie, 29 August, 5, 22 September 1934; questionnaire filled out by PFL, attached to letter from Gordon Sinykin to Sigman, 4 September 1934, box 2, Sigman Papers; PFL to B. L. Bobroff, 5 September 1934, box 27, PFL Papers.

61. PFL to IBL, 10, 11 July 1934, box 135, IBL memoirs, box 165, PFL Papers. Lists of people who attended the conferences at Maple Bluff are in box C509, Family Papers. Tom Amlie to John Kent, 30 July 1934, box 12, Amlie to Hans Amlie, 15 August 1934, box 13, Alfred Bingham to Amlie, 31 May 1934, Amlie to Horace Fries, 2 July 1934, box 12, Amlie Papers; *Milwaukee Journal*, 9, 10, 14 August 1934.

62. Tom Amlie to Ruby A. Black, 17 September 1934, box 13, Amlie Papers.

63. *Progressive*, 26 May 1934.

64. Rexford Tugwell diary, 31 May 1934, box 14, Tugwell Papers; Aubrey Williams to Tom Amlie, 26 May 1934, box 12, Amlie Papers; *Milwaukee Journal*, 31 January 1934; PFL to RML, 14 May 1934, box A43, Family Papers.

65. RML to PFL, 4 June 1934, box A43, Family Papers; FDR Press Conference 133, (27 June 1934), 3:434; *Milwaukee Journal*, 27, 28 June 1934.

66. *Milwaukee Journal*, 12 July, 5, 8 August 1934; Anne McKenzie to PFL, 17 May 1935, box 36, PFL Papers.

67. *Milwaukee Journal*, 9 August 1934.

68. *Madison Capital Times*, 9 August 1936.

69. *Milwaukee Journal*, 9, 10 August 1934; *Progressive*, 11 August, 6 October 1934; *Madison Capital Times*, 29 October 1934.

70. In his memoirs La Follette wrote that Roosevelt later told him that he got the idea for the Civilian Conservation Corps from La Follette's 1931 message to the legislature; *Adventure in Politics*, p. 165. Progressives claimed credit for the CCC idea; *Progressive*, 23 September 1933. But Roosevelt drew his ideas from many sources according to Freidel, *Launching the New Deal*, p. 257; John A. Salmond, *The Civilian Conservation Corps, 1933–1942: A New Deal Case Study* (Durham, N.C.: Duke University Press, 1967), pp. 4–9; and Alfred B. Rollins, Jr., *Roosevelt and Howe* (New York: Knopf, 1962), pp. 402–5. On the lumber agreements, see W. A. Holt to PFL, 6 November 1931, box 12, PFL to Gifford Pinchot, 12 December 1931, box 13, PFL Papers.

71. FDR to RML, 6 September, 1 October 1934, RML and PFL to FDR, 30 September 1934, PPF 1792, FDR Papers; *Milwaukee Journal*, 2 November 1934.

72. *Progressive*, 13 October 1934; RML to Fiorello La Guardia, 15 October 1934, box 29, PFL Papers.

73. Isabel B. La Follette, Harold M. Groves, and Gordon Sinykin, "The Progressive Campaign Worker," 1934 pamphlet, box 26, minutes of the Progressive party platform convention, 2 October 1934, box 29, PFL Papers; *Green Bay Press-Gazette*, 16, 17 October 1934; *Chicago Tribune*, 6 September 1934; *Madison Capital Times*, 2 October 1934.

74. *Wisconsin Blue Book, 1935*, pp. 476–77; *Madison Capital Times*, 15 September 1934.

75. *Wisconsin Blue Book, 1935*, pp. 476–82; *Sheboygan Press*, 30 August 1934; Tom Amlie to O. L. Merrit, 10 December 1934, box 14, Amlie Papers; minutes of Progressive party platform convention, 2 October 1934, box 29, PFL Papers.

76. *Madison Capital Times*, 10 September 1934.

77. Diogenes, "News and Comment from the National Capital," *Literary Digest* 118 (13 October 1934): 12; PFL draft statement, circa 5 November 1934, box 30, PFL Papers; "Report of Contest," [1934], PPF 869-A, FDR Papers; *Wisconsin Blue Book, 1935*, pp. 567–630.

78. PFL to Alfred D. Cookson, 30 October 1934, PFL to S. E. Olson, 12 October 1934, box 29, PFL Papers; *Progressive*, 1 December 1934; William T. Evjue, *A Fighting Editor* (Madison, Wis.: Wells, 1968), p. 554.

79. *Miami Daily News*, 14 November 1934.

Chapter 4: The Wisconsin Works Plan

1. Harry Hopkins to Voyta Wrabetz, 2 December 1933, field reports, Howard O. Hunter to Hopkins, 7, 27 January, 20 March, 6 April, 7 May, 19 June 1934, Record Group 69, "Field Reports of Federal Emergency Relief Administration, Wisconsin," file 406, National Archives.

2. Howard O. Hunter to Harry Hopkins, 14, 27 November 1934, Record Group 69, WPA, file 406.1, National Archives; Hunter to Hopkins, 12 December 1934, 21 January 1935, box 55, Harry Hopkins Papers, FDRL; Hopkins to PFL, 14 January 1935, PFL message to legislature, 21 January 1935, box 32, PFL Papers; *Wisconsin State Journal*, 22 January, 26 February 1935.

3. Harry Hopkins to PFL, 11 March 1935, box 32, PFL Papers; *Wisconsin State Journal*, 28 February, 15 March 1935.

4. Howard O. Hunter to Harry Hopkins, 2 February 1935, Record Group 69, Work Progress Administration, file 406.1, National Archives.

5. PFL to IBL, 7, 8 December 1934, box 135, PFL Papers; FDR Press Conference 163 (7 December 1934), 4:264; *Milwaukee Journal*, 19 June 1935.

6. Wisconsin Regional Planning Committee, *A Study of Wisconsin: Its Resources, Its Physical, Social, and Economic Background*, First Annual Report (December 1934), SHSW; PFL to RML, 8 February 1935, box 31, PFL Papers.

7. *Wisconsin State Journal*, 19, 20 January 1935; *Progressive*, 26 January 1935; PFL memoirs, box 124, PFL Papers; FDR Press Conference 196 (17 April 1935), 5:210.

8. Elliott Roosevelt, ed., *F. D. R.: His Personal Letters, 1928–1945*, 2 vols. (New York: Duell, Sloan and Pearce, 1950), 1:452–53; Henry Morgenthau diary, 4:113–14, Henry Morgenthau Papers, FDRL.

9. Harold L. Ickes, *The Secret Diary of Harold L. Ickes*, 3 vols. (New York: Simon and Schuster, 1953–1954), 2:355–56; *Wisconsin State Journal*, 1 May 1935.

10. *Wisconsin State Journal*, 3, 4 May 1934.

11. Ibid.; FDR Press Conferences 201 (3 May 1935), 5:270 and 217 (3 July 1935), 6:13–14.

12. Rexford Tugwell diary, 5, 7 May 1935, box 14, Rexford Tugwell Papers, FDRL.

13. RML to PFL, 22 April 1935, box 135, PFL Papers; PFL to FDR, 15 May 1935, PPF 6659, FDR Papers; Frank C. Walker to PFL, 16 May 1935, box 36, PFL Papers; *Wisconsin State Journal,* 17 May 1935; FDR Press Conference 205 (17 May 1935), 5:290.

14. *Progressive,* 18 May 1935; *Wisconsin State Journal,* 22 May, 22, 28 June 1935; *Milwaukee Journal,* 22, 25, 29 May, 20 June 1935; Harry W. Bolens radio speech, 7 June 1935, box 6, Harry Bolens Papers, SHSW.

15. *Wisconsin State Journal,* 4 June 1935; *Milwaukee Journal,* 23 May 1935; "Data on the Wisconsin Plan," mimeographed report, 21 May 1935, box 36, PFL Papers.

16. Memorandum, Ralph M. Hoyt to PFL, 14 May 1935, "Data on the Wisconsin Plan," 21 May 1935, box 36, PFL Papers; *Milwaukee Journal,* 19 May, 2 June 1935; *Wisconsin State Journal,* 7 June 1935; Wisconsin State Planning Board, "Wisconsin Work Program," December 1935, SHSW.

17. *Madison Capital Times,* 20 May 1935.

18. PFL radio speeches, 21, 24 May 1935, box 118, PFL Papers.

19. John E. Miller, "Governor Philip F. La Follette's Shifting Priorities: From Redistribution to Expansion," *Mid-America* 58 (April–July 1976):119–26.

20. *Wisconsin State Journal,* 20 May 1935; *Milwaukee Journal,* 23 May 1935; *Proceedings of the 43rd Annual Convention of the Wisconsin State Federation of Labor* (1935), pp. 85, 221; *Madison Capital Times,* 21 July 1935; *Milwaukee Journal,* 21 May, 4, 5, 6, 10 June 1935; Daniel W. Hoan to PFL, 31 May 1935, box 36, PFL to Hoan, 1 June 1935, box 37, PFL Papers.

21. *Milwaukee Journal,* 5, 8 June 1935; PFL radio speech, 7 June 1935, box 118, PFL Papers.

22. *Wisconsin State Journal,* 24, 25, 27 May, 1, 2, 4, 5, 7 June 1935; *Milwaukee Journal,* 29 May 1935.

23. PFL to RML, 14 June 1935, box A44, Family Papers; telephone conversation transcript, Harry Hopkins and PFL, 14 June 1935, box 66, Hopkins Papers; *Milwaukee Journal,* 14, 16 June 1935.

24. *Wisconsin State Journal,* 15, 18 June 1935; *Milwaukee Journal,* 16, 18, 19, 21 June 1935.

25. *Wisconsin State Journal,* 25 June 1935.

26. The vote on the bill was fifteen to fourteen with two Progressives paired with two Democrats according to *Milwaukee Journal,* 25, 29 June 1935; Walter J. Kohler to Harry W. Bolens, 17 June 1935, Bolens Papers.

27. Telephone conversation transcript, Harry Hopkins and Howard O. Hunter, 2 July 1935, box 66, Hopkins Papers; *Milwaukee Journal,* 29 June, 1, 2, 7 July 1935; *Wisconsin State Journal,* 1, 2 July 1935; memorandum, Marvin McIntyre to FDR, 1 July 1935, box 71, OF 300, FDR Papers; PFL, *Adventure in Politics,* pp. 225–26; F. Ryan Duffy to Hopkins, 2 July 1935, Duffy to FDR, 3 July 1935, John W. Kelley to Duffy, 3 July 1935, Record Group 69, WPA, file 630, National Archives.

28. *Milwaukee Journal,* 9, 10, 12 July, 8, 9, 20, 21 August 1935; *Wisconsin State Journal,* 5, 13, 17 July, 31 October, 2, 3 December 1935; Harry Hopkins to Ralph Immell, 19 July 1935, WPA, file 630, Joseph Clancy to F. Ryan Duffy, 30, 31 July 1935, Duffy to Hopkins, 31 July 1935, William H. Shenners to Hopkins, 31 October 1935, Lawrence Westbrook to Shenners, 9 December 1935, Record Group 69, WPA, file 693, National Archives; Immell to Hopkins, 24 August 1935, box 39, PFL Papers.

29. *Milwaukee Journal,* 22 August 1935; *Wisconsin State Journal,* 27 January, 16, 23, 26 February, 8, 16, 21 May, 11 June, 17, 30 August 1935.

30. Francis E. McGovern to FDR, 12 August 1935, PPF 2839, Leo Crowley, "Memorandum to Marvin H. McIntyre upon Wisconsin situation," 5 August 1935, PPF 1004, FDR Papers; *Milwaukee Journal,* 8, 11, 14, 28 July, 23 August 1935; *Wisconsin State Journal,* 28 June, 9 July, 3, 19, 24, 25, 27 August 1935.

31. *Green Bay Press-Gazette*, 16 October 1934; *Wisconsin State Journal*, 9, 10, 15 January 1935.

32. *Wisconsin State Journal*, 27 June, 19 July, 2, 13, 28 August, 18, 19, 29 September 1935.

33. *Wisconsin State Journal*, 20 January, 13 April, 13 May 1935.

34. Ibid., 16, 31 May, 24 June, 1 July, 11, 21 September, 9 November 1935; *Wisconsin Senate Journal* (1935): 2405–28.

35. Joseph Padway to PFL, 16 April 1935, box 35, Padway to Thomas Duncan, 10 May 1935, box 36, PFL to Harold Ickes, 7 August 1935, Ickes to PFL, 12 August 1935, box 39, PFL Papers; *Wisconsin State Journal*, 5 June, 25 July, 1 August, 12 September 1935.

36. *Wisconsin State Journal*, 1 March 1935.

37. Ibid., 18 September 1935.

38. PFL to Harry Hopkins, 7 September 1935, PFL to Howard O. Hunter, 24 August 1935, Hunter to PFL, 26 August 1935, box 39, PFL Papers; Hunter to Hopkins, 22 July 1935, Record Group 69, FERA, box 129, National Archives; *Wisconsin State Journal*, 13 July, 8, 14 August, 16 September 1935; *Milwaukee Journal*, 12 August, 20 September 1935.

39. PFL to Don Teach, 19 November 1935, box 42, press release, 26 November 1935, box 128, PFL Papers; *Wisconsin State Journal*, 25, 26 November, 2, 16 December 1935, 3 January 1936; Ickes, *Secret Diary*, 1: 487.

40. Harry Hopkins, *Spending to Save: The Complete Story of Relief* (New York: Norton, 1936), p. 99.

Chapter 5: Uneasy Alliance with the New Deal

1. Arthur M. Schlesinger, Jr., *The Politics of Upheaval* (Boston: Houghton, Mifflin, 1960), pp. 1–11, 211–14; James M. Burns, *Roosevelt: The Lion and the Fox* (New York: Harcourt, Brace and World, 1956), pp. 220–23; T. R. B., "Washington Notes," *New Republic* 81 (23 January 1935): 302.

2. T. R. B., "Washington Notes," *New Republic* 82 (13 March 1935): 129; *Wisconsin State Journal*, 4, 16, 21 March 1935; Rexford Tugwell diary, 24 February, 3 March 1935, box 14, Rexford Tugwell Papers, FDRL; Henry Morgenthau diary, 18 March 1935, 4: 113–14, Henry Morgenthau Papers, FDRL.

3. Harold L. Ickes, *The Secret Diary of Harold L. Ickes*, 3 vols. (New York: Simon and Schuster, 1953–1954), 1:342; "Gambling on a Boom," *Nation* 140 (8 May 1935): 525; *Madison Capital Times*, 29 May 1935; Schlesinger, *Politics of Upheaval*, p. 274.

4. Ickes, *Secret Diary*, 1:217; *Milwaukee Journal*, 6, 20 May 1935; *Progressive*, 25 May 1935; Raymond Moley, *The First New Deal* (New York: Harcourt, Brace and World, 1966), pp. 92–94; PFL memoirs, box 124, PFL Papers; *Wisconsin State Journal*, 25 June 1935; Ronald L. Feinman, *Twilight of Progressivism: The Western Republican Senators and the New Deal* (Baltimore: Johns Hopkins University Press, 1981), pp. 84–90.

5. *New York Times*, 11 March 1935; *Wisconsin State Journal*, 13 January 1935; Burns, *Roosevelt: Lion and Fox*, p. 214.

6. *Progressive*, 12 January 1935.

7. Schlesinger, *Politics of Upheaval*, p. 53; *Wisconsin State Journal*, 26 January, 28 May, 19 August 1935; PFL to Mrs. Huey P. Long, 10 September 1935, box 40, PFL Papers.

8. *Progressive*, 10 November 1934, 23 March 1935; Schlesinger, *Politics of Upheaval*, pp. 26, 249; *Wisconsin State Journal*, 1, 25 March, 25 April, 10, 28 June, 18 July 1935.

9. *Wisconsin State Journal,* 23 November, 12, 20 December 1935, 11 January, 1 March 1936.

10. RML to PFL, 19 February 1936, box A44, Family Papers; Tom Amlie to Monroe M. Sweetland, 29 February 1936, box 30, Thomas Amlie Papers, SHSW; *Milwaukee Journal,* 6 January 1936.

11. *Wisconsin State Journal,* 19 August 1936.

12. Alfred Bingham to PFL, 29 December 1934, box 31, PFL Papers; Tom Amlie to Bingham, 4 February 1935, box 15, Amlie Papers; Bingham, "Letter to the Editor," *Nation* 140 (3 April 1935): 387; Ernest L. Meyer, *New York Post,* 7 March 1935.

13. Alfred Bingham to Tom Amlie, 24 May, 18 September 1934, 13 February, 15 March 1935, box 12, 13, Amlie Papers; PFL to Bingham, 25 February, Bingham to PFL, 27 February 1935, box 33, PFL Papers.

14. Aldric Revell to A. W. Rees, 17 May 1935, box 36, PFL Papers.

15. *Milwaukee Journal,* 19 May 1935.

16. Ibid., 20 May 1935; *Wisconsin State Journal,* 20, 23 May 1935; "The Week," *New Republic* 83 (29 May 1935): 57; Robert Morss Lovett, "Progressive Birthday," *New Republic* 83 (5 June 1935): 95–96.

17. Wisconsinites in attendance at the Chicago conference included Samuel Soref, Andrew Biemiller, Arnold Zander, Samuel Sigman, Walter Graunke, David Sigman, William Sommers, Al Benson, Harold Groves, and George Schneider. See minutes of Chicago conference on new party, 5–6 July 1935, box 57, Amlie Papers; Schlesinger, *Politics of Upheaval,* pp. 150–51; *Progressive,* 13 July 1935; *Wisconsin State Journal,* 5–8 July 1935; Robert Morss Lovett, "Is It the New Party?" *New Republic* 83 (24 July 1935): 292–97; Donald L. Miller, *The New American Radicalism: Alfred M. Bingham and Non-Marxian Insurgency in the New Deal Era* (Port Washington, N.Y.: Kennikat, 1979), pp. 126–28.

18. Floyd Olson to Tom Amlie, 28 June 1935, box 20, Amlie Papers; *Milwaukee Sentinel,* 8 July 1935; RML to PFL, 23 July 1935, box A44, Family Papers; Selden Rodman to PFL, 11 July 1935, PFL to Rodman, 25 July 1935, PFL to Don Fina, 29 July 1935, box 38, PFL Papers.

19. William E. Leuchtenberg, *Franklin D. Roosevelt and the New Deal, 1932–1940* (New York: Harper and Row, 1963), pp. 147–63; Schlesinger, *Politics of Upheaval,* pp. 291–92; *Madison Capital Times,* 29 May, 8 July 1935.

20. *Milwaukee Journal,* 28 July 1935.

21. Leo Crowley, "Memorandum to Marvin H. McIntyre upon Wisconsin situation," 5 August 1935, PPF 1004, FDR Papers; *Wisconsin State Journal,* 3, 16, 23 August 1935; PFL to Jess H. Stevens, 28 August 1935, box 39, PFL Papers; *Madison Capital Times,* 11 September 1935.

22. PFL, *Adventure in Politics: The Memoirs of Philip La Follette,* ed. Donald Young (New York: Holt, Rinehart and Winston, 1970), pp. 226–28; S. T. E. [Stephen T. Early?], memo for the president, 4 September [1935], PPF 6659, FDR Papers; "The Week," *New Republic* 84 (9 October 1935): 226; *Milwaukee Journal,* 28 September 1935; Monroe Billington, "Roosevelt, The New Deal, and the Clergy," *Mid-America* 54 (January 1972): 20–33.

23. PFL memoirs, box 128, PFL Papers.

24. *Progressive,* 26 October, 2 November 1935; *Wisconsin State Journal,* 18 August, 5, 29 November 1935; PFL to John Gamper, 22 February 1936, box 48, PFL Papers; T. R. B., "Washington Notes," *New Republic* 84 (6 November 1935): 360.

25. Lester F. Schmidt, "The Farmer-Labor Progressive Federation: The Study of a 'United Front' Movement Among Wisconsin Liberals, 1934–1941" (Ph.D. diss., University of Wisconsin, 1954), pp. 50–52.

26. *Milwaukee Journal,* 10 June 1934.

27. *Proceedings of the 43rd Annual Convention of the Wisconsin State Federation of Labor* (1935), pp. 97–98, 212, 232; Schmidt, "Farmer-Labor Progressive Federation," pp. 31–33, 48–50, 88; Thomas N. Duncan to B. C. Vladeck, 7 August 1935, box 39, PFL Papers.

28. Schmidt, "Farmer-Labor Progressive Federation," pp. 55–64; minutes of political unity conference, 30 November–1 December 1935, box 42, PFL Papers.

29. Alfred Bingham to Fred Gram, 16 December 1935, box 26, Amlie Papers; Schmidt, "Farmer-Labor Progressive Federation," p. 32; *Proceedings of the 44th Annual Convention of the Wisconsin State Federation of Labor* (1936), pp. 102, 173, 175, SHSW; interview, Andrew Biemiller, 3 February 1972.

30. Andrew Biemiller to PFL, 19 December 1935, Biemiller to Thomas Duncan, 20 December 1935, box 43, PFL Papers; Biemiller to Tom Amlie, 20 December 1935, box 26, Amlie Papers; *Milwaukee Journal,* 6, 19 December 1935; *Wisconsin State Journal,* 15 April 1936; *Progressive,* 25 January 1936.

31. Gordon Sinykin to Edward McKenzie, 29 May 1936, box 53, PFL Papers; William Sommers to Tom Amlie, 11 June 1936, box 36, Amlie Papers; Schmidt, "Farmer-Labor Progressive Federation," p. 99; *Madison Capital Times,* 6 December 1935, 21 June 1936; *Wisconsin State Journal,* 17 June 1936.

32. *Milwaukee Journal,* 20–22 June 1936; *Progressive,* 27 June 1936.

33. Schmidt, "Farmer-Labor Progressive Federation," pp. 120–21.

34. Ibid., pp. 122, 171–73, 181–82; Tom Amlie to Nathan Fine, 2 July 1936, box 37, Amlie Papers.

35. *Milwaukee Journal,* 10–16, 20, 21, 25 March 1936; *Wisconsin State Journal,* 13–22 March 1936.

36. PFL to Rev. Eugene M. Geimer, 14 March 1936, box 49, PFL Papers; *Milwaukee Journal,* 17 March 1936.

37. PFL, "Capital on Strike," *Common Sense* 3 (July 1934): 6–9; *Progressive,* 27 October 1934.

38. *New York Times,* 2 November 1935; PFL speech, "Can We Pay As We Go?" 9 January 1936, box 118, PFL Papers; *Progressive,* 8 February, 19 September 1936; *Wisconsin State Journal,* 15 March, 30 June 1936.

39. Tom Amlie to PFL, 22 December 1935, 7 February, 30 April 1936, box 43, 48, 52, PFL to Alfred Bingham, 6 July 1936, box 55, PFL Papers; Bingham to Nathan Fine, 8 May 1936, box 34, Bingham to Amlie, 11 March, 29 July 1936, box 31, 37, Bingham to Howard Y. Williams, 10 August 1936, box 37, Amlie Papers; "1936 Is the Time!" *Common Sense* 5 (April 1936): 2–3; "Roosevelt: Radicals' Nemesis," *Common Sense* 5 (June 1936): 3–4; "How Shall I Vote?" *Common Sense* 5 (October 1936): 3–4.

40. *Wisconsin State Journal,* 20 May 1936.

41. Burns, *Roosevelt: Lion and Fox,* pp. 278–79; Leo T. Crowley, "Memorandum to Marvin H. McIntyre upon Wisconsin situation," 5 August 1935, PPF 1004, FDR Papers; John J. Wolf to James A. Farley, 23 September 1936, Otto La Budde to Farley, 20 July 1936, Mary W. Dewson to Farley, 13 August 1936, box 1101, Democratic National Committee Papers, FDRL; *Wisconsin State Journal,* 30 October, 15 December 1935; John N. O'Brien to Farley, 16 December 1938, box 92, OF 300, FDR Papers.

42. FDR to PFL, 30 July 1936, box 56, PFL Papers; Schlesinger, *Politics of Upheaval,* pp. 608–9; Burns, *Roosevelt: Lion and Fox,* pp. 277–81, 520; F. Ryan Duffy to Marvin H. McIntyre, 13 August 1936, PFL to McIntyre, 22, 26 August 1936, McIntyre to PFL, 24, 25 August 1936, OF 200-EE, FDR Papers; F. Ryan Duffy to FDR, 22 September 1936, PPF 6659, FDR Papers.

43. F. Ryan Duffy to James A. Farley, 20 August 1936, Farley to Duffy, 26 August 1936, box 1103, Democratic National Committee Papers, FDRL.

44. *Wisconsin State Journal,* 16 July, 2, 19, 30 October 1936.

45. William B. Rubin to FDR, 14 January 1937, box 71, OF 300, FDR Papers.

46. *Wisconsin State Journal,* 3, 9 April, 20, 21 July, 13 August, 14 December 1935; A. N. Donnellan to "Dear Sir," 29 March 1935, box 34, Thomas J. O'Malley to Peter Spingler, 18 July 1935, attached to Spingler to PFL, 26 December 1937, box 87, PFL Papers.

47. PFL memoirs, box 124, Marguerite Le Hand to PFL, 27 June 1936, box 55, PFL to Tom Amlie, 12 May 1936, box 52, PFL to J. David Stern, 6 July 1936, box 55, PFL Papers; Samuel I. Rosenman, *Working with Roosevelt* (New York: Harper and Row, 1952), p. 103; Schlesinger, *Politics of Upheaval,* p. 582.

48. Ickes, *Secret Diary,* 1: 665; Donald R. McCoy, "The Progressive National Committee of 1936," *Western Political Quarterly* 9 (June 1956): 454–69; Tom Amlie to PFL, 6 July 1936, box 55, PFL to Floyd Olson, 18 August 1936, Olson to PFL, 19 August 1936, box 57, PFL Papers.

49. *Wisconsin State Journal,* 11, 12 September 1936; *Progressive,* 19 September 1936; RML to FDR, 11 September 1936, PPF 1792, FDR Papers; minutes of National Progressive Conference, Chicago, 11 September 1936, box 59, PFL Papers; "Declaration of Principles" adopted at the Chicago conference, 11 September 1936, James H. Causey, "Report of the Progressive National Committee for the Period Sept. 19, 1936–Oct. 19, 1936," Progressive National Committee Papers, Library of Congress; David E. Lilienthal, *The Journals of David E. Lilienthal,* 4 vols. (New York: Harper and Row, 1964–1969), 1: 64.

50. RML and PFL to FDR, 2 November 1936, PFL to FDR, 19, 29 October 1936, FDR to PFL, 26 October 1936, PPF 6659, FDR Papers.

51. Harold M. Wylie to A. W. Zeratsky, 15 October 1936, box 61, Manly D. Hinshaw to Gordon Sinykin, 29 October 1936, box 62, John W. Grobschmidt to Thomas Duncan, 9 December 1935, box 42, PFL to Raymond E. Evrard, 22 April 1935, box 35, PFL to Herbert Fredrich, 28 January 1936, box 47, PFL to Philip Lehner, 18 July 1935, box 38, PFL Papers.

52. PFL to Blance Ryan, 6 August 1936, box 57, PFL to Victor W. Nehs, 8 August 1936, box 57, Gordon Sinykin to RML, 27 April 1935, box 35, Sinykin to A. G. Paffel, 26 August 1936, box 58, Sinykin to William J. Plunkert, 17 December 1936, box 64, W. H. Koelpin to PFL, 13 June 1935, box 37, PFL Papers; *Progressive,* 14 January 1933; *Wisconsin State Journal,* 21 June, 10 July, 14 August 1935.

53. Sam Sigman to George J. Schneider, 7 April, 23 May 1932, box 2, Samuel Sigman Papers, SHSW; William B. Ackerman to PFL, 23 September 1932, box 22, Milton McRae to PFL, 8 January 1936, box 46, PFL to Peter C. Van Nostrand, 5 June 1935, box 37, PFL Papers; PFL to "Dear Ones," 22 July 1930, box A39, Family Papers.

54. J. W. Carow to PFL, 6 November 1935, box 41, PFL Papers. In the PFL Papers see a black 4" x 6" loose-leaf notebook that La Follette carried with him on campaign tours. This collection also contains many lists of Progressive voters in the state. See also Marquis Childs, "How the La Follette Family Has Educated the Voters of Wisconsin," *St. Louis Post-Dispatch,* 12 October 1930; *Wisconsin State Journal,* 16 March 1936.

55. On the internal workings of the Progressive party, the best source is Charles H. Backstrom, "The Progressive Party of Wisconsin, 1934–1946" (Ph.D. diss., University of Wisconsin, 1956).

56. "The La Follette Dynasty," *Literary Digest* 107 (4 August 1930): 9; *Wisconsin State Journal,* 10 April 1935; Henry A. Gunderson to PFL, 10 July 1932, box 20, PFL Papers.

57. Gordon Sinykin to E. L. Schroeder, 19 September 1936, box 59, Sinykin to Michael H. Hall, 23 September 1936, box 60, PFL Papers. Various financial records and expense accounts are contained in box 126, PFL Papers; interview, Gordon Sinykin, 5 November 1971.

58. Robert Morss Lovett, "Progressive Birthday," *New Republic* 83 (5 June 1935): 95; PFL to C. J. B. Wronski, 15 October 1934, box 29, PFL Papers.
59. Gordon Sinykin to L. W. Herzog, 7 October 1936, box 61, PFL Papers; *Madison Capital Times*, 21 October 1936; *Progressive*, 9 February 1935, 20 November 1944.
60. *Milwaukee Journal*, 18, 19 September, 16 October 1936; *Progressive*, 3, 17 October 1936.
61. Winter Everett, "Around the Statehouse," *Wisconsin State Journal*, 25 January 1936; *Madison Capital Times*, 12, 16 October 1936.
62. *Waupaca County Post*, quoted in *Madison Capital Times*, 3 October 1936.
63. Rogin, *Intellectuals and McCarthy*, p. 82; Brye, *Wisconsin Voting Patterns*, p. 328–31; *Wisconsin Blue Book, 1937*, pp. 418–20.
64. Many telegrams circa 2–6 November 1936, PFL to Harry Hopkins, 9 November 1936, FDR to PFL, 21 November 1936, box 63, PFL Papers.
65. Gordon Sinykin to C. G. Warnick, 10 November 1936, box 63, PFL Papers.

Chapter 6: Wisconsin's "Little New Deal"

1. Marquis W. Childs, *Sweden: The Middle Way* (New Haven: Yale University Press, 1936); *Progressive*, 25 April 1936; PFL, *Adventure in Politics: The Memoirs of Philip La Follette*, ed. Donald Young (New York: Holt, Rinehart and Winston, 1970), pp. 228–30; IBL, "A Room of Our Own," *Progressive*, 9 January 1937, 8 January 1938, 23 December 1939; IBL, "Journal of Our Trip," box 162, PFL Papers.
2. IBL political diary, box 161, PFL Papers. On the Glenn Frank episode, see PFL, *Adventure in Politics*, pp. 231–45; Lawrence H. Larsen, *The President Wore Spats: A Biography of Glenn Frank* (Madison: State Historical Society of Wisconsin, 1965), pp. 122–51. Harold Wilkie's list of the charges against Frank is in *Madison Capital Times*, 6 January 1937. A study that takes a sympathetic view of Frank is Steven D. Zink, "Glenn Frank of the University of Wisconsin: A Reinterpretation," *Wisconsin Magazine of History* 62 (Winter, 1978–1979): 91–127.
3. Larsen, *The President Wore Spats*, pp. 46–65; Ernest L. Meyer, "Glenn Frank: Journalist on Parole," *American Mercury* 31 (February 1934): 149–59.
4. *Progressive*, 11 July 1936. See also the letter from "A Faculty Wife," *Nation* 144 (13 February 1937): 195.
5. *Wisconsin State Journal*, 7 January, 11, 15 March 1936; *Milwaukee Journal*, 17 March 1936; PFL, *Adventure in Politics*, p. 238; Zink, "Glenn Frank: A Reinterpretation," pp. 116–17.
6. IBL political diary, box 161, Lewis Gannett to PFL, 17 December 1936, box 64, PFL Papers; *New York Herald Tribune*, 14 December 1936.
7. *Madison Capital Times*, 16 December 1936, 7, 8 January 1937.
8. *Milwaukee Journal*, 17 December 1936; *New York Herald Tribune*, 17 December 1936; Oswald G. Villard, "Issues and Man," *Nation* 143 (26 December 1936): 762 and 144 (23 February 1937): 101.
9. Paul W. Ward, "Frank v. La Follette," *Nation* 143 (26 December 1936): 751–52; "The Shape of Things," *Nation* 144 (16 January 1937): 59; *Madison Capital Times*, 9 January 1937; PFL to Arthur Sulzberger, 16 December 1936, box 64, James B. Conant to PFL, 24 December 1936, box 65, PFL Papers.
10. Curtis P. Nettels to PFL, 19 December 1936, box 65, PFL Papers; George C. Sellery, *Some Ferments at Wisconsin, 1901–1947* (Madison: University of Wisconsin Press, 1960), pp. 85–96; interview, Mark H. Ingraham, University Archives Oral History Project, University of Wisconsin, pp. 79–85; interview, Edwin M. Wilkie, 13 March 1973.
11. RML to Rachel La Follette, 11 January 1937, box A45, Family Papers.

12. *Progressive,* 12 December 1936; *Wisconsin State Journal,* 5 March 1937; PFL to Herbert H. Lehman, 22 January 1937, box 69, Lehman to PFL, 8 February 1937, box 69, Lehman and others to FDR, 28 February 1937, box 71, PFL Papers.

13. *Wisconsin State Journal,* 7 March, 10, 16, 20 April, 21 May 1937; "The Week," *New Republic* 90 (10, 17 March 1937): 122, 149; James M. Shields, *Mr. Progressive: A Biography of Elmer Austin Benson* (Minneapolis: Denison, 1971), pp. 132–33; FDR Press Conference 360, (13 April 1937) 9:264.

14. IBL political diary, 21 May 1937, box 161, PFL to FDR, 3 June 1937, box 76, PFL Papers; PFL to RML, 4 June 1937, box A45, Family Papers; FDR to Harry Hopkins, 8 June 1937, OF 444-C, FDR Papers.

15. PFL to RML, 25 June 1937, box 77, Family Papers.

16. Ronald L. Feinman, *Twilight of Progressivism: The Western Republican Senators and the New Deal* (Baltimore: Johns Hopkins University Press, 1981), pp. 125, 130, 134; *Wisconsin State Journal,* 17 February, 27 April 1937.

17. PFL to Joseph B. Keenan, 1 April 1937, box 73, PFL to J. B. Boscoe, 17 April 1937, box 74, PFL Papers; *New York Times,* 28 February 1937; PFL to RML, 25 June 1937, box A45, Family Papers.

18. George W. Norris to FDR, 28 July 1937, box 78, PFL Papers; *Wisconsin State Journal,* 31 July 1937; Harold L. Ickes, *The Secret Diary of Harold L. Ickes,* 3 vols. (New York: Simon and Schuster, 1953–1954), 2: 182, 190; PFL to FDR, 13 August 1937, PPF 6659, FDR Papers.

19. L. David Carley, "The Wisconsin Governor's Legislative Role: A Case Study in the Administrations of Philip Fox La Follette and Walter J. Kohler, Jr." (Ph.D. diss., University of Wisconsin, 1959), pp. 90–92; *Wisconsin State Journal,* 14, 15 January 1937; interview, Andrew Biemiller, 3 February 1972; interview, Vernon Thomson, 9 February 1972.

20. The legislative lineups were:

	Assembly		Senate	
	1935	1937	1935	1937
Progressive	45	48	13	16
Democrat	35	31	14	9
Republican	17	21	6	8
Socialist	3			

Source: *Wisconsin Blue Book, 1935,* pp. 191–236; *Wisconsin Blue Book, 1937,* pp. 25–70.

21. Walter Hunt to Charles Dow, 9 November [1936], box 63, PFL Papers; *Wisconsin State Journal,* 13 January, 1 May, 30 October, 11 November 1937; Carley, "Governor's Legislative Role," pp. 89–90.

22. *Wisconsin State Journal,* 6 December 1936, 2 April 1937; minutes of state executive board of FLPF, 9 November 1936, PFL Papers; Lester Schmidt, "The Farmer-Labor Progressive Federation: The Study of a 'United Front' Movement Among Wisconsin Liberals, 1934–1941" (Ph.D. diss., University of Wisconsin, 1954), pp. 178–79.

23. PFL to Edward Keating, 6 April 1937, box 73, PFL radio speech, 1 June 1937, box 119, PFL Papers; *Wisconsin Rapids Tribune,* 4 May 1937.

24. *Milwaukee Journal,* 23 April, 20 May 1937; *Wisconsin State Journal,* 23, 27 April 1937; *Chicago Tribune,* 25 April 1937; PFL to Voyta Wrabetz, 21 April 1937, box 74, Edwin E. Witte to PFL, 23 July 1937, box 78, PFL Papers; Nathan P. Feinsinger and William G. Rice, Jr., *The Wisconsin Labor Relations Act,* Bulletin of the University of Wisconsin (June 1937).

25. *Kenosha News,* 20 April 1937; *Milwaukee Journal,* 20 March 1937; F. M. Young to Voyta Wrabetz, 22 June 1937, box 77, PFL Papers.

26. PFL executive budget message, January 1937, box 119, J. B. Borden to Jack Harvey, 30 March 1938, box 95, PFL Papers; *Wisconsin State Journal,* 30 April, 18 June 1937; *Milwaukee Journal,* 12 May 1937.

27. Paul W. Ward, "Washington Weekly," *Nation* 143 (3 October 1936): 383; *Complete Record of Proceedings of the Joint Hearing by the Joint Committee on Finance and the Assembly Committee on State Affairs,* 22 April 1937, 9–11, 15; Samuel Mermin, *Jurisprudence and Statecraft: The Wisconsin Development Authority and Its Implications* (Madison: University of Wisconsin Press, 1963), pp. 7, 18–19; *Milwaukee Leader,* 29 March 1937.

28. *Madison Capital Times,* 14, 15 October 1936, 7 March 1937; John N. Carmody to John A. Becker, 9 November 1936, 21 January 1937, box 86, John Carmody Papers, FDRL; Carmody to PFL, 12 March 1937, box 72, PFL Papers.

29. PFL to Morris L. Cooke, 1 February 1937, box 69, PFL Papers; *Milwaukee Sentinel,* 9 April, 7 May 1937; *Wisconsin State Journal,* 23 April 1937; *Milwaukee Leader,* 10 April 1937; *Madison Capital Times,* 6, 12 May 1937; *Sun Prairie Countryman,* 6 May 1937.

30. *Wisconsin State Journal,* 17 June 1937; *Madison Capital Times,* 17 June 1937.

31. *Wisconsin State Journal,* 13 April 1937.

32. *Progressive,* 1 May 1937; *Wausau Record-Herald,* 26 June 1937.

33. *Report of April 28, 1937 to November 30, 1938,* Edwin E. Witte Papers, SHSW; *Milwaukee Sentinel,* 29 April 1937; Thomas W. Gavett, *Development of the Labor Movement in Milwaukee* (Madison: University of Wisconsin Press, 1965), pp. 164–68; Henry Rutz to Tom Amlie, 13 July 1937, box 46, Amlie Papers; *Racine Journal-Times,* 25 August 1937; *Madison Capital Times,* 3 October 1937; *Wisconsin State Journal,* 27 August, 5 September 1937.

34. *Madison Capital Times,* 5 May, 17 June 1937; *Wausau Record-Herald,* 21 May 1937; *Milwaukee Journal,* 30 May 1937; *Wisconsin State Journal,* 30 March, 2 May, 30 June 1937; Schmidt, "Farmer-Labor Progressive Federation," pp. 225–27.

35. *Milwaukee Sentinel,* 12, 13, 16 June 1937; *Wausau Record-Herald,* 15 June 1937; *Madison Capital Times,* 16 June 1937; *Wisconsin State Journal,* 2, 3 July 1937.

36. *Milwaukee Journal,* 6 June 1937; *Wisconsin State Journal,* 25, 26 June 1937; *Madison Capital Times,* 25 June, 10 July 1937; PFL to RML, 25 June 1937, box A45, Family Papers.

37. *Wisconsin State Journal,* 3 August, 12, 13 September 1937.

38. *Milwaukee Sentinel,* 25 August 1937; *Milwaukee Journal,* 1 October 1937; *Madison Capital Times,* 1, 4 October 1937; *Wisconsin State Journal,* 1, 4, 6, 7 October 1937.

39. *Milwaukee Journal,* 16, 17 October 1937.

40. *New York Times,* 28 February 1937.

41. PFL radio speech, "Democracy Functions in Wisconsin," 16 October 1937, box 119, C.W. Hoyt to PFL, 21 February 1938, box 92, William F. Ashe to PFL, 28 October 1938, box 111, PFL Papers.

42. PFL radio speech, "Democracy Functions in Wisconsin," 16 October 1937, box 119, PFL Papers.

43. *Madison Capital Times,* 19 October 1937.

44. IBL political diary, 25 May 1937, box 161, PFL Papers.

45. PFL speech at Harvard University, "Orderly Progress," 18 June 1937, box 119, PFL to Arthur Hays Sulzberger, 16 June 1937, box 77, PFL speech at Northwestern University, 22 July 1937, box 119, PFL Papers.

46. PFL speech, "Orderly Progress," box 119, PFL Papers.

47. In his first fireside chat of 1934 President Roosevelt had used similar terminology: "It is this combination of the old and the new that marks orderly peaceful progress," FDR, *Public Papers and Addresses* (1934), 3: 318. *Stevens Point Journal,* 4 May 1937; *Wisconsin Rapids Tribune,* 4 May 1937; *Progressive,* 26 June 1937.

48. *Appleton Post-Crescent,* 8 September 1937; *Wisconsin State Journal,* 15 July 1937; *Milwaukee Journal,* 27 June 1937; *Fort Atkinson Union,* 23 July 1937; *Cochrane Recorder,* 29 July 1937.

49. IBL political diary, 23 February 1937, box 161, PFL Papers; *Stoughton Courier-Hub,* 27 July 1937.

50. *New York Times Magazine,* 3 January 1937; *Wisconsin State Journal,* 19 May 1937; *Milwaukee Journal,* 20 May 1937.

51. PFL, *Adventure in Politics,* pp. 251–52; William T. Evjue, "Memorandum of conversation with Governor La Follette on April 22, 1938," William T. Evjue Papers, SHSW; IBL political diary, 19 August 1937, box 161, FDR to PFL, 16 August 1937, box 80, PFL Papers; *Wisconsin State Journal,* 29 July 1937.

52. IBL political diary, 19 August 1937, box 161, PFL Papers; *Madison Capital Times,* 24, 27 July, 2 September 1937; *Wisconsin State Journal,* 31 July, 1 August, 5, 17 September 1937; *New York Herald Tribune,* 1 September 1937. Arthur Schlesinger, Jr., concluded that if Roosevelt thought of any of the progressives as his successor, it was RML, *Politics of Upheaval* (Boston: Houghton Mifflin, 1960), p. 136; Stanley High, *Roosevelt—And Then?* (New York: Harper, 1937), pp. 273–74, 310.

53. *Prairie du Chien Press,* 29 July 1937; *Milwaukee Journal,* 1 August 1937; *Wisconsin State Journal,* 27 July, 7, 18 August 1937; "A Political Realignment in Wisconsin," *New Republic* 92 (1 September 1937): 89; *Columbus Democrat,* 20 August 1937; *Medford Star-News,* 12 August 1937; *Omaha News,* 6 September 1937; PFL to Francis Brown, 10 September 1937, box 82, PFL Papers.

54. Marvin H. McIntyre to PFL, 3 October 1937, box 83, PFL Papers; *Milwaukee Wisconsin News,* 5 October 1937; *Milwaukee Journal,* 5 October 1937.

55. *Madison Capital Times,* 1 August 1937; PFL to George W. Norris, 17 August 1937, box 80, PFL Papers; *Milwaukee Journal,* 7 September 1937; *Mondovi Herald-News,* 17 September 1937; *Green Bay Press-Gazette,* 7 September 1937; *Oshkosh Northwestern,* 19 September 1937; *New York Post,* 21 September 1937; *Milwaukee Wisconsin News,* 21 September 1937; *United States News Service,* 19 July 1937.

56. *New York Herald Tribune,* 10 October 1937; Max Lerner, "A Third Party for 1940?" *Nation* 145 (4 September 1937): 234.

57. IBL, "A Room of Our Own," *Progressive,* 4 December 1937, 29 April 1946; *Madison Capital Times,* 1, 11, 22 November 1937; PFL to Alex Gumberg, 11 November 1937, box 14, Alex Gumberg Papers, SHSW.

58. PFL to RML, 27 November, 5, 20 December 1937, RML to PFL, 7 December 1937, box A45, Family Papers; David K. Niles to PFL, 6 December 1937, box 86, PFL Papers.

59. Interview, Norman Clapp, 2 March 1973; interview, Gordon Sinykin, 4 May 1973.

60. Harry O. Kovenock to PFL, 5 April 1938, box 96, PFL Papers.

61. Thurman W. Arnold, *The Symbols of Government* (New Haven: Yale University Press, 1935), pp. iii, 9, 17, 229; idem, *The Folklore of Capitalism* (New Haven: Yale University Press, 1937), p. 115.

62. Stuart Chase, "Spring Book Selection," *Common Sense* 5 (April 1936): 24–25; Chase to PFL, 30 August 1937, box 81, 13 April 1938, box 96, PFL to Chase, 10 September 1937, box 82, 21 February 1938, box 92, PFL Papers.

63. Louis Adamic, "A Talk with Phil La Follette," *Nation* 140 (27 February 1935): 243.

Chapter 7: The National Progressives of America

1. *Madison Capital Times,* 4 January, 18 February 1938. In 1937 La Follette had found it necessary to deny that he was grooming Immell as his successor. *Milwaukee Journal,* 11 April 1937; *Progressive,* 1 May 1937.

2. *Madison Capital Times,* 11 January 1938; *Progressive,* 22 January 1938.

3. IBL memoirs, box 165, PFL Papers; interview, Isabel B. La Follette, 14 May 1972; William T. Evjue to FDR, 6 October 1936, FDR to Evjue, 20 October 1936, PPF 4029, FDR Papers.

4. *Milwaukee Journal,* 20 February 1938; Andrew Biemiller to Tom Amlie, 8 February 1937, box 41, Thomas Amlie Papers, SHSW; *Madison Capital Times,* 13, 24, 27 January 1938.

5. *Minneapolis Journal,* 13 February 1938; PFL speech, 28 February 1938, PFL Papers; *Madison Capital Times,* 29 February 1938.

6. "The Week," *New Republic* 93 (23 December 1937): 209–10; Max Lerner, "Fear Hits the New Deal," *Nation* 145 (20 November 1937): 551–52; "Is Roosevelt on the Run?" *Nation* 145 (27 November 1937): 576–77; *Madison Capital Times,* 10 November 1937, 11 January, 8, 27 February 1938; *New York Times,* 6 February, 7 March 1938.

7. *Madison Capital Times,* 27 March 1938; *Wisconsin State Journal,* 25 February 1938.

8. Max Otto to PFL, [circa 14 March 1938], box 94, IBL political diary, 29 March 1938, box 161, PFL Papers.

9. *Wisconsin State Journal,* 15–18 April 1938; copies of the four April radio speeches are in box 119, PFL Papers.

10. *Wisconsin State Journal,* 22, 24, 25 April 1938; *New York Times,* 25, 26 April 1938; *Madison Capital Times,* 24, 25 April 1938; IBL political diary, 23, 30 April 1938, box 161, PFL Papers.

11. *New York Times,* 28 April 1938; *Milwaukee Sentinel,* 27 April 1938.

12. *Wisconsin State Journal,* 24, 28 April 1938; *New York World-Telegram,* 25 April 1938; FDR Press Conference 454 (26 April 1938), 11:387.

13. William T. Evjue, "Memorandum of conversation with Governor La Follette," 3, 22 April 1938, William T. Evjue Papers, SHSW; Evjue, "Wisconsin: A State that Glories in Its Past," in *Our Sovereign State,* ed. Robert S. Allen (New York: Vanguard, 1948), pp. 228–36; *Madison Capital Times,* 28 April 1938, 23 August 1965.

14. Ruben Levin, "A New Party Is Launched," *Common Sense* 7 (June 1938): 17–19; Robert Morss Lovett, "April Hopes in Madison," *New Republic* 95 (11 May 1938): 13–14; *Wisconsin State Journal,* 29 April 1938; *Madison Capital Times,* 29 April 1938.

15. PFL speech, "A New Movement," 28 April 1938, box 119, PFL Papers.

16. "Progressives, What Now?" *Common Sense* 7 (June 1938): 3–5; *Milwaukee Sentinel,* 3 May 1938.

17. *Wisconsin State Journal,* 3 May 1938; *Madison Capital Times,* 3, 7 May 1938.

18. *Madison Capital Times,* 30 June 1938; *Common Sense* 7 (June 1938): 4; Geoffrey Parsons, Jr., to PFL, [circa 2 May 1938], box 99, Geoffrey Parsons, Sr., to PFL, 3, 11 May 1938, boxes 99 and 100, IBL political diary, 30 April 1938, box 161, PFL to William R. Hearst, 27 April 1938, box 97, PFL Papers.

19. Reprinted in *New York Times,* 20 April 1938.

20. "New Deal or New Party?" *Common Sense* 6 (September 1937): 3–5; "Progressives, What Now?" *Common Sense* 7 (June 1938): 3–5; Alfred Bingham to Tom Amlie, 7 May 1938, box 55, Amlie Papers; Donald L. Miller, *The New American Radicalism: Alfred M. Bingham and Non-Marxian Insurgency in the New Deal Era* (Port Washington, N.Y.: Kennikat, 1979), pp. 141–42.

21. Tom Amlie to Oscar Ameringer, 9 May 1938, Amlie to C. C. Cunningham, 8 May 1938, Amlie to Henry P. Fairchild, 27 May 1938, Amlie to Alfred Bingham, 8 May 1938, boxes 55 and 56, Amlie Papers.

22. Heywood Broun, "Phil La Follette Sounds Off," *New Republic* 95 (11 May 1938): 16; *Madison Capital Times,* 4, 6, 8 May 1938.

23. "A Third Party in 1940?" *New Republic* 94 (4 May 1938): 382–83; "The Progressives and the Future," *New Republic* 95 (11 May 1938): 3–4; Bruce Bliven to PFL, 10 May 1938, PFL to Bliven, 13 May 1938, box 100, PFL Papers; "La Follette Thunder," *Nation* 146 (30

April 1938): 492–93; "The New Progressives," *Nation* 146 (7 May 1938): 519–20; "The Shape of Things," *Nation* 146 (28 May 1938): 603.

24. Oswald G. Villard, "Issues and Men," *Nation* 146 (14 May 1938): 561; David C. Coyle to PFL, 29 April 1938, box 97, PFL Papers; *Madison Capital Times*, 23, 24 May 1938; *Progressive*, 4 June 1938; Paul Y. Anderson, "La Follette's Bid for Power," *Nation* 146 (7 May 1938): 524–25.

25. *Milwaukee Leader*, 6 May 1938.

26. *New York Times*, 1, 5, 27 May 1938; *Milwaukee Journal*, 1, 14 May 1938; *Madison Capital Times*, 2, 3, 14, 15 May 1938; *Phil La Follette's New Party*, pamphlet (Socialist Party of the United States, 1938), Socialist Party Papers, Milwaukee County Historical Society.

27. *Madison Capital Times*, 1, 2, 12 May 1938; *Wisconsin State Journal*, 24, 30 April 1938; *Progressive*, 16 July, 9 November 1938; "Political Paragraphs," *Common Sense* 7 (June 1938): 23–34; Upton Sinclair to PFL, 15 June 1938, H. L. Nunn to PFL, 3 May 1938, William Allen White to Hugh P. Greely, 1 June 1938, Gerald Boileau to PFL, 12 April 1938, B. J. Gehrmann to PFL, 14 April 1938, Harry Sauthoff to PFL, 30 March 1938, George Schneider to PFL, 26 April 1938, Tom Amlie to PFL, 4 April 1938, Gardner Withrow to PFL, 5 April 1938, boxes 95–102, PFL Papers.

28. Harold L. Ickes, *The Secret Diary of Harold L. Ickes*, 3 vols. (New York: Simon and Schuster, 1953–54), 2:378–80, 385.

29. *Madison Capital Times*, 28 April 1938; Elliott Roosevelt, ed., *F. D. R.: His Personal Letters, 1928–1945*, 2 vols. (New York: Duell, Sloan, and Pearce, 1950), 2: 785; *New York Times*, 6 May 1938.

30. Ickes, *Secret Diary*, 2: 393–95; Rexford Tugwell, *The Democratic Roosevelt: A Biography of Franklin D. Roosevelt* (New York: Doubleday, 1957), p. 412.

31. Fola La Follette to George Middleton, 15 May 1938, box A45, Family Papers; IBL political diary, 13 May 1938, box 161, PFL Papers; *New York Times*, 14 May 1938; *Madison Capital Times*, 14, 16 May 1938.

32. William T. Evjue, "Memorandum of conversation with Herman L. Ekern, 1 May 1938," Evjue Papers; *Wisconsin State Journal*, 30 April, 16 September 1938.

33. Ernest K. Lindley, *The Roosevelt Revolution: First Phase* (New York: Viking, 1933), pp. 10–11 and *Half Way with Roosevelt* (New York: Viking, 1937), p. 67; Bernard Bellush, *Franklin D. Roosevelt as Governor of New York* (New York: Columbia University Press, 1955), pp. 4–5; James M. Burns, *Roosevelt: The Lion and the Fox* (New York: Harcourt, Brace and World, 1956), p. 198; Tugwell, *The Democratic Roosevelt*, pp. 412, 415, 436, 454, 530, 546; Bernard Sternsher, *Rexford Tugwell and the New Deal* (New Brunswick, N.J.: Rutgers University Press, 1964), pp. 309–11; Ickes, *Secret Diary*, 2: 533; Arthur M. Schlesinger, Jr., *The Coming of the New Deal* (Boston: Houghton Mifflin, 1958), pp. 504–5.

34. Samuel I. Rosenman, *Working with Roosevelt* (New York: Harper and Brothers, 1952), pp. 176–80; Ickes, *Secret Diary*, 2: 256–57; Stanley High, *Roosevelt—And Then?* (New York: Harper, 1937), pp. 278–82; Burns, *Lion and Fox*, pp. 358–60; Tugwell, *The Democratic Roosevelt*, pp. 461, 468–76; IBL political diary, 7 September 1938, box 161, PFL Papers.

35. "Washington Notes," *New Republic* 95 (27 July 1938): 333; Burns, *Lion and Fox*, pp. 360–66, 402–3.

36. PFL, *Adventure in Politics: The Memoirs of Philip La Follette*, ed. Donald Young (New York: Holt, Rinehart and Winston, 1970), p. 254; *Madison Capital Times*, 7 September 1938.

37. On Roosevelt's continued desire for political realignment, see Rosenman, *Working with Roosevelt*, pp. 463–70; Tugwell, *The Democratic Roosevelt*, pp. 658–59, 663, 676–77; and James M. Burns, *Roosevelt: The Soldier of Freedom* (New York: Harcourt Brace Jovanovich, 1970), pp. 510–13.

38. *Wisconsin State Journal,* 1 May 1938.

39. John F. Wirds to PFL, 17 September 1937, box 81, PFL to Wirds, 24 September 1937, box 82, 1 July 1938, box 104, PFL to George F. Buresh, 26 August 1938, box 107, W. Howard Chase to PFL, 20 September 1938, box 109, PFL Papers; *Wisconsin State Journal,* 30 April, 31 July, 15 August, 11, 15 September, 8 November 1938.

40. Elmer Benson to PFL, 14 February 1938, box 92, 18 April 1938, box 97, PFL Papers; James M. Shields, *Mr. Progressive: A Biography of Elmer Austin Benson* (Minneapolis: Denison, 1971), pp. 150–53, 157; "Dark Angel?" *Time* 31 (23 May 1938): 8–9; Jack Alexander, "The Third Party Gets a Rich Uncle," *Saturday Evening Post* 211 (3 September 1938): 5–7, 56–59; *Madison Capital Times,* 11 May, 30, 31 August, 25 September 1938; *Wisconsin State Journal,* 29 April, 1, 20 May, 19 September 1938; Elmer Benson to author, 12 December 1972.

41. *New York Times,* 1, 12 May, 1 June 1938; Arthur H. Harlow to PFL, 24 May 1938, box 101, PFL to James H. Causey, 13 May 1938, box 100, PFL Papers.

42. *New York Times,* 4 June 1938; *Madison Capital Times,* 4–6 June 1938; IBL political diary, 26, 28 July 1938, box 161, PFL Papers.

43. William Benton to PFL, 7, 16 February, 22 July, 23 August 1938, PFL to Benton, 10 February, 19, 22, 23 April, 19 May 1938, boxes 91–107, PFL Papers; Sidney Hyman, *The Lives of William Benton* (Chicago: University of Chicago Press, 1969), pp. 204–5; Jack Howard to author, 31 January 1972; James K. Libbey, *Alexander Gumberg and Soviet-American Relations, 1917–33* (Lexington: University Press of Kentucky, 1977), pp. 108–18, 151.

44. *New York Times,* 23 June 1938; *Madison Capital Times,* 22 June 1938; *Progressive,* 2 July 1938; PFL to Ernest W. Gibson, Jr., 1 July 1938, box 104, PFL Papers.

45. Alfred J. Snyder to PFL, 29 June 1938, PFL to Snyder, 1, 5 July 1938, Mary Farquaharson to IBL, 14 May 1938, Farquaharson to Ralph M. Immell, 5 July 1938, Immell to Gilmour Young, 27 May, 7 June 1938, Young to Immell, 2 June 1938, Ped Watkins to PFL, 24 May, 16 June, 17 August 1938, PFL to Watkins, 29 May, 3, 26 August 1938, boxes 100–107, PFL Papers; *Madison Capital Times,* 11 June 1938; *Seattle Times,* 12 May 1938.

46. Paul Douglas to PFL, 16, 21 July 1937, Raymond Haight to PFL, 28 September, 11, 15 December 1937, PFL to Haight, 19 July 1937, J. R. Richards to PFL, 26 November 1937, Frank W. Hooper to PFL, 15 January 1938, E. A. Crocker to PFL, 27 December 1937, Jerry Voorhis to PFL, 6, 27 May 1938, PFL to Voorhis, 18 May 1938, Culbert L. Olson to Elmer Benson, 2 May 1938, Benson to PFL, 14 February, 5 May 1938, Herman L. Ekern to PFL, 31 March 1938, Olson to PFL, 4, 23 September 1938, Al Sessions to PFL, 4 May 1938, boxes 78–109, PFL Papers; *Wisconsin State Journal,* 29, 30 November 1937, 18, 26 September 1938.

47. Jay Franklin, *1940* (New York: Viking, 1940), p. 94; Sheldon R. Brewster to PFL, 20 November 1937, 24 June 1938, Ray McKaig to PFL, 17 May, 20 July 1938, PFL to McKaig, 20 May 1938, Leslie J. Aker to PFL, 11 August 1938, M. L. Alsup to PFL, 16 August 1938, boxes 85 and 100–7, PFL Papers; *Madison Capital Times,* 13, 18 September 1938.

48. PFL to Roy Frazier, 11 May 1938, box 100, L. J. Wehe to Gordon Sinykin, 24 May 1938, box 101, Sinykin to PFL, 4 May 1938, box 99, PFL Papers; *Madison Capital Times,* 16 July 1938.

49. Elmer Davis, "The Wisconsin Brothers: A Study in Partial Eclipse," *Harper's* 178 (February 1939): 268–77.

50. Hadley Cantril and Mildred Strunk, *Public Opinion 1935–1946* (Princeton: Princeton University Press, 1951), pp. 576–77; *Wisconsin State Journal,* 29 April, 27 May 1938; "The Fortune Survey: The La Follette Progressives," *Fortune* 18 (October 1938): 90–92.

51. *Madison Capital Times,* 8 May 1938.

52. Ibid., 24 June, 3, 8, 11, 22, 24 July 1938.
53. Jerry Voorhis, "Legislative Abundance," *Common Sense* 7 (February 1938): 13–14; *Wisconsin State Journal*, 7 June 1938; Tom Amlie to PFL, 3 November 1937, box 84, PFL Papers.
54. *Madison Capital Times*, 4, 7, 9, 11–13, 17 September, 14 November 1938; Mordecai Ezekiel, "Democratic Economic Planning," *Common Sense* 7 (July 1938): 8–10; *Wisconsin State Journal*, 6 September 1938; notes on Amlie's address, 19 August 1938, box 39, Herman Ekern Papers, SHSW.
55. *Madison Capital Times*, 3 September 1938.
56. Ibid., 18 September 1938; interview, Gordon Sinykin, 4 May 1973.
57. *Madison Capital Times*, 21 September 1938; Tom Amlie to Herman Ekern, 21 September 1938, Evjue Papers.
58. *Wisconsin State Journal*, 2 October 1938.
59. Ibid., 5 October 1938.
60. Ibid., 4 October, 3 November 1938.
61. John King to Gordon Sinykin, 4 October 1938, box 110, Mrs. John Ockerlander to PFL, 13 February 1938, box 92, R. J. Cuskey, "Progressive versus Paffelism," *Washburn County Farmer-Labor Club Bulletin* 3, 14 September 1938, box 108, Lawrence Larson to PFL, 14 July 1938, box 105, Atlee H. Maedke to PFL, 6 August 1938, box 106, Clyde Schloemer to Sinykin, 7 November 1938, box 112, PFL Papers.
62. Roy Empey to Gordon Sinykin, 7 November 1938, box 112, PFL Papers; RML to Mary La Follette, 6 September 1938, box A46, Family Papers; *Wisconsin State Journal*, 19 October 1938.
63. Gordon Sinykin to PFL, 29 September 1938, box 109, PFL Papers; *Madison Capital Times*, 6, 28 October 1938; *Milwaukee Journal*, 4 October 1938.
64. *Progressive*, 15 October 1938; *Milwaukee Journal*, 6 October 1938; *Madison Capital Times*, 23 August, 20 October 1938; PFL to "Dear Friends," 2 November 1938, box 112, PFL Papers.
65. *Madison Capital Times*, 7, 11, 24, 26 October, 2 November 1938.
66. Louise Givan to James A. Farley, 31 October 1938, OF 300, box 92, William B. Rubin to Farley, 22 October 1938, OF 300, box 88, FDR Papers.
67. *Madison Capital Times*, 5, 12, 14 October, 2 November 1938; F. M. Corry to James A. Farley, 17 December 1938, William J. Brennan to Farley, 15 December 1938, William B. Rubin to Farley, 2 November 1938, OF 300, box 92, FDR Papers; *Wisconsin State Journal*, 25 July 1938; FDR to Leo Crowley, 4 February 1938, Evjue Papers.
68. *Madison Capital Times*, 31 August, 20, 26 November 1938.
69. F. Ryan Duffy to James A. Farley, 15 November 1938, OF 300, box 92, FDR Papers; James Donoghue, *How Wisconsin Voted, 1848–1972* (Madison: Bureau of Government, University of Wisconsin Extension Division, 1974), pp. 113, 129; Robert R. Dykstra and David R. Reynolds, "In Search of Wisconsin Progressivism, 1904–1952: A Test of the Rogin Scenario," in *The History of American Electoral Behavior*, ed. Joel H. Silbey, Allen G. Bogue, and William H. Flanigan (Princeton: Princeton University Press, 1978), p. 305.
70. *Wisconsin Blue Book, 1940*, pp. 559–621; David L. Brye, *Wisconsin Voting Patterns in the Twentieth Century, 1900 to 1950* (New York: Garland, 1979), pp. 400–402, 410.
71. PFL, "They Wanted Something New," *Nation* 147 (3 December 1938): 586–87; *Madison Capital Times*, 11, 12 November 1938; *Wisconsin State Journal*, 12 November 1938; IBL political diary, 10 November 1938, box 161, PFL Papers.
72. FDR Press Conference 499 (11 November 1938), 12:222–23; James A. Farley, *Jim Farley's Story: The Roosevelt Years* (New York: McGraw-Hill, 1948), pp. 148–49; Burns, *Lion and Fox*, pp. 365–67; Elliott Roosevelt, ed., *F. D. R.: His Personal Letters, 1928–1945*, 2: 827; *Wisconsin State Journal*, 12 November 1938.
73. *Madison Capital Times*, 10, 25 November 1938.

74. PFL to Alexander Zasoba, 19 November 1938, PFL to Mrs. Stanley Chudy, 18 November 1938, Edward G. Littel to Grace Lynch, 9 November 1938, William O. Douglas to PFL, 19 November 1938, Ernest W. Gruening to PFL, 9 November 1938, Lloyd Garrison to PFL, 11 November 1938, G. C. Sellery to PFL, 10 November 1938, W. F. Ashe to PFL, 9 November 1938, box 113, PFL Papers; *Progressive,* 19 November 1938.

75. IBL to Fola La Follette, 28 November 1938, box A45, Family Papers.

76. "Election Returns," *Common Sense* 7 (December 1938): 6; *Madison Capital Times,* 13, 14, 22 November 1938; *Wisconsin State Journal,* 16 November 1938; *Progressive,* 19 November 1938.

77. *Wisconsin State Journal,* 9, 13, 16 November 1938; *Madison Capital Times,* 9 November, 7 December 1938.

Chapter 8: The Political Outsider

1. PFL, *Adventure in Politics: The Memoirs of Philip La Follette,* ed. Donald Young (New York: Holt, Rinehart and Winston, 1970), pp. 257–59; PFL to "Dear Ones," letters in box 135, PFL Papers and in box A47, Family Papers; *Madison Capital Times,* 11 May, 8 August 1939; PFL, "Between the Lines—in Italy," *The Commentator* 5 (May 1939): 3–7; subsequent issues deal with France (June 1939: 51–54); Germany (July 1939: 70–75); and England (August 1939: 19–22).

2. *New York Times,* 22 April 1939; *Madison Capital Times,* 19, 22 April 1939.

3. Alex Gumberg to Raymond Robins, 24 April 1939, box 16, Alex Gumberg Papers, SHSW; PFL, *Adventure in Politics,* pp. 259–62; PFL to Robert Vansittart, 24 April 1939, box 116, PFL Papers.

4. *New York Times,* 23, 25 September 1939; RML to Rachel La Follette, 23 September 1939, box A47, Family Papers; *Madison Capital Times,* 4 October 1939; IBL political diary, 9 February 1941, box 161, PFL Papers.

5. PFL radio speech, "The Defense of America," 6 July 1940, box 120, PFL Papers; *Madison Capital Times,* 6 March 1941.

6. *Madison Capital Times,* 13, 23 April, 25 November, 17 December 1939, 20 February 1940; *Progressive,* 20 June 1939, 3 February 1940; *New York Times,* 3 April 1939; *Janesville Gazette,* 22 December 1939; *Milwaukee Journal,* 30 July 1939, 11 January, 14 June 1939; PFL to Joseph R. Farrington, 5 June 1939, box 116, PFL Papers.

7. Interview, Gordon Sinykin, 4 May 1973; PFL radio speeches, 20 June, 6, 7, 8 July 1940, box 120, IBL political diary, 9 February 1941, box 161, PFL Papers; *Madison Capital Times,* 7–9 July, 27 September 1940; *Progressive,* 21, 28 September, 5 October, 9 November 1940; Jack Kyle to FDR, 2 October 1940, FDR to Kyle, 4 October 1940, PPF 6916, FDR Papers; Patrick J. Maney, *"Young Bob" La Follette: A Biography of Senator Robert M. La Follette, Jr., 1895–1953* (Columbia: University of Missouri Press, 1978), pp. 242–43.

8. *Milwaukee Journal,* 23 October 1940; *Progressive,* 13 January, 17 February, 16 November 1940; *Madison Capital Times,* 17, 18 April, 7 May, 20 August 1939; *Janesville Gazette,* 2 May 1939; *Wisconsin State Journal,* 15 August 1945.

9. PFL to C. E. Venne, 7 July 1939, box 116, PFL Papers; *Madison Capital Times,* 23 January 1939; Tom Amlie, "The Time Has Come for the Farmer-Laborites to Go into the Democratic Party," 24 November 1941, Amlie to Benjamin Sonnenberg, 19 November 1941, box 62, Sam Sigman to Amlie, 25 September, 2 October 1942, box 63, Thomas Amlie Papers, SHSW; Amlie to William T. Evjue, 8 March 1946, Evjue, "Memo of conversation with Sen. Robert M. La Follette, Jr., July 24, 1943," William T. Evjue Papers, SHSW;

Progressive, 5 April, 4 October 1941; *Milwaukee Sentinel,* 24 September 1941; interview, Andrew Biemiller, 3 February 1972.

10. Harold L. Ickes, *The Secret Diary of Harold L. Ickes,* 3 vols. (New York: Simon and Schuster, 1953–1954), 2: 654; *Madison Capital Times,* 24, 30 April, 13 May, 15, 18, 19, 21 June 1939; *Milwaukee Journal,* 16 May, 19 June 1939; *Progressive,* 24 June 1939; Gustave Keller to Edward J. Flynn, 29 May 1942, box 1140, Democratic National Committee Papers, Roosevelt Library; interview, Miles McMillin, 11 December 1972.

11. PFL to Marguerite Le Hand, 17, 18 May 1940, Lauchlin Currie to FDR, 29 May 1940, PPF 6659, FDR Papers; FDR to Currie, 28 May 1940, Elliott Roosevelt, ed., *F. D. R.: His Personal Letters,* 2: 1933; PFL to RML, 25 May 1940, box 136, PFL Papers; RML to PFL, 27 May 1940, PFL to RML, 2 June 1940, box A47, Family Papers.

12. Robert E. Wood to PFL, 5 July 1940, R. Douglas Stuart to PFL, 30 July 1940, PFL to Chester Bowles, 16, 24 August 1940, Wood to PFL, 26 December 1940, PFL to Wood, 30 December 1940, Stuart to PFL, 24 May 1941, boxes 136–38, PFL Papers; PFL to RML, 1 May 1941, box A48, Family Papers; Wayne S. Cole, *America First: The Battle Against Intervention, 1940–1941* (Madison: University of Wisconsin Press, 1953), pp. 13–14, 23–25.

13. Cole, *America First,* pp. 8–9, 70–72; PFL, *Adventure in Politics,* pp. 263–66; *Madison Capital Times,* 4 February 1941; see Sidney Hyman, *The Lives of William Benton* (Chicago: University of Chicago Press, 1969), pp. 238–39.

14. *Wisconsin State Journal,* 21 September 1941; Charles Holmberg to William T. Evjue, 29 July 1941, Evjue, "Memorandum on Conversation with Aldric Revell," 18 September 1941, Robert S. Allen to Evjue, 21 June 1941, William T. Evjue Papers; *Chicago Tribune,* 29 July 1941; *New York PM,* 15 May 1941; John Roy Carlson [Arthur Derounian], *Under Cover: My Four Years in the Nazi Underworld of America* (New York: Dutton, 1943), pp. 242–44.

15. *Madison Capital Times,* 6 January 1941; *Chicago Tribune,* 6, 8 January 1941; *Progressive,* 11 January 1941.

16. PFL to RML, 6 September 1941, box A48, Family Papers; Cole, *America First,* pp. 181–82; *Milwaukee Sentinel,* 2 September 1941; *New York Times,* 4 December 1941; *Progressive,* 15 November 1941.

17. *Milwaukee Journal,* 7 December 1941.

18. PFL to IBL, 3, 30 August 1942, box 139, PFL Papers; PFL, *Adventure in Politics,* p. 266.

19. PFL to IBL, 28 April 1942, box 139, PFL Papers.

20. Carolyn J. Mattern, "The Man on the Dark Horse: The Presidential Campaigns for General Douglas MacArthur" (Ph.D. diss., University of Wisconsin, 1976), pp. 43–44; PFL to RML, 22 January 1943, box A48, Family Papers.

21. PFL to RML, 12 February, 17 March 1943, box A48, Family Papers; PFL to RML, 14 June 1943, IBL to PFL, 2 July 1943, box 140, PFL Papers.

22. PFL to IBL, 18 June 1943, RML to PFL, 2, 20 February, 24 June 1943, box 140, PFL Papers; RML to PFL, 9, 11 March 1943, PFL to RML, 25 February 1943, box A49, Family Papers.

23. IBL political diary, 29 March, 30 April, 8, 13 May 1938, box 161, PFL Papers.

24. IBL to PFL, 12 May 1943, PFL to IBL, 18 June 1943, 25 May 1944, boxes 140–42, PFL Papers; *Progressive,* 29 June 1940.

25. PFL to IBL, 3 September 1943, box 141, PFL Papers.

26. IBL political diary, 13 May 1938, box 161, PFL to IBL, 18 March 1944, box 142, PFL Papers.

27. Mattern, "Man on the Dark Horse," p. 34.

28. *Madison Capital Times,* 26, 28 October 1943; *New York PM,* 7 November 1943; "The Shape of Things," *Nation* 157 (20 November 1943): 570; *Progressive,* 29 March, 3 May 1943, 10 January 1944; PFL to RML, 10, 25 November 1943, box A49, Family Papers; IBL to PFL, 28 October 1943, PFL to IBL, 16 November 1943, box 141, PFL Papers.

29. PFL to IBL, 24, 30 June, 2, 21 July, 3 August 1943, IBL to PFL, 1, 7, 25, 28 July 1943, Mary Rubin to PFL, 21 June 1943, Robert E. Wood to PFL, 6, 22, 23 July, 7 September, 7 December 1943, Wood to Douglas MacArthur, 2 December 1943, RML to PFL, 5 July 1943, boxes 140–41, PFL Papers.

30. Concerning the 1944 Wisconsin primary and MacArthur's bid for the presidency, see Mattern, "Man on the Dark Horse," pp. 86–126; Lansing Hoyt to IBL, 2 July 1943, Hoyt to PFL, 3 January 1944, IBL to PFL, 4, 10, 29 July 1943, 3 February 1944, PFL to IBL, 25 January 1944, Robert E. Wood to PFL, 25 June 1943, Wood to IBL, 8 July 1943, 22 March 1944, boxes 140–42, PFL Papers.

31. RML to PFL, 28 November 1942, box A48, Family Papers; RML to PFL, 14 December 1942, PFL to IBL, 24 December 1942, 3 January 1943, box 140, PFL Papers.

32. PFL memoirs, box 124, PFL Papers.

33. PFL, "MacArthur has B-R-A-I-N-S," *Freeman* 1 (7 May 1951): 506–7.

34. IBL to PFL, 24 March, 17 May 1944, RML to PFL, 27 March 1944, PFL to IBL, 8 April, 1 May 1944, box 142, PFL Papers; PFL to RML, 29 March, 8 April 1944, box A49, Family Papers; PFL memoirs, box 124, PFL Papers.

35. PFL to IBL, 14 March, 29 April 1944, 22 March 1945, boxes 142–43, PFL Papers.

36. PFL to IBL, 15 July 1943, 12 March, 3 April, 12 October, 26 November 1944, 5 April, 9 May 1945, boxes 140–43, PFL Papers.

37. PFL to IBL, 2, 3 May, 14 November 1943, 4 November 1944, 5 April 1945, boxes 140–43, PFL Papers; PFL to RML, 22 October 1944, box A49, Family Papers.

38. PFL to IBL, 16 March, 13, 14 April 1945, box 143, PFL Papers.

39. *Progressive,* 15 May 1944; *Madison Capital Times,* 18, 22, 23 September, 9 October 1945; *Peoria Journal-Transcript,* 12 December 1945; *Milwaukee Sentinel,* 27 September 1945; *Milwaukee Journal,* 13 November 1945; PFL speech, "A Sound American Policy," 13 October 1946, box 120, PFL Papers.

40. PFL, *Adventure in Politics,* pp. 273–75; Roger T. Johnson, *Robert M. La Follette, Jr. and the Decline of the Progressive Party in Wisconsin* (Madison: SHSW, 1964), pp. 109–22.

41. RML to PFL, 10 November 1943, box A49, Family Papers; IBL political diary, 16 March 1952, box 161, PFL Papers; PFL, *Adventure in Politics,* pp. 274–78; PFL to Robert M. La Follette III, 21 March 1946, box 143, PFL Papers. On the rise of the liberal Democrats, see Richard C. Haney, "A History of the Democratic Party of Wisconsin Since World War Two" (Ph.D. diss., University of Wisconsin, 1970), and "The Rise of Wisconsin's New Democrats: A Political Realignment in the Mid Twentieth Century," *Wisconsin Magazine of History* 58 (Winter 1974–1975): 90–106.

42. IBL to PFL, 11 December 1948, box 146, PFL Papers.

43. PFL memoirs, box 124, IBL political diary, 16 March 1952, box 161, IBL to PFL, 24 April, 29 November 1948, box 146, PFL Papers; *Wisconsin State Journal,* 25 September 1947; *New York Times,* 8 October 1947; *Progressive,* 18 February 1946; interview, IBL, 14 May 1972.

44. IBL political diary, 16 March 1952, box 161, IBL to PFL, 24 April 1948, box 146, PFL Papers; Mattern, "Man on the Dark Horse," pp. 188–229; Howard B. Schonberger, "The General and the Presidency: Douglas MacArthur and the Election of 1948," *Wisconsin Magazine of History* 57 (Spring 1974): 201–19.

45. *Madison Capital Times,* 7 December 1959.

46. Interview, IBL, 14 May 1972; Maney, *"Young Bob" La Follette,* pp. 311–12.

Appendix

1. Michael P. Rogin, *The Intellectuals and McCarthy: The Radical Specter* (Cambridge, Mass.: M. I. T. Press, 1967), pp. 59–103.

2. Ibid., pp. 65, 82; Robert R. Dykstra and David R. Reynolds, "In Search of Wisconsin Progressivism, 1904–1952: A Test of the Rogin Scenario," in *The History of American Electoral Behavior*, ed. Joel H. Silbey, Allen G. Bogue, and William H. Flanigan (Princeton: Princeton University Press, 1978), pp. 300–301, 325.

3. David L. Brye, *Wisconsin Voting Patterns in the Twentieth Century, 1900 to 1950* (New York: Garland, 1979), pp. 280, 298, 301.

4. *Wisconsin Blue Book, 1933*, pp. 103–8.

5. Ibid.

6. Brye, *Wisconsin Voting Patterns*, p. 325. Donald Pienkos demonstrates that Polish voters in Milwaukee were more progressive in orientation than has generally been acknowledged. Examples of this were Robert M. La Follette, Sr.'s better showing in 1922 in Polish wards than in Milwaukee as a whole and PFL's duplication of the feat in 1930, "Politics, Religion, and Change in Polish Milwaukee, 1900–1930," *Wisconsin Magazine of History* 61 (Spring 1978): 179–209.

Bibliographical Essay

Most important as a source for this study are the more than 150 boxes of letters, memoranda, reports, speeches, clippings, memoirs, and miscellaneous materials in the Philip F. La Follette Papers at the State Historical Society of Wisconsin. La Follette's wide-ranging correspondence with leaders in Wisconsin and around the country provides a richly detailed picture of his political operations. Since, as one of his friends noted, Phil La Follette was a person who "played his cards close to his chest," the political diary sporadically kept by his wife Isabel ("Isen") constitutes a valuable supplementary source. Her papers are housed along with her husband's. Her political astuteness and close working relationship with her husband made her weekly column in the *Progressive,* "A Room of Our Own," an unusually enlightening source on his thinking and on the Progressive movement in general from 1930 to 1947. Phil's correspondence with Isen and the rest of the family during World War II is considerably more voluminous and informative about his thinking than most of his letters written during the thirties. In addition, the La Follette Family Papers at the Library of Congress are especially useful, containing many letters not to be found in the Philip F. La Follette Papers between Phil and Isen and other members of the family—Belle Case, Bob, Fola, and Mary La Follette, Ralph Sucher, and George Middleton. The Robert M. La Follette, Jr., Papers, housed with the Family Papers, contain little information relating to this study that is not in the collections already mentioned.

Phil La Follette's memoirs were published posthumously as *Adventure in Politics: The Memoirs of Philip La Follette,* edited by Donald Young (New York: Holt, Rinehart and Winston, 1970). Unfortunately, La Follette, whose speaking style was direct and scintillating, failed to capture on paper the excitement and controversy that swirled around his political career. A considerable amount of material not included in the book is contained in drafts located in the Philip F. La Follette Papers. Reminiscences by other family members are contained in Robert M. La Follette, Sr., *La Follette's Autobiography: A Personal Narrative of Political Experiences* (Madison: University of Wisconsin Press, 1960); in Belle Case and Fola La Follette, *Robert M. La Follette: June 14, 1855 to June 18, 1925,* 2 vols. (New York: Macmillan, 1953); and in George Middleton, *These Things Are Mine: The Autobiography of a Journeyman Playwright* (New York: Macmillan, 1947).

At the Roosevelt Library in Hyde Park, New York, the Franklin D. Roosevelt Papers contain many important items illuminating his relationship with the La Follettes and the Progressives. Other useful sources are the transcripts of Roosevelt's press conferences, *The Public Papers and Addresses of Franklin D. Roosevelt,* edited by Samuel I. Rosenman (New York: vols. 1–5, Random House, 1938; vols. 6–9, Macmillan, 1941; vols. 10–13, Harper & Brothers, 1950), and the letters edited by Elliott Roosevelt, *F. D. R.: His Personal Letters,* 4 vols. (New York: Duell, Sloan and Pearce, 1947–1950). The Democratic National Committee Papers at the Roosevelt Library contain many letters and reports documenting the interaction between the national administration and Wisconsin's Democrats and Progressives. Other useful collections at the Roosevelt Library are the papers of Harry Hopkins, Rexford G. Tugwell, and Aubrey Williams.

At the National Archives in Washington, D.C., Record Group 69, including records of the Federal Emergency Relief Administration, the Civil Works Administration, and the Works Progress Administration, contains a large number of memoranda, field reports, and documents describing the Wisconsin situation and the interaction between the administration and Wisconsin government officials. The records of the Social Security Administration (Record Group 47) and the National Resources Planning Board (Record Group 187) also contain considerable material on Wisconsin. Less useful are the National Youth Administration (Record Group 119) and the National Recovery Administration (Record Group 9) files.

The State Historical Society of Wisconsin holds the papers of a number of state political leaders, including several top Progressives and La Follette associates and some of their opponents. The Thomas R. Amlie Papers contain a multitude of letters that delineate the conflict between farmer-labor groups and moderate or traditional Progressives. They constitute an excellent and detailed source on the efforts of the Wisconsin congressman to promote a national third party. Other perspectives on radical Progressivism are provided in the Samuel Sigman Papers and the Harold Groves Papers. The William T. Evjue Papers are a valuable source; especially interesting are the numerous summaries Evjue recorded of conversations. The Edwin E. Witte Papers and the Frank Kuehl Papers provide insights into other men who were close to the movement. Only minimally helpful for this study were the papers of John J. Blaine, Orland Loomis, Joseph D. Beck, and Herman L. Ekern. The Alex Gumberg Papers are the best source on Phil La Follette's friendship with Gumberg, James Causey, and Boyd Hatch. The Democratic point of view is represented in the papers of Harry W. Bolens, Charles E. Broughton, Emanuel F. Brunette, and William B. Rubin.

The papers of the Wisconsin Farmer-Labor Progressive Federation at the Milwaukee County Historical Society contain minutes, letters, and other materials on this left-wing faction.

Articles in magazines and newspapers sometimes provide perceptive insights into Phil La Follette's thoughts and actions. Notable are articles by Louis Adamic, "La Follette Progressives Face the Future" and "A Talk with Phil La Follette," *Nation* 140 (20 February 1935): 213–15 and (27 February 1935): 242–45. La Follette called himself a "radical" in an interview with Fred C. Kelly in the *Milwaukee Journal*, 28 July 1935. While still a student at the University of Chicago, Sidney Hyman elicited many revealing remarks from the governor in an interview published in the *Progressive* on 12 December 1936. On the subject of the formation of the National Progressives of America, two articles stand out: Max Lerner, "Phil La Follette—An Interview," *Nation* 146 (14 May 1938): 552–55, and Reuben Levin, "A New Party Is Launched," *Common Sense* 7 (June 1938): 17–19. Highly penetrating in its analysis of Wisconsin politics and the La Follettes is Elmer Davis, "The Wisconsin Brothers: A Study in Partial Eclipse," *Harper's* 178 (February 1939): 268–77.

I relied heavily on newspapers for information about Progressive politics. Most frequently consulted were the *Madison Capital Times,* the *Wisconsin State Journal,* and the *Milwaukee Journal.* Analyses by Aldric Revell, whose sympathetic column "All Around Wisconsin" appeared in the *Capital Times* and the *Progressive,* and by Winter Everett, whose generally critical column "Around the Statehouse" was carried daily by the *Wisconsin State Journal* and other papers, are especially informative about day-to-day political developments. Indispensable are the weekly issues of the *Progressive,* which was edited by William T. Evjue during the 1930s until he severed his relationship with the paper in 1940 because of his disagreements with the La Follettes over foreign policy. Two years later, Morris Rubin took over editorial duties and began making it into the national publication that it is today.

Few historical subjects have attracted more attention from scholars than the New Deal. The places to start for Roosevelt's political leadership are James M. Burns's volumes *Roosevelt: The Lion and the Fox* (New York: Harcourt, Brace and World, 1956), and *Roosevelt: The Soldier of Freedom* (New York: Harcourt Brace Jovanovich, 1970), which devote considerable attention to Roosevelt's interaction with political leaders in various states and to his continued desire to liberalize the Democratic party. Further insight on these issues is provided by the books and articles of Rexford G. Tugwell, who writes as an administration insider about Roosevelt's progressive inclinations and his attempts to woo the Progressives into a liberalized Democratic party, especially in *The Democratic Roosevelt: A Biography of Franklin D. Roosevelt* (New York: Doubleday, 1957). Also indispensable for studying the relationship between the Progressives and the national administration are the three completed volumes of Arthur M. Schlesinger, Jr., *The Age of Roosevelt* (Boston: Houghton Mifflin, 1957–1960).

Wisconsin: A History (Madison: University of Wisconsin Press, 1973) by Robert C. Nesbit supersedes previous texts on Wisconsin history and deftly portrays political developments, to which it gives special emphasis. Leon D. Epstein's *Politics in Wisconsin* (Madison: University of Wisconsin Press, 1958) remains the starting point for any student of state politics. Now standing as the most important historical analysis of state politics since 1900 is David L. Brye's *Wisconsin Voting Patterns in the Twentieth Century, 1900 to 1950* (New York: Garland, 1979), in which the author uses the techniques of the "new political history" to develop a sociocultural interpretation of voting determinants. Also useful are Michael P. Rogin's "Wisconsin: McCarthy and the Progressive Tradition" in *The Intellectuals and McCarthy: The Radical Specter* (Cambridge, Mass.: M. I. T. Press, 1967), and Robert R. Dykstra and David R. Reynolds, "In Search of Wisconsin Progressivism, 1904–1952: A Test of the Rogin Scenario," in *The History of American Electoral Behavior,* edited by Joel H. Silbey, Allen G. Bogue, and William H. Flanigan (Princeton: Princeton University Press, 1978). Voting statistics may be found in James Donoghue, *How Wisconsin Voted, 1848–1972* (Madison: Bureau of Government, University of Wisconsin Extension Division, 1974), and in the biennial *Wisconsin Blue Books.*

There is a voluminous literature on the Wisconsin progressive movement, including the standard treatments by Robert S. Maxwell, *La Follette and the Rise of the Progressives in Wisconsin* (Madison: State Historical Society of Wisconsin, 1956), and Herbert F. Margulies, *The Decline of the Progressive Movement, 1890–1920* (Madison: State Historical Society of Wisconsin, 1968). Recent studies of La Follette progressivism have been influenced by the increasingly critical attitude taken in studies of the national movement. Stanley P. Caine minimizes the results of one kind of state reform in *The Myth of a Progressive Reform: Railroad Regulation in Wisconsin, 1903–1910* (Madison: State Historical Society of Wisconsin, 1970). Eugene A. Manning analyzes the senior La Follette's manipulative use of rhetoric in "Old Bob La Follette: Champion of the People" (Ph.D. diss., University of Wisconsin, 1966). David P. Thelen argues that Old Bob La Follette emerged into the limelight as a conventional political figure and that he remained more a follower than a leader of public opinion in *The Early Life of Robert M. La Follette, 1855–1884* (Chicago: Loyola University Press, 1966) and in *The New Citizenship: Origins of Progressivism in Wisconsin, 1885–1900* (Columbia: University of Missouri Press, 1972). His short biography, *Robert M. La Follette and the Insurgent Spirit* (Boston: Little, Brown, 1976), emphasizes La Follette's innovativeness during his later career and his championing of a rising consumer consciousness. Making good use of the La Follette Papers, which were opened to scholars in 1970, Fred Greenbaum has written a succinct political biography, *Robert Marion La Follette* (Boston: Twayne, 1975). In "Belle Case La Follette: Progressive Woman" (Master's thesis, University of Maryland, 1976), Ann J. Brickfield presents a brief sympathetic account of an astute political adviser and campaigner.

A critical evaluation of both generations of La Follettes by a reporter who covered politics for the *Milwaukee Journal,* a continual La Follette antagonist, is Craig Ralston's "The La Follette Dynasty" (manuscript, n.d., Manuscripts Division, State Historical Society of Wisconsin). Few writers have attempted to cover the entire span of progressivism in Wisconsin. Edward N. Doan's *The La Follettes and the Wisconsin Idea* (New York: Rinehart, 1947) is laudatory and uncritical and concentrates mainly on the senatorial careers of Old Bob and Young Bob La Follette. Four Wisconsin elections are singled out as transitional by Karl Ernest Meyer in "The Politics of Loyalty from La Follette to McCarthy in Wisconsin: 1918–1952" (Ph.D. diss., Princeton University, 1956).

The relationship between progressivism and the New Deal has generated considerable scholarly debate. In the last chapter of *The Age of Reform: From Bryan to F. D. R.* (New York: Knopf, 1955), Richard Hofstadter asserts that New Deal liberalism differed considerably in tone and aim from old-style progressivism. Utilizing the collective biography approach, Otis Graham tests the discontinuity thesis in *An Encore for Reform: The Old Progressives and the New Deal* (New York: Oxford University Press, 1967) and comes to much the same conclusion. More general treatments of the relationship between the states and the federal government are James T. Patterson, *The New Deal and the States: Federalism in Transition* (Princeton: Princeton University Press, 1969), and John Braeman, Robert H. Bremner, and David Brody, editors, *The New Deal,* 2 vols. (Columbus: Ohio State University Press, 1975). In *Twilight of Progressivism: The Western Republican Senators and the New Deal* (Baltimore: Johns Hopkins University Press, 1981), Ronald L. Feinman chronicles the process by which New Deal Democrats supplanted progressive Republicans as the vanguard of liberal reform. He identifies George W. Norris and Robert M. La Follette, Jr., as the most advanced of the twelve progressives in the Senate bloc from 1930 to 1945. Ronald Mulder, in *The Insurgent Progressives in the United States Senate and the New Deal, 1933–1939* (New York: Garland, 1979), argues that while insurgent Republicans and Democrats were generally enthusiastic about Roosevelt personally, they were ambivalent about or hostile toward most of his programs, except for those enacted during the "second New Deal" of 1935. They broke sharply with the administration over the Court-packing fight and after that increasingly revealed their antiurban, antispending, and antibureaucratic biases. Mulder agrees with Feinman that Bob La Follette was an exception in this regard and that he and George Norris were the only members of this group that remained sympathetic to the New Deal after 1937.

The Wisconsin progressive movement is located securely within the tradition of Midwestern agrarian radicalism in Russel B. Nye, *Midwestern Progressive Politics: A Historical Study of Its Origins and Development, 1870–1958* (New York: Harper & Row, 1959). Donald R. McCoy discusses the National Progressives of America within the context of radical third-party politics in the thirties in *Angry Voices: Left-of-Center Politics in the New Deal Era* (Lawrence: University of Kansas Press, 1958), and in "The National Progressives of America, 1938," *Mississippi Valley Historical Review* 44 (June 1957): 75–93. The best treatment of the internal structure and dynamics of the Progressive party is Charles H. Backstrom, "The Progressive Party of Wisconsin, 1934–1946" (Ph.D. diss., University of Wisconsin, 1956). Lester Schmidt focuses on the radicals within the movement in "The Farmer-Labor Progressive Federation: The Study of a 'United Front' Movement among Wisconsin Liberals, 1934–1941" (Ph.D. diss., University of Wisconsin, 1954). Insight into the national third-party movement is provided in Robert E. Kessler, "The League for Independent Political Action, 1929 to 1933" (Master's thesis, University of Wisconsin, 1969). And an important segment of the Progressive coalition in the state during the late 1930s is discussed by Frederick I. Olson in "The Milwaukee Socialists, 1897–1941" (Ph.D. diss., Harvard University, 1952). The exhilaration as well as the frustration of radical crusading, thirties style, is captured in Donald L. Miller's excellent intellectual biography, *The New American Radicalism: Alfred M. Bingham and Non-Marxian Insurgency in the New Deal Era* (Port Washington, N.Y.: Kennikat, 1979). The state movement that most nearly resembled Wisconsin Progressivism is described in *Minnesota Farmer-Laborism: The Third-Party Alternative* (Minneapolis: University of Minnesota Press, 1979) by Millard L. Gieske, who, in analyzing ideological inconsistencies in the Farmer-Labor movement, the pragmatic opportunism practiced by Gov. Floyd B. Olson, internecine conflict between moderates and radicals, and moves for coalition with the Democrats, touches upon themes that closely parallel the Wisconsin experience.

Phil La Follette's techniques of party leadership are studied in L. David Carley, "The Wisconsin Governor's Legislative Role: A Case Study of the Administrations of Philip Fox La Follette and Walter J. Kohler, Jr." (Ph.D. diss., University of Wisconsin, 1959). Donald R. McCoy discusses the Progressives' political calculations in "The Formation of the Wisconsin Progressive Party in 1934," *Historian* 14 (Autumn 1951): 70–90, which draws upon his "The Development of the Wisconsin Progressive Party of 1934 to 1946'' (Master's thesis, University of Chicago, 1949). He also describes the La Follettes' role in Roosevelt's reelection in "The Progressive National Committee of 1936," *Western Political Quarterly* 9 (June 1956): 454–69. John G. Burnett's "The Progressive Party in Wisconsin" (Honors thesis, Princeton University, 1947) briefly outlines the background and development of the Progressive party. Alan E. Kent focuses on foreign policy issues in "Portrait in Isolationism: The La Follettes in Foreign Policy" (Ph.D. diss., University of Wisconsin, 1956). A suggestive analysis of Phil La Follette's political philosophy is contained in Walter B. Raushenbush, "Wisconsin under Governor Philip La Follette" (Honors thesis, Harvard College, 1950).

An excellent biography of Robert M. La Follette, Jr., and arguably the best book to date about Wisconsin progressivism, is Patrick J. Maney's *"Young Bob" La Follette: A Biography of Senator Robert M. La Follette, Jr., 1895–1953* (Columbia: University of Missouri Press, 1978). The senator's ideas are sensitively outlined in "The Ideology of Senator Robert M. La Follette, Jr." (Master's thesis, University of Wisconsin, 1966) by Theodore Rosenof, who also helps to locate the ideas of the La Follette brothers within the shifting ideological matrix of the thirties in *Dogma, Depression, and the New Deal: The Debate of Political Leaders over Economic Recovery* (Port Washington, N.Y.: Kennikat, 1975). Jerold S. Auerbach demonstrates the importance of the La Follette-labor connection in *Labor and Liberty: The La Follette Committee and the New Deal* (Indianapolis: Bobbs-Merrill, 1966).

A number of studies investigate special aspects of Wisconsin politics between 1928 and 1946. The background of progressive ideas is set in Alfred Slatin, "Wisconsin Progressivism in Transition: A Study of Progressive Concepts, 1918–1930" (Master's thesis, University of Wisconsin, 1952). That possibilities for cooperation between progressives and Democrats existed even before the advent of the Great Depression is clearly demonstrated by Thomas J. Schlereth in "The Progressive-Democrat Alliance in the Wisconsin Presidential Election of 1928" (Master's thesis, University of Wisconsin, 1965). Progressive backing for Franklin Roosevelt and other Democratic candidates is described in John E. Miller, "The Elections of 1932 in Wisconsin" (Master's thesis, University of Wisconsin, 1968). The activities of the Democratic administration that rode into office on New Deal coattails are chronicled in Robert E. Long, "Wisconsin State Politics, 1932–1934: The Democratic Interlude" (Master's thesis, University of Wisconsin, 1962), and Wayne E. Laufenberg, "The Schmedeman Administration in Wisconsin: A Study of Missed Opportunities" (Master's thesis, University of Wisconsin, 1965). Additional studies of the thirties include Peter Carstensen, "The Progressives and the Declining Role of State Government in Wisconsin, 1930–1938" (Honors thesis, University of Wisconsin, 1964), and Francis J. Moriarty's account of Phil La Follette's third term, "Philip F. La Follette: State and National Politics, 1937–1938" (Master's thesis, University of Wisconsin, 1960). Roger T. Johnson provides detailed information about the internal operations of the Progressive party and about Bob La Follette's reluctance to lead it in *Robert M. La Follette, Jr. and the Decline of the Progressive Party in Wisconsin* (Madison: State Historical Society of Wisconsin, 1964). Richard C. Haney demonstrates the continuity that existed between Progressivism and the revitalized Democratic party in Wisconsin by tracing the careers of top Democratic leaders to their roots in Young Progressive organizations in "A History of the Democratic Party of Wisconsin Since World War Two" (Ph.D. diss., University of Wisconsin, 1970), and "The Rise of Wisconsin's New Democrats: A Political Realignment in the Mid Twentieth Century," *Wisconsin Magazine of History* 58 (Winter 1974–1975): 90–106. Howard B. Schonberger relates La Follette's role in MacArthur's 1948 bid for the presidency in "The General and the Presidency: Douglas MacArthur and the Election of 1948," *Wisconsin Magazine of History* 57 (Spring 1974): 201–19. A much more detailed analysis, which emphasizes the special importance of the role Phil La Follette played in MacArthur's 1944 and 1948 campaigns, is Carolyn J. Mattern's "The Man on the Dark Horse: The Presidential Campaigns for General Douglas MacArthur" (Ph.D. diss., University of Wisconsin, 1976).

Several Wisconsin Progressives joined Phil La Follette in writing memoirs of their political experiences. William T. Evjue's *A Fighting Editor* (Madison, Wis.: Wells, 1968) derives largely from the files of his own *Capital Times* but, although quite long, reveals little about the man or the movement. The unpublished autobiography of Harold Groves, "In and Out of the Ivory Tower," which is located in his papers at the State Historical Society of Wisconsin, contains the observations of a university professor who was close to La Follette and who served in the legislature.

Numerous studies have been made of individual Progressives, including Robert E. Long, "Thomas Amlie: A Political Biography" (Ph.D. diss., University of Wisconsin, 1969); Alfred R. Schumann's laudatory biography of Progressive state treasurer Sol Levitan, *No Peddlers Allowed* (Appleton, Wis.: Nelson, 1948); Albert Erlebacher, "Herman L. Ekern: The Quiet Progressive" (Ph.D. diss., University of Wisconsin, 1965), which touches only briefly on the thirties; Richard H. Davis, Jr., "Merlin Hull: A Wisconsin Progressive and the New Deal" (Master's thesis, University of Wisconsin, 1964), about a nonideological Progressive and Republican congressman; Kent H. Keeth, "The Profile of a Progressive: The Political Career of Orland S. Loomis, 1897–1942" (Master's thesis, University of Wisconsin, 1961), about the only Progressive besides Phil La Follette to be elected governor; and Theron Schlabach, *Edwin E. Witte: Cautious Reformer* (Madison: State Historical Society of Wisconsin, 1969), about an academician who worked closely with Phil La Follette during the early 1930s.

Two important episodes of Phil La Follette's last term in office have received book-length treatment. In *Jurisprudence and Statecraft: The Wisconsin Development Authority and Its Implications* (Madison: University of Wisconsin Press, 1963), Samuel Mermin deemphasizes Governor La Follette's personal role in the project, attributing greater importance to more general forces and bureaucratic tendencies that were operating during the period. La Follette is treated more gently than he was by many of his contemporary critics, and the university president is portrayed as a politically minded educator who should not have been surprised by a political move to oust him, in Lawrence H. Larsen's *The President Wore Spats: A Biography of Glenn Frank* (Madison: State Historical Society of Wisconsin, 1965).

Index